Liberating Praxis

CRITICAL STUDIES IN EDUCATION AND CULTURE SERIES

Liberating Praxis

*Paulo Freire's Legacy for Radical
Education and Politics*

PETER MAYO

Critical Studies in Education and Culture Series
Edited by Henry A. Giroux

**Westport, Connecticut
London**

Library of Congress Cataloging-in-Publication Data

Mayo, Peter, 1955–
  Liberating praxis : Paulo Freire's legacy for radical education and politics / Peter Mayo.
    p. cm.—(Critical studies in education and culture series, ISSN 1064–8615)
  Includes bibliographical references and index.
  ISBN 0–89789–786–2 (alk. paper)
  1. Freire, Paulo, 1921– 2. Education—Philosophy.   3. Critical pedagogy.
  I. Title. II. Series.
  LB880.F732M39   2004
  370.11'5—dc22   2004004533

British Library Cataloguing in Publication Data is available.

Library of Congress Catalog Card Number: 2004004533
ISBN: 0–89789–786–2
ISSN: 1064–8615

First published in 2004

Praeger Publishers, 88 Post Road West, Westport, CT 06881
An imprint of Greenwood Publishing Group, Inc.
www.praeger.com

Printed in the United States of America

The paper used in this book complies with the
Permanent Paper Standard issued by the National
Information Standards Organization (Z39.48–1984).

10 9 8 7 6 5 4 3 2 1

Copyright Acknowledgments

Contents

Acknowledgments

There are a number of people whose help I should like to acknowledge. In the first place, I must express my gratitude to members of my family, Josephine, Annemarie, and Cecilia, for having put up with me, especially during the summer months when I spent the best part of almost every day and night logged on to my computer working on the manuscript for this book or alternatively reading those last few books that I felt deserved a thorough read before I could do justice to them in the book. They also deserve gratitude for the way they put up with the constantly increasing towers of books and papers that have become a feature of our house.

I should also like to express a big "thank you" to a colleague and good friend, Carmel Borg, with whom I have coauthored several papers, for reading and commenting on a draft version of the entire manuscript and for giving me permission to use material from interviews we carried out together and from papers we coauthored and published together. A big "thank you" is also due to another friend and colleague, Paula Allman, who was ever so willing to read drafts of chapters for this book. Both Carmel and Paula provided me with invaluable feedback and very good tips to improve the text. I should also like to thank Noah Lissovoy, from UCLA, for his feedback on a number of draft chapters I sent him, and Antonia Darder, from the University of Illinois, and Joseph Buttigieg, from Notre Dame University, for their instant feedback on chapter 5. I also want to express my gratitude to Daniel Schugurensky, a longtime friend, for having discussed and clarified issues taken up in this book through e-mail exchanges.

I should also like to thank the participants in the M.Ed. course with specialization in Adult Education and the participants in the diploma in adult education course with whom I discussed several issues pertinent to this book in courses on Freire. The same applies to students in the B.Ed. course who followed the optional credits in adult education. Works by Freire featured prominently in these courses.

Finally, any remaining shortcomings in this book are my responsibility.

Series Foreword

Educational reform has fallen upon hard times. The traditional assumption that schooling is fundamentally tied to the imperatives of citizenship designed to educate students to exercise civic leadership and public service has been eroded. The schools are now the key institution for producing professional, technically trained, credentialized workers for whom the demands of citizenship are subordinated to the vicissitudes of the marketplace and the commercial public sphere. Given the current corporate and right wing assault on public and higher education, coupled with the emergence of a moral and political climate that has shifted to a new Social Darwinism, the issues which framed the democratic meaning, purpose, and use to which education might aspire have been displaced by more vocational and narrowly ideological considerations.

The war waged against the possibilities of an education wedded to the precepts of a real democracy is not merely ideological. Against the backdrop of reduced funding for public schooling, the call for privatization, vouchers, cultural uniformity, and choice, there are the often ignored larger social realities of material power and oppression. On the national level, there has been a vast resurgence of racism. This is evident in the passing of anti-immigration laws such as Proposition 187 in California, the dismantling of the welfare state, the demonization of black youth that is taking place in the popular media, and the remarkable attention provided by the media to forms of race talk that argue for the intellectual inferiority of blacks or dismiss calls for racial justices as simply a holdover from the "morally bankrupt" legacy of the 1960s.

Poverty is on the rise among children in the United States, with 20 percent of all children under the age of eighteen living below the poverty line. Unemployment is growing at an alarming rate for poor youth of color, especially in the urban centers. While black youth are policed and disciplined in and out of the nation's schools, conservative and liberal educators define education through the ethically limp discourses of privatization, national standards, and global competitiveness.

Many writers in the critical education tradition have attempted to challenge the right wing fundamentalism behind educational and social reform in both the United States and abroad while simultaneously providing ethical signposts for a public discourse about education and democracy that is both prophetic and transformative. Eschewing traditional categories, a diverse number of critical theorists and educators have successfully exposed the political and ethical implications of the cynicism and despair that has become endemic to the discourse of schooling and civic life. In its place, such educators strive to provide a language of hope that inextricably links the struggle over schooling to understanding and transforming our present social and cultural dangers.

At the risk of overgeneralizing, both cultural studies theorists and critical educators have emphasized the importance of understanding theory as the grounded basis for "intervening into contexts and power . . . in order to enable people to act more strategically in ways that may change their context for the better."[1] Moreover, theorists in both fields have argued for the primacy of the political by calling for and struggling to produce critical public spaces, regardless of how fleeting they may be, in which "popular cultural resistance is explored as a form of political resistance."[2] Such writers have analyzed the challenges that teachers will have to face in redefining a new mission for education, one that is linked to honoring the experiences, concerns, and diverse histories and languages that give expression to the multiple narratives that engage and challenge the legacy of democracy.

Equally significant is the insight of recent critical educational work that connects the politics of difference with concrete strategies for addressing the crucial relationships between schooling and the economy, and citizenship and the politics of meaning in communities of multicultural, multiracial, and multilingual schools.

Critical Studies in Education and Culture attempts to address and demonstrate how scholars working in the fields of cultural studies and the critical pedagogy might join together in a radical project and practice informed by theoretically rigorous discourses that affirm the critical but refuse the cynical, and establish hope as central to a critical pedagogical and political practice but eschew a romantic utopianism. Central to such a project is the issue of how pedagogy might provide cultural studies theorists and educators with an opportunity to engage pedagogical practices that are not only transdisciplinary, transgressive, and oppositional, but also connected to a wider project designed to further racial, economic, and political democracy.[3] By taking seriously the relations between culture and power, we further the possibilities of resistance, struggle, and change.

Critical Studies in Education and Culture is committed to publishing work that opens a narrative space that affirms the contextual and the specific while simultaneously recognizing the ways in which such spaces are shot through with issues of power. The series attempts to continue an important legacy of theoretical work in cultural studies in which related debates on pedagogy are understood and addressed within the larger context of social responsibility, civic courage, and the reconstruction of democratic public life. We must keep in mind Raymond Williams's insight that the "deepest impulse (informing cultural politics) is the desire to make learning part of the process of social change itself."[4] This series challenges the current return to the primacy of market values and simultaneous retreat from politics so evident in the recent work of educational theorists, legislators, and policy analysts. Professional relegitimation in a troubled time seems to be the order of the day as an increasing number of academics both refuse to recognize public and higher education as critical public spheres and offer little or no resistance to the ongoing vocationalization of schooling, the continuing evisceration of the intellectual labor force, and the current assaults on the working poor, the elderly, and women and children.[5]

Emphasizing the centrality of politics, culture, and power, *Critical Studies in Education and Culture* will deal with pedagogical issues that contribute in imaginative and transformative ways to our understanding of how critical knowledge, democratic values, and social practices can provide a basis for teachers, students, and other cultural workers to redefine their role as engaged and public intellectuals. Each volume will attempt to rethink the relationship between language and experience, pedagogy and human agency, and ethics and social responsibility as part of a larger project for engaging and deepening the prospects of democratic schooling in a multiracial and multicultural society. *Critical Studies in Education and Culture* takes on the responsibility of witnessing and addressing the most pressing problems of public schooling and civic life, and engages culture as a crucial site and strategic force for productive social change.

Henry A. Giroux

NOTES

1. Lawrence Grossberg, "Toward a Genealogy of the State of Cultural Studies," in Cary Nelson and Dilip Parameshwar Gaonkar, eds. *Disciplinarity and Dissent in Cultural Studies* (New York: Routledge, 1996), 143.

2. David Bailey and Stuart Hall, "The Vertigo of Displacement," *Ten 8* 2:3 (1992), 19.

3. My notion of transdisciplinary comes from Mas'ud Zavarzadeh and Donald Morton, "Theory, Pedagogy, Politics: The Crisis of the 'Subject' in the Humanities," in *Theory Pedagogy Politics: Texts for Change,* Mas'ud Zavarzadeh and Donald Morton, eds. (Urbana: University of Illinois Press, 1992), 10. At issue here is neither ignoring the boundaries of discipline-based knowledge nor simply fusing different disciplines, but creating theoretical paradigms, questions, and knowledge that cannot be taken up within the policed boundaries of the existing disciplines.

4. Raymond Williams, "Adult Education and Social Change," in *What I Came to Say* (London: Hutchinson-Radus, 1989), 158.

5. The term "professional legitimation" comes from a personal correspondence with Professor Jeff Williams of East Carolina University.

CHAPTER 1

Paulo Freire: The Educator, His Oeuvre, and His Changing Contexts

Paulo Reglus Neves Freire has been one of the most significant educationists of the last 30 years. His work is cited freely in the literature on education and social thought, emerging not only from the Third World that provided the context for most of his pedagogical ideas and practice, but also from the world's most industrially developed centers.

He continues to enjoy iconic status among educators. Argentinean scholar Daniel Schugurensky says, with reference to adult education, that: "in Latin America, Paulo Freire constitutes a watershed. There is before and after Freire" (Schugurensky, 1996, p. 344). Several years earlier, another Argentinean scholar, Carlos Alberto Torres, remarked: "We can stay with Freire or against Freire, but not without Freire" (Torres, 1982, p. 94). And although Freire is undoubtedly one of the most heralded educators of the twentieth century, who inevitably has his detractors, his influence extends beyond the field of education to be felt in a variety of areas, including sociology, political theory, development studies, theology, philosophy, cultural studies, anthropology, language studies, and communication.

He was, first and foremost, a man of action who suffered imprisonment and exile for his efforts in planning what was perceived as being a subversive approach to literacy in Brazil in the early sixties, was frequently called on by revolutionary governments to assist them in developing and evaluating educational projects, used his 16-year period of exile to engage in projects with a variety of groups in different parts of the world, and also ventured into the complex area of municipal educational administration in one of the world's largest cities. He was, however, a most prolific writer, with many of his works having been translated into English and other languages. Freire's better-known work is regarded by many to be exemplary in the way it provides reflections on his many worlds of action in a process that also involves constant recourse to theoretical for-mulations deriving from a variety of sources. Remaining steadfast till the very end to his cherished principles of radical humanization and democ-racy, Freire has, throughout his life, produced work that provides those who share his political–pedagogical philosophy with resources of hope and a strong sense of agency.

With the posthumous publication of a number of his last writings, Paulo Freire's oeuvre is almost complete. It therefore seems to be an appropriate time to take stock of a substantial and representative part of Freire's work with a view to, among other things, tracing the evolution of his thought and its contemporary significance.

PAULO FREIRE (1921–1997)

The greatest and most enduring aspect of Freire's work is his emphasis on the political nature of all educational activity, as this book will show. In Freire's view, there is no such thing as a neutral education. Education can either domesticate or liberate; in the latter case, as I shall argue in chapter 3, it can foster the disposition among learners to engage in a dialectical relationship with knowledge and society.

One-way teacher–student transmission, often a reflection of a wider prescriptive process of communication, constitutes a domesticating edu-cation. Freire advocates a process involving a dialogical approach to knowledge, an approach that warrants much elaboration in that it entails a number of conditions and features, as I shall demonstrate further on in this book. Although they are not on an equal footing, teacher and learner learn from each other as they coinvestigate dialectically the object of knowledge. This entails a process of *praxis,* a key term in Freire's work. It is central to Paulo Freire's educational philosophy and will be elaborated on in chapter 3 where I will also discuss its varying uses and foci in Freire's work, including, in the latter case, the areas of communal living, production (as in Marx's *Capital,* Vol. 1), and temporary abode during periods of exile.

One aspect of Freire's pedagogical approach to be emphasized through-out this book is that educators have to be *directive* in their approach. This will be a recurring theme throughout the book, starting from chapter 2, in which I review a selection of works, in the English language, that attempt to analyze Freire's work holistically, each in a book-length single study. Quite important in this context will be the discussions surrounding the tension between authority and freedom, which, as I shall argue, draws parallels with Gramsci and especially the distinction in Freire between authority and authoritarianism, a distinction that recurs throughout his

work, especially his work from the mid-1980s onward. This is all in keeping with a rigorous approach to teaching that eschews all forms of laissez-
faire pedagogy and that is predicated on a very complex notion of
dialogue. It is an approach characterized by a sense of authority that rests
on other important qualities that deserve elaboration in the chapters that
follow, notably chapter 4. Included among them are those of humility and
love (Freire, 1970b, 1993, pp. 89–90; Freire, 1995b, p. 20). Humility is a feature often attributed to Freire himself. The lay Dominican friar, Carlos
Alberto Libanio Christo, better known as Frei Betto[1] and one of Brazil's
foremost contemporary left-wing intellectuals, has this to say about Paulo
Freire:

During many periods of our lives I was on intimate terms with Paulo Freire and I
consider myself his disciple. For more than 20 years I worked in popular education
based upon his method and we wrote a book together, with the participation of
journalist Ricardo Kotscho. The first thing that impressed me about Paulo Freire
was that, ever since his experience with workers in the State of Pernambuco, he
allowed himself to be educated by the workers, before presuming to be their educator. . . . He was a simple person, an unpretentious intellectual, who never
wished to show off his erudition, who did not favor one person over another in
any relationship. I remember him telling me how he had entered a store that sold
neckties in Switzerland and could not get anyone to help him. After some time he
complained and the employee said that nobody paid attention to him because he
would not have enough money to buy any of those ties. He related this anecdote
as a joke, laughing, to show the prejudices that exist in Europe regarding Latin-
Americans. (Betto, 1999, p. 44)[2]

A Freirean approach to knowledge is not concerned solely with the cognitive aspects of learning (Darder, 2002, p. 98). It involves conceiving of
the educators and learners as "integral human beings" (p. 94) in an educational process that has love at its core (p. 91).[3] An e-mail message by
Valerie Scatamburlo posted on the Progressive Sociologists network soon
after Freire's death on May 2, 1997, eventually to reappear in a special
issue of the journal *Taboo*, reproduces a remark said to be uttered by Freire
only a few days before his death:

I could never think of education without love and that is why I think I am an educator, first of all because I feel love. . . . [4]

In response to Carlos Alberto Torres's question regarding his legacy to
humanity, Paulo Freire stated that he would like to think that people
would say the following about him:

Paulo Freire was a man who loved, who could not understand a life existence
without love and without knowing. Paulo Freire lived, loved and he tried to know.
(Freire, 1995c, p. 181)

The humanizing relationship between teacher and taught (teacher–student and student–teacher, in Freire's terms) is a relationship of love. It is love that drives the progressive Freire-inspired educator forward in teaching and working for the dismantling of dehumanizing structures. Antonia Darder states, quoting Freire, that he

> was thoroughly convinced that the process of dialogue, central to his pedagogical project, could not exist "in the absence of a profound love for the world and for people."[5] . . . it was through such love, he surmised, that teachers could find the strength, faith, and humility to establish solidarity and struggle together to transform the oppressive ideologies and practices of public education. (Darder, 2002, pp. 91–92)

It is love that lies at the heart of the struggle to solve the contradiction of opposites that is part and parcel of a dialectical approach to learning, a point that deserves much elaboration in any serious account of Freire's work and that will be taken up in chapter 3, where I will draw on, among other sources, the work of Paula Allman. The entire process advocated by Freire rests on the trust he had in human beings and in creating "a world in which it will be easier to love" (Freire, 1970b, 1993, p. 40; see Allman et al., 1998, p. 9). This concept has strong Christian overtones as well as revolutionary ones, some of the influence in the latter case deriving from Ernesto "Che" Guevara, who, according to Freire, "did not hesitate to recognize the capacity of love as an indispensable condition for authentic revolutionaries" (Freire, 1970a, p. 45).

The emphasis on dialectics and on a dialectical mode of thinking, certainly reflected in Paulo Freire's own style of conceptualization (Allman, 1988, 1994, 1999), immediately recalls Hegel and Marx, the latter constituting, as I shall argue, one of the greatest influences on Freire, especially following the Brazilian's period of exile in Chile (see Gajardo, 1998, p. 44; Schugurensky, 1998, p. 19).[6] Marx's early writings are constantly referred to and provide the basis for Freire's social analysis in his most celebrated work, *Pedagogy of the Oppressed.* This book was conceived of and written during the first six years of his long period of exile involving spells in Bolivia, Chile, the United States, and Geneva. Freire has often acknowledged, in this regard, the influence of his first wife, Elza (died in 1986), and such close collaborators as fellow Brazilian exiles Plinio Sampaio, Paulo de Tarso Santos, Ernani Fiori, Francisco Weffort, and the Chilean Marcela Gajardo (Freire, 1994), the last mentioned being a colleague who, among other things, introduced him to the writings of a very important source of influence, namely Antonio Gramsci, and specifically to an anthology of Gramsci's cultural writings, *Letteratura e vita nazionale* (see Morrow and Torres, 1995, p. 457).[7]

Freire was exiled following the multinationals-backed military coup of 1964 that overthrew the administration of Joao Goulart. At the time of the coup, Freire was about to coordinate a nationwide literacy program that would have rendered several thousand Brazilians (peasants and city dwellers alike) literate and therefore eligible to vote. Because of this and the fact that his approach involved a process of reading the word and the world (Freire and Macedo, 1987), Freire's work was perceived as posing a threat to the status quo.[8] Asked in London whether his adult literacy work in Brazil would have succeeded had no coup been staged, Freire had this to say:

At least some Brazilians, in their negative criticism of my work, were able to find something positive by saying that one of my major pieces of luck was the coup d'état. In their view the coup spared me a tremendous disaster. I am not sure about that. On the contrary, I think that if the coup d'état had not happened we would have been very successful all over Brazil. We had examples of success. In Brasília, for example, for three or four months we had the opportunity to work with thousand of illiterate workers. We organized three hundred cultural circles, around Brasília in the satellite towns, with excellent results. The first experience in Northeast Brazil, in Angicos, in the state of Rio Grande do Norte, was also very good. I had there three hundred illiterate workers reading and writing just before the coup d'état. (Freire, 1995b, p. 65)

The Marxist–humanist element is all pervasive in Freire's work, which is, however, often judged to be eclectic in that it draws on a broad range of writings, including the work of Leszek Kolakowski, Karel Kosik, Eric Fromm, Antonio Gramsci, Karl Mannheim, Jean Paul Sartre, Herbert Marcuse, Pierre Furter, Mao, Che Guevara,[9] Franz Fanon, Albert Memmi, John Dewey, Lev Vygotsky, Amilcar Cabral, Martin Buber, Teilhard de Chardin, Jacques Maritain, Karl Jaspers, the Christian Personalism theory of Emanuel Mounier, and Tristian de Atiade (see Jarvis, 1987; Elias, 1994; Gadotti, 1994; Schugurensky, 1998; Taylor, 1993; Torres, 1993; Youngman, 1986) and the "secular, dialogical hermeneutics" of Eduardo Nicol[10] (Morrow and Torres, 2002, p. 26). The list is not exhaustive.

Pedagogical activity is discussed not in a vacuum but in the context of an analysis of power and its structural manifestations. There are those who often miss this key point and consequently adulterate his work by reducing it to a method or technique (Allman, 1996; Aronowitz, 1993; Macedo, 1994; Macedo in Freire and Macedo, 1995). In his early work, the focus is primarily on the Latin American context in which Freire, who was born in Recife (he always had a special passion for this city) in the northeast state of Pernambuco, drew on his experiences as an adult educator, the vocation he embraced after having studied law and taught Philosophy of Education. The context of his adult education work is the Nord-Este itself, one of the world's most impoverished areas.

Freire initially worked in a region characterized by semifeudal relations of production, which campesinos had to accept to gain access to land (Ireland, 1987). They therefore lived and worked in a situation of abject thralldom. The rural landowning class is engaged in a historical alliance with the national indigenous bourgeoisie located in the southeast, the São Paulo area (Ireland, 1987). The country is characterized by huge contrasts. In a discussion involving Fidel Castro, Frei Betto, and the Brazilian correspondent on economic affairs, Joelmir Beting, the country was dubbed "Belindia," that is to say, Belgium and India side by side (Betto, 1986, p. 33). It was stated at the time that, in Brazil, there were no less than 32 million consumers with a per capita income equivalent to that of Belgium. They thus constituted a huge market. Another 40 million lived in relative poverty, whereas 30 million lived in absolute misery. In between the affluent 32 million and the 70 million poor existed a working class living at basic subsistence level. The 70 million poor were said to live in a situation comparable to India, hence the tag "Belindia," which captured the sharp social contrast characterizing Brazilian society at the time (Betto, 1986, pp. 33–34).

The situation is one of stark contrast in access to material goods and power, in a country whose fortunes have been guided by colonial and neocolonial interests. Echoing Brazil's well-known sociologist, Fernando Henrique Cardoso,[11] later to become President of Brazil, Freire stated that the coup d'état brought about a "recapitulation to an ideology of development based on the handing of the national economy to foreign interests, an ideology in which 'the idea of the great international enterprise replaces the idea of the state monopoly as the basis for development'" (Freire, 1970a, pp. 41–42). The issue concerning the very poor distribution of resources in Brazil and the rest of Latin America rendered discussions regarding social class an important feature of such works as *Pedagogy of the Oppressed.* As Freire himself has admitted, this feature is conspicuously missing from his first published work, *Education as the Practice of Freedom* (published in English as part of Freire, 1973) (see Gajardo, 1998, p. 44; Schugurensky, 1998, p. 14).

Social class analysis constitutes an important feature of the radical Brazilian religious movement with which Freire is strongly associated. A "man of faith," Freire was certainly influenced in the development of his ideas by the radical religious movements that made their presence felt in Brazil in the late 1950s and early 1960s (Dekadt, 1970). There is a strong convergence between his views on education and the education document produced by the Latin American bishops for the Episcopal conference in Medellin, Colombia (this conference represents a landmark in Liberation Theology), a point to which I shall return in chapter 3. In a conversation with Carmel Borg and me, the then São Paulo cardinal, Paulo Evaristo Arns, stated categorically that, in his view, Paulo changed not only people's lives but also the Church; he made reference, in this context, to the 1968 Medellin conference.[12] This connection between Freire and the Liberation Theology movement persisted throughout his life. A year after Freire's death, Frei Betto (1999) had this to say about the state of the movement:

On the one hand, Liberation Theology is weak at the moment. After the fall of the Berlin Wall and the pressures from the Vatican, there have been no great advances and in some measure it "dis-articulated" itself because of a lack of support. On the other hand, themes that belonged exclusively to Liberation Theology are today addressed even in documents by the Pope. Suddenly, the Vatican publishes a document about Land Reform which could be signed by any liberation theologian. We now say that Liberation Theology is no longer a ghetto in the Church, but a leaven that has been "irradiated" so that one can no longer perceive the leaven because it has irradiated itself. Anyone who can cook can distinguish the leaven from the dough at the moment of mixing, but afterwards this is no longer possible. In a way, Liberation Theology is present as a method, as a sensibility towards social questions and the poor in the general Church theology, because the Vatican's disappointment with neo-liberalism, with the situation of the countries of the late Soviet Bloc, induces it to favor this concern about destitution and poverty. I would say that Liberation Theologians were marginalized, but Liberation Theology ended up by being incorporated into the official theology of the Church with all the contradictions that this official theology has, because it still carries great conservative weight.

On the issue of poverty, and therefore social stratification, Freire claimed to have made no less than 33 references to social class in *Pedagogy of the Oppressed* (Freire in Freire and Macedo, 1993, p. 172), and this led to some severe criticisms leveled at him, primarily by North American feminists who pointed to the invisibility of women and their experiences in his project of liberation. This criticism seems to have had a telling effect on Freire's later writings, including work that was born out of contact with the North American educational milieu. Issues concerning gender, race, and social movements began to feature prominently in his work, as I will show in chapter 4, where I also discuss the issue of progressive social movements and political party. One ought to remark that, in published dialogues, the Cape Verde-born scholar Donaldo Macedo, from the University of Massachusetts at Boston, with whom Freire had a fruitful association (Freire and Macedo, 1987, 1993, 1995, 2000), pushed him hard on such issues.

Writers such as Kathleen Weiler (1991) sought to fuse his ideas with those representing different strands within feminism. Probably one feminist writer who openly embraces his ideas, not allowing his earlier "phallocentric paradigm of liberation" (hooks, 1993, p. 148) to stand in the way, is Gloria Watkins, alias bell hooks (see also hooks, 1989, 1994a). She incorporates Freire's pedagogical ideas within the best critical traditions of African American writing. Freire's work, with its emphasis on libera-

tory pedagogy, appealed to other African American activists and intellectuals, including Cornell West (1994, p. xiii), who hailed him "as the exemplary organic intellectual of our time." From the mid-1980s onward, Freire
engaged in talking books (dialogical books) and coauthored texts with a
number of writers and educators, including the radical adult educator
Myles Horton (founder of the Highlander Folk High School, Tennessee),
fellow Latin American exile Antonio Faundez, Frei Betto (Betto and Freire,
1986), a group of academics from UNAM, Mexico City (Escobar, Fernandez, and Guevara-Niebla, 1994), and the American critical pedagogue Ira
Shor, whom Freire first met in a pizza parlor at Amherst in 1984 (Shor,
1998, p. 75) and with whom he wrote an important book (Shor and Freire,
1987). Ira Shor is one of a number of important critical pedagogues from
North America who are inspired by Freire's work. They include one of
Freire's earliest friends in North America, Jonathan Kozol, and such critical pedagogues as Henry A. Giroux (Giroux, 1985, 1996) and Peter
McLaren, the last mentioned having produced four books on Freire
(McLaren, 2000; McLaren and Lankshear, 1994; McLaren and Leonard,
1993; Steiner, Krank, McLaren, and Bahruth, 2000). In one of the last
works, which saw the light a few months after he passed away, Freire
responded to a number of North American–based critics who reflected on
his work in the same volume (Freire et al., 1997).

Despite his large output as a writer in Portuguese and English, Freire
did not forsake direct political activity. When in exile in Geneva, working
for the World Council of Churches, he engaged in activities with trade
unionists and other social activists from Spain and Italy (Freire, 1994) and
as a consultant to governments in such former Portuguese colonies in
Africa as Guinea Bissau (Freire, 1978; Freire and Faundez, 1989; Freire and
Macedo, 1987),[13] Cape Verde, and São Tome' and Principe. He later served
as consultant to the organizers of literacy campaigns in Nicaragua (see
Arnove, 1986; Carnoy and Torres, 1990) and Grenada (Hickling-Hudson,
1999; Jules, 1995; Torres, 1986).

His lifelong commitment to social justice culminated in his being a
founder member of the Partido dos Trabalhadores (Workers' Party—PT)
that was founded in 1979 through a left-wing coalition of unions, leftist
organizations, and social movements (Gandin and Apple, 2002, p. 100)
and is headed by Luiz Inacio "Lula" da Silva. As a result of this commitment to social justice, Freire served, on behalf of this party, as Education
Secretary in the São Paulo Municipal Government when Luiza Erundina
de Souza, a social worker, was mayor. There he engaged in reforming the
public education sector through the development of popular public
schools and adopting innovative measures in developing schools as learning communities with all personnel involved, from teachers to janitors
and cooks, being prepared as educators (Freire, 1991). He also developed
a strong adult education program, Mova São Paulo—Movimento de Alfa-

betização de Adultos e Jovens (Adult and Youth Literacy Movement). Grassroots organizations were invited and were actively engaged in the process (Freire, 1991, 1993; O'Cadiz, Wong, and Torres, 1998; Saul, 1995; Stromquist, 1997; Torres, 1993, 1994). These approaches, although dismantled for a while in São Paulo after the PT lost the elections there, were adopted in other municipalities governed by the PT, notably Porto Alegre in Rio Grande do Sul, where, since 1989, the PT has been leading a coalition of leftist parties (Gandin and Apple, 2002, p. 100). One should also refer, in this context, to the municipalities (including São Paulo) and states in which the PT gained power following the elections of the fall 2000.

Freire's writing continued unabated till the end with a number of works and interviews appearing in the months before his death and even posthumously, one of his most recent works in Portuguese being *Pedagogia da Indignação* (Pedagogy of Indignation).

He was due to visit Cuba in the first fortnight of May 1997 to collect an award from Fidel Castro, an event to which he had naturally been looking forward. At 5:30 A.M. (Brazilian time) on Friday, May 2, 1997, Paulo Freire passed away at the Albert Einstein Hospital in São Paulo, where he had been admitted because of heart problems. In an interview with Carmel Borg and me, Paulo's widow, Ana Araujo (Nita) Freire, stated,

All of a sudden, when he was full of engagements, projects and life, there came the heart attack that took him away. He smoked many cigarettes a day. His organism was compromised, undermined by nicotine. One of the kidneys was not functioning any more; he had a brain ischemia and his blood pressure was controlled by drugs. Unfortunately his whole circulatory system was weakened, but we never thought he could die so soon. (Nita Freire in Borg and Mayo, 2000b, p. 118)[14]

The spirit of this remarkable figure, however, lives on. It is constantly felt by those like me, who often seek refuge and solace in his works to recuperate that sense of hope and agency that can easily be lost as we are constantly assailed by the dominant hegemonic discourse of technical rationality and marketability. This sense of hope is communicated through the constant fusion of reason and emotion that constitutes one of the most distinguishing features of Paulo Freire's style as writer and speaker.

HOW MUCH IS LOST IN TRANSLATION?

An appreciation of the constant fusion in Freire between reason and emotion would lead to the consideration of a much-related issue—the issue of translation. The great majority of the works from which I quote and to which I refer in this book are in the English language, often translations of works originally written by Paulo in Portuguese. Those who read his works in English must keep in mind that this is only a part, albeit a substantial and, I would argue, a representative one, of Freire's output. Some works still await translation. We also have to ask ourselves an important question: How much is lost in translation? Carmel Borg and I posed the question, in the same interview, to Nita Freire. She replied unequivocally that those who read Paulo only in translation miss much of the beauty and emotional resonance of his work.

He used words of such beauty and plasticity, organized in phrases and these in turn in the context of the totality of the text, with such aesthetic and political force that, I repeat, they cannot be transposed so easily into other languages because a language cannot be translated literally. And it is important to emphasize that his language is extraordinarily beautiful, rich and full of his particular way of being. . . . Another problem for translators who did not know Paulo well is the fact that his language is loaded with his feelings, since he never provided a dichotomy between reason and emotion. Paulo was a radically coherent man: what he said contained what he felt and thought and this is not always easy to translate. There are emotions whose meaning can only be well perceived, understood and felt inside a certain culture. And we Brazilians are unique in this way. I think this is so, isn't it? Without any prejudice, I think it is difficult for translators who have only studied the Portuguese language, albeit accurately, to express Paulo in all his aesthetic and even cultural-ideological richness. (Nita Freire, in Borg and Mayo, 2000b, pp. 110–111)

The emphasis on Freire's constant fusion between reason and emotion is underlined. As I have intimated earlier, many of us experience this sense of an absolute fusion between the two human elements, even when reading Freire in translation. One can imagine how great our sense of this fusion would be if we read Paulo in the beautiful Brazilian variant of Portuguese. And yet I have come across a few North American feminists who refer to the "separation between reason and emotion" as one of the problematic polarities in Freire's work. There are those who would argue that his work promotes the rational to the exclusion of other domains of experience and knowing.[15] One wonders whether they would hold the same opinion were they to read him in the original.

PERSONAL REFLEXIVE STATEMENT

This fusion of reason and emotion became apparent to me from my very first contact with Freire's work, a first contact that, however, did not occur at an early stage in my experience as a professional educator. I had been teaching in the Maltese state school system for a number of years, equipped with a mixed theoretical baggage of behavioral and progressivist notions concerning teaching, before I encountered Paulo Freire's writing. The occasion for this encounter was the first semester of graduate studies at the University of Alberta in Canada. This experience was to change my attitude toward teaching, knowledge, and society. Freire's work, together with that of Marx, Gramsci, Nyerere, and a number of exponents of critical pedagogy and the new sociology of education, helped bring about such a change. I would daresay that his was a very significant influence on my view of the world from then onward. Although many other writers appealed to me mostly at a cerebral level, he was among a small band of writers who spoke to me also at an emotional level. The emotional impact of Freire's work is such as to render it distinct from that of many other male writers whose work influenced me profoundly.

Freire has taught me or consolidated in me several things. He helped me develop a sensitivity to the politics of knowledge and to confront a very disturbing question: On whose side am I when I teach or act? He has also taught me to appreciate the virtues of and ethical issues involved in dialogical education and to realize that this approach to learning, once again based on a dialectical engagement with the material world, implies not a laissez-faire pedagogy but a pedagogy that is directive. He also taught me that one should not shy away from working for change within the system, provided one keeps one foot inside and another outside the system. In short, one should be tactically inside and strategically outside the system, a theme to which I return time and time again in this book, especially in my focus on sites of practice in the last chapter. I have since begun to regard this as an important consideration for teachers engaged in the public schooling sector, who require support and sustenance from sources lying beyond the school walls. It is also heartening to note, in Freire, something on which several writers have been harping all along, namely that although social class considerations retain their importance within a critical approach to education (one should guard against the now-fashionable tendency, typical of certain reactionary and nihilistic currents within contemporary social theory, to throw out the class baby with the class bath water), there are other considerations of social difference to be borne in mind. In this regard, one cannot but appreciate Freire's engagement with feminist and antiracist issues in his later work.

For someone like me who was brought up and still lives in a country with a long history of direct colonialism, to use Edward Said's term (Said, 1993, p. 8) applied to situations characterized by the presence of an occupying force, reading Freire meant something else. It meant much to read Freire extensively and intensively after having been brought up reading texts primarily by mainstream European (mainly British) and American authors. Reading Freire, a "southern" author, and other majority world writers taught my colonized mind a lot about the social dimensions of knowledge and the need for its decolonization through reading, thinking, and acting beyond the exclusively Eurocentric framework.

Finally, for someone coming from a country with a dominant Catholic culture, Freire's writings on the prophetic church, with its basis in Liberation Theology, have helped in my conception of this church as a site of struggle. These and other elements in Freire's work resonate with my experience and hopefully the experience of several readers of this book. This is what has compelled me over the years to write a substantial amount of papers on the work of one of the twentieth century's most significant educators. The purpose of this book is to bring these writings together and develop them into a coherent piece in which I take stock of a representative corpus of work by this writer produced over a 28-year period. I also attempt to go beyond this task and demonstrate the relevance of his ideas for a specific southern regional context, very much the context in which I have lived and worked for practically all my life. The focus will be on the Mediterranean regional context. The attempt here is to give prominence to areas that do not feature strongly in the English language literature with regard to contextual reinventions of Freire's work,[16] given the preponderance of writings on Freire and Freirean ideas developed within the UK–Australian–North American contexts and the obvious Latin American one. My choice of the Mediterranean region as focus is also part of my attempt to make sense of the contexts in which I act as educator, researcher, and citizen. To this end, I conclude the work with a chapter in which I reflect on a few, varied "on the ground" projects with which I have had a connection as researcher, educator, or in the case of two of these projects, member of the coordinating team.

NOTES

1. Frei Betto is from Belo Horizonte and was very active in the Brazilian student movement. He has been active in the Christian Base Communities; among other things, he was in charge of the workers' pastoral at the Metallurgical center of São Bernardo do Campo. He suffered imprisonment (1969–1973) at the hands of the military regime in Brazil (Betto, in Betto and Freire, 1986, pp. 39–52) and has written extensively on various subjects, including religion in revolutionary contexts (Betto, 1986).

2. Taped interview with Frei Betto carried out by Carmel Borg and me in São Paulo on April 28, 1998, and reproduced in a Maltese Sunday newspaper. The transcript was translated by Lillia de Azevedo, whereas Frei Joao Xerri, who set up the interview, helped with on-the-spot translations during the interview from Maltese to Portuguese and vice versa.

3. Antonia Darder (2002) eloquently and lucidly underlined these points in a book on Freire aptly subtitled *A Pedagogy of Love*.

4. Quote also reproduced by Peter McLaren (2002).

5. Freire considers love "the foundation of dialogue" (Freire, 1970b, 1993, p. 89).

6. Plinio Sampaio, a good friend and collaborator of Freire, disclosed in a taped interview in English with Carmel Borg and me, held at his residence in São Paulo,

in April 1998, that he and a number of other exiles, including Freire, gained greater exposure to Marxist class analysis during the Chilean experience. This exposure added a new and significant dimension to the level of analysis hitherto derived by Sampaio from writings by authors to the left of Christian democratic politics. Before the coup, Sampaio was a congressman in Brazil who, like the Minister of Education, Paulo de Tarso Santos, stood to the left of the Christian Democratic party. His left-leaning brand of politics had, until the Chilean experience, been mainly influenced by the social teachings of the Catholic Church and the writings of such figures in Christian-democratic politics as the Italian center-left economist and political leader Amintore Fanfani. Information provided in the taped interview. Freire refers to Sampaio in at least three books (Freire, 1970b, 1993; Freire, 1994; Freire, 1996).

7. For an exploration of relations between the thought of Gramsci and Freire, see Coben (1998), Allman (1999), and Mayo (1999a, 2002).

8. Interestingly enough, Plinio Sampaio told us in the same interview that he had forewarned Freire of a probable coup, attributing this intuition to his experience of being a politician. Trusting his politician's instinct, Sampaio left Brazil before the coup took place.

9. On this influence and connections between Freire's thought and that of Che, see McLaren's excellent comparative work (McLaren, 2000).

10. See, for instance, Freire's reference to Eduardo Nicol's *Los Principios de la Ciencia* (Mexico, Fondo de Cultura Económica, 1965) with respect to the point, concerning the nonviability of a neutral education, that "the mere awareness of the fact does not constitute a full knowledge of it" and that one must transcend mere awareness of it to obtain precise knowledge of it through apprehending "the reason for its being" (Freire, 1972, pp. 174–175). He also referred to Nicol when making the point that the "dialogical relation does not, as is sometimes thought, rule out the possibility of the act of teaching" and this act is founded and "sealed" in its "correlative, the act of learning" (Freire, 1994, p. 117). The reference is to the same work by Eduardo Nicol.

11. Freire cites Cardoso's work, "Hegemonia Burguesa e Independencia Economica: Raizes Estruturias da Crise Politica Brasileira" from the *Revista Civilacao Brasileira*, no. 17 of January 1968.

12. This conversation was held in English in the Sacristy of São Paulo Cathedral, April 1998, in the presence of Frei Joao Xerri.

13. See also the videotaped interview, *Guns and Pencils*, featuring Paulo Freire, Alan Thomas, and J. Roby Kidd.

14. The interview took place in São Paulo, April 24, 1998. It was transcribed by Frei Sergio Abreu and translated by Lilia Azevedo. Frei Joao Xerri acted as interlocutor throughout the interview.

15. Antonia Darder's work (Darder, 2002) provides a most valuable corrective in this regard, as the earlier quotes from her book in this chapter immediately suggest.

16. There is much activity and research, from a Freirean perspective, going on in this region and in neighboring countries that, though geographically not bordering the Mediterranean (e.g., Portugal), have strong cultural affinities with this

region. The three Freire Forums to date, organized by the Instituto Paulo Freire in collaboration with the host institution and held in São Paulo (1998), Bologna (2000), and Los Angeles (2002), have shed light on the work emerging from this part of the world. Represented in these forums were such countries as Italy, Spain (Catalonia in particular), Portugal (there are such organizations as the Paulo Freire Institute in Oporto and the Paulo Freire Center for Social Research, University of Evora), and Malta. It is quite significant that the next forum will be held in Oporto (September 2004).

CHAPTER 2

Holistic Interpretations of Freire's Work: A Critical Review

In the preface to a book containing one of Freire's later pieces (Freire et al., 1997), published soon after the Brazilian's death on May 2, 1997, the American scholar Joe L. Kincheloe wrote: "I suppose Paulo Freire is the closest thing education has to a celebrity. Known or loved (or not) throughout the world, Paulo commands a presence unequaled by anyone who calls himself or herself an educator" (p. vii).

Evidence for Kincheloe's claim derives from the fact that publications and conferences celebrating Freire's ideas and evaluating their relevance to different fields and forms of social activism never ceased throughout the last 20 years or so. In addition to Freire's considerable output, we have been witnessing a series of studies concerning the application of Freire's ideas in different contexts. These studies include the ones by Shor (1987) with respect to the United States, Kirkwood and Kirkwood (1989) with respect to Scotland, and Roberts (1999) with regard to New Zealand. There have also been comparative studies linking Freire's work, or, in one case (Coben, 1998), refuting the linkage of Freire's work with that of other theorists or activists. The one theorist whose ideas figure prominently alongside Freire's in comparative work is Antonio Gramsci, and we have witnessed three books on this topic. In addition to the book by Diana Coben, who considers Gramsci's work more useful to radical adult educators than Freire's, we come across work focusing on Gramsci and Freire by the present author (Mayo, 1999a) and Paula Allman (1999). These last two works are very sympathetic toward Freire and seek to strengthen the connections between Gramsci and Freire. My work represents an attempt at a synthesis of the ideas of these two key figures in the radical debate on adult education whereas Allman's work affirms the indebtedness of both Gramsci and Freire to Marx (his work is given extensive treatment in this book) and specifically Marx's theory of consciousness in which the respective works of the Brazilian and the Sardinian are anchored. These positions were elaborated on by Allman and me in a number of papers that each of us published in journals or as chapters in books. Papers and chapters linking Freire's work to Gramsci abound, and one can mention here the work of Marjorie Mayo (1997), who links the Brazilian's work with that of Gramsci and Ettore Gelpi in the context of adult education for social transformation and that of Raymond Morrow and Carlos Alberto Torres (1995, 2002). Morrow and Torres consider the work of Freire and Gramsci in relation to Latin American popular education; Freire is one of the foremost exponents of popular education, that type of education on which Gramsci's thought has exerted considerable influence (Ireland, 1987; La Belle, 1986).[1]

There is a substantial amount of literature dealing with popular education in Latin America. Popular education takes on different forms in different contexts, and its rhetoric betrays a strong Marxist influence. It is often undergirded by theoretical formulations that combine Christian precepts with Marxist class analysis. This kind of popular learning activity has often been described as a form of "Catholic populism" (Paiva, 1995). The Christian Base Communities provide the context for much of this work that is closely connected to Liberation Theology (see Mayo, 2000). Ideas from popular education abound throughout the related and broader field of community development. This is an area in which Freire has been very influential. Margaret Ledwith (1997, 2001) explored Freire's work alongside that of Gramsci in the context of a critical approach to community development.

Literature linking Freire's thinking with that of Gramsci does not end there. It is widespread and has been developed outside the strictly educational field. Paul Ransome (1992), for instance, explores such a linkage, albeit briefly, in a discussion on Gramsci and intellectuals whereas Peter Leonard (1993) explores this linkage in the context of a critical and nonconventionally welfarist approach to social work. We are here dealing with education in its broader context. Other figures that feature prominently in the literature on Freire are the Argentinean revolutionary Ernesto "Che" Guevara, the German social philosopher Jürgen Habermas, and the American philosopher John Dewey. John Dewey seems to be an obvious figure with whom to contrast Freire's work, and there are those who would argue, often in a manner intended to detract from Freire's stature, that there is little in Freire's pedagogical thought that is not found in Dewey. Among recent works connecting Freire's thought with that of Dewey, in a manner that certainly does not detract from Freire, are papers by Feinberg and Torres (2001) and Abdi (2001).[2]

Dewey's influence on Freire, probably via the mediating Brazilian influence of Anísio Texeira (Gadotti, 1994, p. 117), who studied with the American pragmatist philosopher at Columbia University (Morrow and Torres, 2002, p. 3), is also dealt with in a book systematically comparing and contrasting Freire's work with that of Jürgen Habermas. In this book, the two authors, Raymond Morrow and Carlos Torres (2002), posit a complementarity thesis regarding Freire and Habermas, claiming that they "share a conception of the human sciences, the crisis of modern societies, theory of the subject, and pedagogical practice" and that, when viewed conjointly, their work can help "provide a framework for further developing and radicalizing the themes relating philosophy, education, and democracy joined in the great American pragmatist John Dewey . . . " (Morrow and Torres, 2002, p. 3). Among other things, this book serves to connect Freire with the critical social theory tradition and reconnect this theoretical tradition with Latin America.

The Latin American context is foregrounded in a book connecting Freire with another figure, Ernesto "Che" Guevara. That Freire's thought has potential for the development of a pedagogy of revolution, triggered by some of the recent historical experiences in the Latin American context, both in terms of guerilla warfare and in terms of peasant movements such as the Frente Zapatista in Chiapas, can be seen from this comparative work. To my mind, this work comprises one of the most thorough discussions on Freire available in the English language. The book in question was written by Peter McLaren, a prolific writer on Freire (this will be borne out throughout the book and elsewhere in this chapter), critical pedagogy, and Marxist politics. This linkage between Che and Freire occurs in a work that, like that of Paula Allman, stresses the Marxian and Marxist underpinning to Freire's thought with a view to highlighting the relevance of historical materialist thinking for a global strategy against global capitalism.

In addition to these conjoint analyses, we come across several books that contain at least one chapter focusing exclusively on Freire. The list here cannot be exhaustive, and among such chapters that come to mind is Frank Youngman's analysis of the suitability of Freire's work for a socialist pedagogy. This occurs in what I regard as one of the finest texts in English to date that provides a comprehensive analysis of the potential contribution of historical materialist tenets to the development of a socialist approach to adult education. The book contains, among other things, a brilliant and lucid second chapter, "Marxism and Learning." In one particular chapter, Youngman assesses Freire's suitability against the template he constructs earlier on in the book, a template consisting of a number of concepts he deems suitable for a socialist pedagogical approach. I shall return to Youngman's assessment of Freire's work and ideas in chapter 4.

One other prolific writer who engages Freire's work is Henry A. Giroux, a key figure in the American critical pedagogy movement who is on record as having stated: ". . . that anyone who took up that field [i.e., critical pedagogy], in some way, had to begin with him [Freire] whether they liked him or not" (Giroux, in Torres, 1998b, p. 141). Apart from writing what I consider to be a memorable introduction to Freire's *Politics of Education*, subsequently republished in Giroux (1988), he has also written on the relevance of Freire to postcolonial politics (Giroux, 1996) and on Freire's relevance to a process of revitalization of the public sphere in a period when this sphere is subjected to corporate encroachment and commodification and when a veritable war is being waged, in this sphere, on youth and children (Giroux, 2000).

Other examples of essays on Freire appearing as chapters in books dealing with more general themes include bell hooks' essay in her anthology, *Teaching to Transgress*. In this essay, hooks discusses the notion of an inclusionary politics of liberation and embraces Freire's ideas, as she does in other works, finding them instructive and inspirational, despite the "phallocentric paradigm of liberation" they reflect.

It is virtually impossible to do justice to all the essays on Freire that have appeared throughout the last 20 years. It is even impossible to do justice to essays on Freire that appeared from the 1990s onward. Some of these essays reappeared in edited volumes focusing exclusively on Freire, notably the two volumes for which Peter McLaren has acted as coeditor, namely *Paulo Freire: A Critical Encounter*, which he coedited with Peter Leonard (McLaren and Leonard, 1993), and *Politics of Liberation: Paths from Freire*, which he coedited with Colin Lankshear (McLaren and Lankshear, 1994). They follow the earlier well-known anthology of essays edited by Robert Mackie and published in Australia: *Literacy and Revolution—the Pedagogy of Paulo Freire*.[3] The first volume by McLaren brings together some of the best British and American names in critical pedagogy. Among the finest white male exponents of this approach in North America are Henry Giroux, Ira Shor, Stanley Aronowitz, Roger I. Simon, and Peter McLaren. Four of these authors provide articles in this volume. African American and women writers are hardly evident, bell hooks being the only one to contribute a chapter, with Cornel West writing a very brief, one-page preface. The piece by hooks, referred to earlier (hooks, 1994a), appears also in this volume alongside other memorable pieces. These include Carlos Alberto Torres's reworked essay on Freire, originally published in the University of Botswana's *Education and Production*, which provides excellent background material for an appreciation of Freire's work. The piece has been updated to include, among other things, Freire's work as Education Secretary in São Paulo. There are also Paulo Freire's conversation with Donaldo Macedo, Stanley Aronowitz's discussion of Freire's radical humanism, and the joint piece by Tomaz Tadeuz da Silva and Peter

McLaren on adapting Freire's theoretical insights for an engagement with the politics of redemptive memory.

As far as gender is concerned, the situation in the second volume, coedited by McLaren, is much better. There are six of the many women who engage with Freire's ideas in their work. Three of them coauthor their pieces with male contributors. Included is Kathleen Weiler's memorable piece that originally appeared in the *Harvard Educational Review* (Weiler, 1991). After underlining the important absences in Freire's project of liberation and outlining as well as analyzing different strands within feminism, Weiler explored possibilities for a fusion of Freire's insights and those of a feminist pedagogy. Other memorable pieces in this volume are the ones focusing on Latin America, notably the chapter by Edgar Gonzalez Gaudiano and Alicia de Alba, which examines the way Freire's work is taken up in Guatemala and Mexico and which assesses Freire's role within the tradition of Latin American great intellectuals, including Simon Rodriguez (Bolivar's teacher), José Vasconcelos, José Mariategui, Julio Antonio Mella, and Farbundo Martí. Equally revealing is an interview that McLaren carried out with left-wing Argentinean educationist Adriana Puiggros. Here, Freire's work is discussed against the backdrop of the history of education in Argentina, characterized by such historical developments as the process of nation building, relations between church and state, populist regimes, and dictatorships.

Other anthologies on Freire involving different authors from different contexts include two volumes published soon after Freire's death. The first of these, entitled *Mentoring the Mentor*, involved Freire as editor together with a host of other contributors, mainly authors based in North America. This book was in press before Freire passed away, but it was published soon after. It includes a memorable piece by Freire that consists of a response to issues raised by the various contributors to the volume. Freire elected to provide a more general response rather than answer each author directly. This essay sheds light on Freire's thinking concerning the issue of identity and difference, with specific reference to issues concerning class, race, gender, and the area of multiple, layered, and contradictory identities or subjectivities. Reference to this important essay will be made in this book, especially when I discuss the later Freire in chapter 4. The volume includes essays by established authors such as Donaldo Macedo and Peter McLaren besides lesser known ones. Among the essays that stand out is a piece on the relevance of Freire's ideas for struggles in Africa, penned by the Massachusetts-based Eritrean scholar, Asgedet Stefanos (1997). She wrote about education in the context of the struggle for liberation in Guinea Bissau, where Freire served as consultant to the PAIGC government, and the struggle for liberation in Eritrea (for a more recent elaboration of her thinking in this regard, see Stefanos, 2002). There is an insightful and revealing piece by Marilyn Frankenstein concerning the relevance of Paulo Freire's pedagogical approach to the teaching of mathematics, a theme she had broached in an earlier volume concerning the reinvention of Paulo Freire in a classroom context (Shor, 1987).

The other volume published after Freire's death is a special issue of the prominent adult education journal, *Convergence,* produced by the International Council for Adult Education (ICAE) with which Freire had strong connections, having served, until his death, as Honorary President. Freire wrote a memorable piece published in *Convergence,* titled "To the Coordinator of a Cultural Circle" (Freire, 1971, pp. 61, 62). I would consider this very short piece inspirational for practitioners seeking to reinvent his work in a nonformal adult education setting. In 1990, *Convergence* featured an interview, published in Spanish, that Moema Viezzer had conducted with Paulo Freire. The interview, which was subsequently included in *Pedagogy of the City* (Freire, 1993), focused for the most part on his work as Education Secretary in the Municipal Government of São Paulo (Viezzer, 1990). Soon after Freire's death, the then editor of *Convergence,* Deborah Wise Harris, assembled a team of guest editors, consisting of Paula Allman (Senior Research Fellow, University of Nottingham), chris cavanagh (popular educator from the Catalyst Center, Toronto), Chan Lean Heng (University of Malaysia), Sergio Haddad (a colleague of Paulo Freire in the Department of Curriculum at the Pontifical Catholic University of São Paulo), and the present author, to help prepare a special issue of *Convergence* that would provide a tribute to Freire. The final product was a collection of articles dealing with different aspects of Freire's work.

Some deal with more general issues, such as the introductory essay (Allman et al., 1998), which traces the evolution of Freire's thought, the overview provided by Daniel Schugurensky, and the analysis of some of Freire's key concepts provided by one of his closest collaborators, Marcela Gajardo. Others provide revealing biographical anecdotes. These include the pieces by Ira Shor, Budd Hall, and D'Arcy Martin,[4] as well as the preface, which provides important insights regarding the act of listening, penned by Freire's widow, Ana Maria (Nita) Araujo Freire. The piece, aptly titled "The Million Paulo Freires," by Rosa Maria Torres, deals with the different interpretations of Freire's work, whereas the article by popular educator Deborah Barndt focuses on a specific aspect of Freire's pedagogical approach—the codification.

There is an excellent discussion on Freire's relevance to people from the south working in northern contexts and facing the legacies of colonial struggles (Egli Martinez), besides a chapter on the impact of Freire's thought on African scholars (Prosper Godonoo). One comes across discussions on Freire's relevance to work within the Canadian labor union (D'Arcy Martin), work for social justice in a nonpoor context (Lange), popular legal education in Chile (Susan Macdonald), and feminist struggles in different parts of the world (Leith Dunn, Kate Pritchard Hughes).

The foregoing provides an indication of the range of available writings on Freire. This is by no means an exhaustive list and is selected from only one section of the vast literature on Freire, specifically literature in the English language. This review does not take into account literature written in other languages, including Freire's native Portuguese. Given that it covers a wide range of writings, the account perforce consists of simply an overview. In addition to the foregoing collective works, however, we have seen, during the last 12 years, five comprehensive and book-length single studies on Freire in English. These are the books by Taylor (1993), Gadotti (1994), Elias (1994), Roberts (2000), and Darder (2002). My book would fall into this category of writings on Freire, and it is for this reason that I feel that these book-length single studies deserve to be analyzed in some depth. I will also add to the preceding books another book-length single study that focuses on Freire. It differs from the ones just mentioned in that it focuses exclusively on one aspect of his work and not on his entire oeuvre. This is the study by Maria del Pilar O'Cadiz, Pia Lindquist Wong, and Carlos Alberto Torres (1998) on the educational reforms introduced by Paulo Freire in the city of São Paulo.

PAUL V. TAYLOR'S *THE TEXTS OF PAULO FREIRE*

The first book-length single study to appear in English in the 1990s is Paul V. Taylor's *Texts of Paulo Freire* (Taylor, 1993). Paul Taylor started by providing a comprehensive "biotext" of Freire's life, relying, in the absence of a fully developed Freire biography, on biographical references made by Freire throughout his large corpus of writings. The range of writings on which Taylor draws is impressive and includes primary, secondary, and background sources written in Spanish, Portuguese, and French. Taylor's knowledge of these different languages, very much in evidence in this work, constitutes one of the book's strengths.

It is surprising, however, that no sustained reference is made to some of Freire's later volumes in the English language, such as *We Make the Road by Walking*. I single out this book because it appeared two years before Taylor's book was published. Taylor's book came out before *Pedagogy of Hope* and well before *Letters to Cristina*, two books from which anyone seeking to provide a biographical account of Freire's life would have benefited, given the ample biographical material contained in them.

The introductory and second chapters of the Horton and Freire book include ample biographical material on which Taylor could have drawn to enrich his "biotext." This includes discussions concerning Freire's formative years in which the various influences on the development of his ideas are outlined. The Horton and Freire book, therefore, would also have been useful to Taylor for the purpose of developing his otherwise excellent chapter, "Backgrounds and Borrowings." In this chapter, the author does a great job of acknowledging, among other influences, the "European heritage," including important French connections, in Freire's thought. Omitted from this discussion, apart from the Horton and Freire book, is the important article on Freire and feminism by Kathleen Weiler (Weiler, 1991). This article raises important issues regarding gender that would have been relevant to the study under review, considering that Taylor is at pains to underline the sexist nature of Freire's early writing and the patriarchal nature of literacy programs, including many of the pictures used as codifications in Freire's work (Taylor, 1993, p. 93).

The chapter on "education and liberation" provides a good exposition of Freire's pedagogical ideas, yet it relies too heavily on earlier works by Freire, making few references to later ones. These later works mark significant developments in and provide important elaborations on Freire's ideas. One of these developments is Freire's rendering explicit the belief that educators and learners are not on an equal footing in the learning process, a point developed within the context of his discussion of the tension between authority and authoritarianism. *The Politics of Education,* as well as the Horton and Freire (1990) and the Shor and Freire (1987) books, are instructive in this regard. In my view, this point should have been borne in mind by Taylor in his discussion of one of the situations in his otherwise in-depth analysis of Freire's decodification process. Probably consideration of Freire's points concerning directivity and authority and freedom, on which I shall elaborate in the next chapter, would have made him refrain from producing such a statement as, "The most obvious (contradiction) is the overtly directive manner of the teaching. There is no hint here of a learning partnership, of a dialogue between equals. Rather, what is evident is the clear distinction between the teacher and the taught" (Taylor, 1993, p. 129).

The author, nonetheless, provides an excellent discussion that highlights the contradictions in Freire's pedagogy. The point regarding the need to write the wor(l)d, rather than merely read it, is well argued and can generate much debate. This is one of the key insights I drew from Taylor's discussion. However, given the author's background as an educator who adopted Freire's method and philosophy in community work, I was somewhat disappointed not to discover, at the end of the penultimate chapter ("A reconstruction of literacy"), any practical suggestions for the reconstitution of Freirean pedagogy in future literacy and community work.

Such criticisms notwithstanding, I would argue that the text demonstrates erudition on the author's part and is extremely informative and very thought provoking. It challenges Freire-inspired adult educators to reflect critically on their practice and on the basic tenets of the pedagogical theory on which they draw, encouraging them to recognize the contradictions involved.

MOACIR GADOTTI, *READING PAULO FREIRE*

In *Reading Paulo Freire,* which is a translation of a work in Portuguese that appeared a few years earlier in Brazil, Moacir Gadotti provides an introduction to Freire's work. This introduction is written by someone who, for 20 years, had worked at close quarters with Paulo Freire, having also been Chief of Cabinet during the time when Freire was Education Secretary for the city of São Paulo. Gadotti is now Director of the Instituto Paulo Freire based in São Paulo.

This book stands out among the books in English on Freire precisely for the accuracy of its contextualization of the key concepts we have come to associate with Freire. It also provides insider's knowledge regarding certain projects in which Freire was involved, in view of the fact that Gadotti collaborated with him on many of them. This applies in particular to work carried out by Freire following his return to Brazil after 16 years of exile. Written by a Brazilian, this book captures aspects of Brazilian culture that contributed substantially to the development of certain concepts in Freire's work. It also provides useful insights deriving from exchanges involving the author and Freire.

The book is quite comprehensive in scope, starting from Freire's early work in Angicos, proceeding with the plans for the national literacy program in Brazil that Freire had been discussing with Brazilian government authorities, the period surrounding the coup and Freire's eventual arrest, his period of exile in Bolivia, Chile, the United States, and Geneva, his African experience, and his return from exile. It also provides accounts of Freire's work with the Education and Society Centre of Studies (CEDES) in Campinas of which he had been a founder while still in exile. Light is also shed on Freire's work as Education Secretary in São Paulo comprising his curricular reforms involving interdisciplinarity, his efforts to create partnerships between state educational agencies and social organizations, and his contribution to setting up a literacy program for young people and adults in São Paulo (MOVA-SP). The book provides an overview of the entire range of Freire's writing in Portuguese and English as well as his intellectual influences, including the authors he had been reading in the early 1990s, which coincided with Gadotti's preparation of the manuscript for the original version of this book in Portuguese. Gadotti stated that classic and contemporary Marxist writers continued to feature among the authors Freire read. Freire's Christian faith is emphasized alongside his indebtedness to Marxist and other authors. Gadotti furthermore compared Freire's work with that of other educators and educationists, providing passing references to Janusz Korczak, Theodore Brameld, Pichon-Riviere, Pierre Bovet, Celestine Freinet, and Jean Jacques Rousseau.

In an number of short sections, Gadotti dwelled on four writers whose work invites comparisons with that of Freire, namely Carl Rogers, Ivan

Illich, John Dewey, and Lev Vygotsky. In each case, he brought out the points of convergence and contrast between Freire's ideas and those of each of these thinkers. For instance, in contrast with Illich, Freire believed that institutions such as the church and the school constitute sites of struggle and allow scope for transformative work. Instead of doing away with schooling in favor of learning webs, as Illich had suggested, Paulo Freire argued that work can be carried out within and outside the school to transform it into a popular public institution, something Freire sought to carry out during his tenure as Education Secretary in São Paulo and something that his party carried out when in government in other municipalities throughout Brazil. Gadotti argued that Dewey's notion of culture is "simplified" without the anthropological connotation that Freire's notion has, a notion that renders imperative considerations regarding structures of class, race, and ethnic oppression. He also saw Dewey's and Freire's respective educational goals as being different, with the Brazilian thinker linking education to "a structural change in the oppressive society" (Gadotti, 1994, p. 118).

This book also has the merit of shedding light on some of the works by and on Freire published in Brazil. Certain works are mentioned only briefly and perhaps, given that this is an introductory book targeted at an English-speaking readership with no knowledge of Portuguese, some further elaboration on these works would have been appropriate. Brevity and conciseness characterize the writing in this introductory book in which the author restricted himself to providing the reader with just a broad introductory overview of the background material that would help enhance one's understanding of Freire's work. Serious students of Freire's work are expected to deepen their knowledge by following up on the sources indicated in this book.

JOHN L. ELIAS, *PAULO FREIRE: PEDAGOGUE OF LIBERATION*

Gadotti's introductory book came out the same year that *Paulo Freire: Pedagogue of Liberation* by John Elias was published. Elias's book provides us with an overview of Freire's work. It focuses on the events that led to Freire's formation as a revolutionary educator, the pedagogical method he used in his cultural circles, the many sources of intellectual influence on which he drew (certainly in his early work), the fusion of Christian and Marxist ideals that underpin his writings and inspire his practice, the theory of knowledge that emerges from his various writings, his contribution to social theory, the revolutionary theory that can be gleaned from his writings, his critique of traditional teaching methods, his alternative of an education for liberation based on conscientization through dialogue, and his interrelated roles as liberation theologian and educator.

I feel that the sections dealing with the philosophical and religious influences on Freire are the strongest ones in this book. The author does a very good job of delineating and indicating, with sufficient documentation, the two main strands in Freire's thought, namely the Marxist–humanist one and that of Liberation Theology. That the religious dimension of Freire's writing features prominently and strongly in this book is hardly surprising, given that the author is a specialist in religion and education and has published several books in the area. He attaches due importance to the particular chapter in *The Politics of Education* in which Freire (1985) distinguished between different types of churches, a point to be dealt with in the chapter that follows. Elias also stressed the influence that Freire exerted on Latin American Liberation Theologians, notably Gustavo Gutierrez and Juan Segundo.

As far as the Marxist–humanist side of Freire is concerned, one welcomes the extensive reference to the work of Leszek Kolakowski, presented as an important source of influence on Freire. One, however, would have expected a number of pertinent quotations from the early Marx (and Engels), notably from such works as the *Holy Family*, the *Theses on Feuerbach, The German Ideology* and the *Economic and Philosophic Manuscripts*, to emphasize this important aspect of Freire's work.

One would also have expected an avoidance of such statements as "Freire, however, does not accept the economic determinism that Marx espoused" (Elias, 1994, p. 43). In my view, what Freire did not accept, as indicated in his interview with Donaldo P. Macedo (Freire, 1985), is the overly economistic readings of Marx by orthodox Marxists, as I shall show in chapter 3. I feel that Freire's work is imbued with that strong sense of agency that is also a feature of Marx's work.

As with Taylor's book, this work is quite comprehensive in its coverage of Freire's ideas over the years. The lack of reference to Freire's 1993 book, *Pedagogy of the City*, is understandable. Elias's work must have already been in press when this particular volume dealing with Freire's work as Education Secretary in the Municipal Government of São Paulo, Brazil, came out. Elias, therefore, could not have been exposed to the excellent analytic accounts by Carlos Alberto Torres of Freire's work in São Paulo (see Torres, 1993, 1994). This aspect of Freire's work is hardly given any treatment in the chapter, "The Making of a Revolutionary." Nevertheless, sufficient information concerning Freire's work in São Paulo was available[5] to enable it to draw more than just a passing comment that, in effect, constitutes a howler: "Freire is presently a Minister of Education in Rio de Janeiro" [*sic*] (Elias, 1994, p. 13).

As regards texts by Freire, the range of literature drawn on is quite extensive, with references also made to his later talking books. Once again, as with Taylor's book, the talking book with Myles Horton is overlooked. This book was published in sufficient time for some of its ideas concerning commitment, pedagogy, and the system to be taken up and analyzed in Elias's study. Two sources on which Elias draws are Freire (1985) and Shor and Freire (1987), works in which one discovers a deepening of some of the insights provided in Freire's earlier work regarding a liberatory practice of education.

This book completely overlooks the emphasis on directivity in Freire's later work (I would argue in the next chapter that this emphasis was always present in Freire's work) as well as the complexity of Freire's views on the relations between teacher and learner, not to mention the distinction between authority and authoritarianism and the tension between freedom and authority, alluded to in the introductory chapter and to be elaborated on in the one that follows. It is because of these considerations that Elias's statement that there are "areas which entail careful teaching and even testing" (Elias, 1994, p. 116), intended as a criticism of Freire, is problematic.

Neither does Elias's book take into account the multiple sources of oppression that Freire exposed in later works. The author also repeated the by then already dated criticism that conscientization does not necessarily result in action for social transformation. My major criticism of this book, therefore, is that it fails to provide a holistic analysis of Freire's work. Elias does not take into account points made in Freire's later writings regarding the need for teachers to work in wider contexts outside the school or educational settings and the opportunities provided by social movements and, in later discussions, political parties in this regard. I shall return to this point in subsequent chapters because it represents a key element in the development of Freire's pedagogical thinking. Elias goes so far as to state, "The works after *Cultural Action for Freedom,* which was published in 1970, do not add anything substantive to Freire's social and educational philosophy" (Elias, 1994, p. 14). I hope the chapters that follow can suggest otherwise. A more holistic reading of Freire's corpus is called for.

MARIA DEL PILAR O'CADIZ, PIA LINDQUIST WONG, AND CARLOS ALBERTO TORRES, *EDUCATION AND DEMOCRACY: PAULO FREIRE, SOCIAL MOVEMENTS, AND EDUCATIONAL REFORM IN SÃO PAULO*

Of the five books that I am reviewing in this chapter, this is the only study that combines theoretical and empirical work. It is very much a study about the *Pedagogy of the Oppressed* in action, featuring the presence of Paulo Freire himself. It focuses not only on Paulo Freire's actual work as Education Secretary in the city of São Paulo but also on his legacy in this regard.[6]

This is a well-researched book that provides a very detailed and in-depth analysis of the policies and actions of the PT government in democratizing the system of education in the Brazilian megalopolis through a concerted effort to improve the quality of public schools, democratize access, and most importantly, democratize in a concrete way the social relations of education and the knowledge content of what is taught in these schools. Furthermore, the process of democratization was extended to the administrative setup in schools, involving the revival of the school councils that had a pivotal role to play in the school's regeneration. It also involved efforts to encourage the active participation of all the potential and actual stakeholders in the public education sector, including teachers, students, parents, educational administrators, and community representatives. This massive reform of the previously neglected and largely underfunded public sector (the emphasis then was on privatization for those who aspired to a good quality and materially rewarding education) also included improving the conditions and financial situation of the hitherto underpaid teachers in this sector, with better pay being reserved for those electing to teach in the less-popular areas of the city. The improvement in the teachers' conditions of work was also intended to be matched by greater teacher resourcefulness and by a qualitative change in the nature of teaching that is conceived of no longer as an isolated activity but as an activity involving teamwork, research, and ongoing reflection on action. Importance was attached, in this context, to ongoing teacher formation through the setting up of *Grupos de Formação*. These reforms in the public education sector were complemented by a strong adult and youth literacy program, which, as already indicated, involved efforts to forge a partnership between the state, as reflected in the PT municipal government, and social movements.

The adult literacy program naturally and, as expected, was to comprise many of the elements one has come to associate with Freire-inspired popular education. However, the same can be said of the public school system that the Secretariat sought to develop, a system that was to take on board many aspects of popular education.[7]

The foregoing points strike me as being the main features of the reforms to emerge from this account. The book also provides the reader with excellent background material consisting of a historical and sociological analysis of Latin American and, specifically, Brazilian education. It indicates the landmarks in the development of public education in Brazil, provides a discussion concerning Freire and popular education, and offers the reader a concise and succinct historical account of the development of the PT. It provides a brief overview of the educational achievements of the PT administration in São Paulo and goes on to provide a brief account of the neoliberal turn after the PT was defeated in the 1992 municipal elections. The book also provides a fine discussion regarding theories of the state and then dwells, at considerable length, on the role of social movements in the struggle for power, with specific reference to Latin American social movements.[8] The authors also provide a highly illuminating account of state–social movement relationships in Brazil and the kind of relationships the Freire secretariat sought to establish with respect to the process of educational reform in São Paulo. I consider this to be one of the most important discussions in the book that dwells on transformative education being carried out in the context of broader social movements. The study also conveys the idea that those engaged in the desired process of curriculum reform can constitute a social movement.[9]

Most of the salient features of the process of educational reform in São Paulo, provided at the outset of this review, and the idea of a curriculum reform movement are described and expounded on in the chapter, "Creating the Popular Public School." This chapter is followed by an equally in-depth discussion on the interdisciplinary curriculum project, based on generative themes derived from the pupils' own social environment, developed within the participating schools. A number of documents and other sources normally used in the context of policy studies are availed of here.

The longest and arguably the most revealing chapter is the almost 100-page-long qualitative research study that exposes us to the realities experienced inside a number of participating São Paulo schools. Many are located in poor communities. Others are located in areas marked by crime and murder, whereas one school is characterized by the presence of a middle-class residential area on one side and a favela on the other. The voices of people involved in this reform process also emerge from this account, which, as with most ethnographic work, features numerous quotes from interviews with key actors in the project, tables outlining school subjects and generative themes, and the occasional thick description of teacher–student dialogic interactions (O'Cadiz, Wong, and Torres, 1998, pp. 176–182).

The interviews mainly privilege teachers' voices, and perhaps the study could have been enhanced by a greater presence of voices pertaining to other important stakeholders, notably students and parents. It would have also been enhanced with more thick descriptions from field notes of the type mentioned earlier. Furthermore, it would have been interesting to see some revealing disclosures by teachers and other personnel regarding not only the handling of social themes emerging from the pupils' immediate surroundings but also the learning process occurring with respect to those subjects and their content areas, which somehow relate to the dominant culture. Whenever discussions revolve around Freire and his ideas, the focus with regard to content is often on the popular, and these schools are no exception; they are, after all, designated popular public schools. This is as it should be, given the need to strengthen the school's link with the pupils' immediate culture as a result of which these pupils can experience a sense of ownership of the school and identify with the culture it fosters. And yet Freire has always insisted that the popular constitutes only the starting point of the educational process. I will return to this point later in this book. What also strikes me as missing from this book is some discussion concerning the tensions, contradictions, and obstacles arising from different systems operating within the same sector, the public sector in this case, and across sectors (a reformed and nonselective public-sector system existing alongside a competitive and elitist private-sector system).

The detailed accounts of life within schools are honest. They capture the complexities with which the secretariat had to deal. This process of reform met with a variety of responses ranging from approval, especially by teachers such as Francisco, who had shared the pupils' poverty earlier on in life, to resistance and suspicion, especially in the latter case by teachers who did not support the PT and therefore regarded the generative themes focusing on social issues as vehicles for the promotion of PT propaganda. Teachers who misconstrued the reforms' underlying philosophy often applauded them for the wrong reasons. Then there are those who were attracted to the project of the popular public school by the extra pecuniary remuneration (p. 173), and some of them made no bones about the fact that they were determined to keep on teaching the way they liked in the privacy of the classroom. Others complained that participation in the project entailed an increase in the amount of work they needed to carry out.

Equally honest and disheartening are the revelations that, despite the secretariat's intentions to create a nonselective public-sector system, teachers carried out internal tracking within the privacy of their classrooms. This is not unique to the São Paulo experience. It seems that certain teachers might find it extremely hard to break away from the selectivity and what can be called the streaming (tracking) mind-set. Others also fear the freedom to experiment, create their own teaching resources, and engage in preliminary research.[10]

The foregoing indicates that the discussion throughout this book is grounded in the realities of practice at different levels. It should be a key source of reference for any account of Freire's later work, one that dwells not only on theory but also on the relationship between this theory and the realities of administering education within a specific municipality's public sector. It also serves as a lucid and revealing account of curriculum reform within a specific context, with due attention attached not only to the process of developing curricular guidelines and their underlying philosophy but also, and most importantly, to the way the reform is interpreted or mediated by and reinvented through the multiple realities of school and classroom practice. This book ought to be recommended to policy makers and curriculum specialists, as well as to prospective and present educational administrators. It offers a refreshingly southern perspective and a welcome respite from the onslaught of imported ideas in educational administration emanating from northern contexts that often favor an unmistakably technical–rational approach.[11]

PETER ROBERTS, *EDUCATION, LITERACY, AND HUMANIZATION: EXPLORING THE WORK OF PAULO FREIRE*

The book on the São Paulo reforms was followed by a largely theoretical study on Freire by the New Zealand–based scholar Peter Roberts. Earlier, I showed how the Paul V. Taylor and John Elias books have their strengths. I feel, however, that Roberts's more recent *Education, Literacy, and Humanization* (Roberts, 2000) surpasses them in breadth of analysis. Of course, because his book was published quite recently, Peter Roberts had the advantage of being able to incorporate some of Freire's latest work. One ought to remark, here, that there are still more works by Freire to be published posthumously in English. Even so, the major shortcoming of the otherwise valuable books by Elias and Taylor is their failure to take sufficient account of Freire's work that was published in English in the late 1980s and early 1990s. We have seen that Elias disregarded the early 1990s work completely.

Peter Roberts differs in this respect. He gives due consideration, in the evolution of Freire's ideas, to both early and later books in English, thus providing a welcome holistic reading of Paulo Freire. This is important, given that in his later work, Freire stressed and elaborated on a number of points, some of which were already present in his early work but were not rendered explicit. In a collaborative piece (Allman et al., 1998), it was argued that "these positions were also revised in the light of the new experiences of oppression and emancipation to which he was exposed in the later years of a highly eventful life as educator, activist, consultant to revolutionary governments (Guinea Bissau, Nicaragua, Grenada) and ultimately educational policy maker and administrator" (Allman et al., 1998, p. 9).

Freire has offered us ideas and conceptual tools that constantly warrant further elaboration in view of the new experiences and challenges encountered across different borders. It is this aspect of the book by Roberts that gives it its strength, allowing the author sufficient material to engage adequately with some of the criticisms leveled at Freire by a number of writers.

In focusing on the evolution of Freire's ideas throughout his 30-year oeuvre, Roberts is careful not to go over material that had already been well documented before. This includes material concerning two of Freire's major sources of influence: Liberation Theology and Marxism. The book by Elias (1994) and Retamal's (1981) monograph, for instance, have dealt adequately with the former, whereas, as indicated, Paula Allman provided a most thorough exposition of the Marxian influence on Freire (All-man, 1999). There was no point for Roberts to repeat such arguments, even though he did take the concepts involved on board and used them to good effect throughout his text.

Roberts' holistic discussion, which reflects an intimate familiarity with all of Freire's texts that were available in English at the time of his writing, enabled him to underline the most important developments in Freire's thinking. Included are those elements that were implied in the early work but that Freire had to emphasize in his later ones to set the record straight, given the several misconceptions surrounding his view of education.

The one obvious point that Freire emphasized, time and time again, from the mid-1980s onward (it was always present in his work but required greater emphasis) is once again the directive nature of socially transformative education. This leads to one of the best discussions in the book under review, Roberts's engagement with Chet Bowers and Peter Berger on the interventionist nature of education. Once again, the distinction in Freire between authority and authoritarianism is key, and Roberts did a great job of illustrating this aspect of Freire's work, indicating that the kind of democratic relations advocated by the Brazilian educator is a complex one. Once again, the issue of authority and the danger of lapsing into laissez-faire pedagogy are brought to the fore.

Considerations such as these led Peter Roberts to defend Freire's notion of an interventionist pedagogy. In his critique, Roberts targeted not only Bowers and Berger but also postmodern feminists such as Elizabeth Ellsworth and Kathleen Weiler. Perhaps Roberts could have extended his critique to engage with other writers who have taken up issue, in a systematic way, with Freire. These include, as I have indicated, Diana Coben and Frank Youngman, the latter critiquing Freire for reasons that are much different from those that prompted the criticisms of Bowers, Berger, Ellsworth, Weiler, and Coben.

Apart from emphasizing the directive or interventionist nature of Freirean pedagogy, Roberts rightly stressed the collective dimension of learning in Freire's work. This, in my view, is of crucial importance, given the constant misappropriation of Freire's ideas by many who use and distort them within a liberal, individualistic learning framework. Although also emphasizing Freire's tendency to overlook race, gender, and other forms of difference in earlier work, Roberts foregrounded the Brazilian educator's later positions on these issues by taking on board the discussions concerning identity and coherence that feature prominently in Freire's later works, issues that will be discussed in chapters 4 and 5.

One element, however, that is missing from Peter Roberts's analysis and other analyses of Freire's work (my previous work included) is the recognition that Freire's discussions on transformative learning and difference remain encapsulated within the anthropocentric framework. I shall return to this point in chapter 4, drawing on writers who have added the bio-difference dimension to the critical pedagogy literature.

Peter Roberts's book does not romanticize Freire. Throughout this book, Peter Roberts portrayed Freire as someone who is inspiring, who has influenced generations of teachers and other cultural workers, but who, to use an important Freire expression, is incomplete, as is the case with all human beings. The flaws in Paulo Freire's thinking are a reflection of this incompleteness, which renders his call for an ongoing struggle for greater coherence all the more urgent.

ANTONIA DARDER, *REINVENTING PAULO FREIRE: A PEDAGOGY OF LOVE*

The latest book-length single study on Paulo Freire to reach me in time for inclusion in this chapter, dealing with the English language literature on the Brazilian educator, is Antonia Darder's lucid account of the relevance of some of Freire's concepts for contemporary struggles at the macro- and microlevels. Darder does not spend time and space rehashing the literature concerning the origins of certain concepts developed by Freire. Neither does she dwell on Freire's formative influences. Much has been written and published on these aspects, as this chapter will have shown by now. As the title of her book suggests, she is concerned about the way Freire's concepts can be reinvented in a predominantly U.S. context as part of the struggle by progressive teachers and other cultural workers for greater social justice, a struggle meant to occur within the context of larger progressive social movements. She heeded Freire's warning that experiments and concepts cannot be transplanted from one context to another, otherwise they would constitute yet another form of cultural invasion. They ought to be reinvented.

Darder focused on some of the basic concepts in Freire's pedagogical approach and elaborated on them. She dealt with Freire's advocacy of basic human virtues such as humility, love, tolerance, courage, hope, decisiveness, security, and patience (or rather, patient impatience, a point that Gadotti also stressed and that is a key theme in Freire's later works). She elaborated on these points by interspersing personal anecdotes with accounts concerning other teachers' or activists' day-to-day struggles in and outside classrooms and in the larger public sphere. It is evident from the very start that this book provides no dichotomy between theory and practice but is concerned with praxis throughout. Theoretical insights from Freire are elaborated on in light of the personal everyday experiences of progressive teachers. In fact, the voices of progressive teachers are reproduced in this work that ends with a long final chapter consisting of first-person narratives by various educators of different class, ethnic, and gender background.

"Walking the talk" is a key concern throughout this book, penned by an educator with a reputation for her activism in the struggle for social justice. Throughout her writing, reason is never divorced from emotion and the other noncognitive domains of being, a key insight gleaned from Freire. The kind of progressive education called for by Darder is intended toward seeing educators and educatees, the two key elements in the dialogical process, develop, through coinvestigation of the object of knowledge, into more integral human beings. And yet, this development is to occur by means of a process—authentic dialogue—in which conflicts are not avoided but confronted. Yet what distinguishes the confrontation involved in Freire's conception of dialogue from other types of confrontations is that the interaction occurs within a context characterized by a genuine love for humanity and a sense of solidarity with others for the creation of a more humane, more socially just world.

The emphasis on the lived experiences of teachers of different ethnic and gender background in this book has not led Darder to overlook the larger macrolevel issues that impinge on people's everyday lives. She analyzed these experiences against a scenario marked by the intensification of globalization and neoliberalization of policies that affect the work of people engaged as teachers, learners, and citizens. In the opening chapters, the author provided a very illuminating account of some of these processes and their encroachment on public or private lives. Particular emphasis is placed on the lives of people from traditionally subaltern ethnic groups, which reflects the author's own location as a Puerto Rican, a person hailing from a country still experiencing direct colonialism. Echoing Freire, Darder maintained that progressive educators and cultural workers must develop a strong knowledge of political economy to be able to, among other things, fully recognize the limited situations of their work and to connect their work with larger struggles.

The emphasis on courage is key because the effusive and enthusiastic nature of her writing on Freire, though continuing to render her book inspiring and imbued throughout with the message of hope that Freire himself always sought to convey, is tempered with a strong sense of realism. This realism derives from the authors' own experience as an activist involved in various struggles concerning social justice, struggles that involve victories and losses and, as always, reprisals. Her writing on the issue of political backlash is quite insightful in this regard; these insights are reechoed, in one of the first-person narratives, by a teacher who suffered reprisals from the school board for engaging in a struggle on the side of the students during her first experience as a fully fledged teacher. It takes courage and an unswerving sense of justice to persist with such potentially transformative action. Freire's account of the risks taken by popular educators in certain parts of Latin America, who risked life and limb to carry out their dangerous work (see Freire's and Horton's account of the situation concerning popular educators in Nicaragua during the Contra War), while serving as a stark reminder of the price to be paid for teaching or working against the grain, can also serve as a source of inspiration.

This book, written in a very lucid and flowing style, appeals to both academics and practitioners. Perhaps I might here be accused of reproducing the sort of false dichotomy that this book by Antonia Darder should have led me to avoid. *Reinventing Freire* provides a clarion call for activism and scholarly work to be combined—a process of praxis characterized by the inextricable intertwining of action and reflection for further transformative action. It deals with Freire's work holistically, with substantial material derived from both the early and later Freire. Key quotes from *Education for Critical Consciousness, Pedagogy of the Oppressed,* and *Pedagogy in Process* coexist with equally key and substantive quotes from *Pedagogy of the Heart, Pedagogy of Hope, Pedagogy of Freedom,* and significantly, given that Darder is constantly appealing to progressive teachers, *Teachers as Cultural Workers: Letters to Those Who Dare Teach.*

One quibble that I have is that the book could have been concluded with a short chapter in which the author provided an analysis of the first-person narratives and the themes that they introduced, connecting these issues with the larger issues from Freire's work and other sources taken up in the earlier chapters. Perhaps I am once again being conventionally academic here. I do feel, however, that such a concluding analysis would have certainly enhanced the sense of praxis that runs throughout the book in which reflection and action are intertwined.

CONCLUSION

This chapter was intended to provide an overview of some of the literature on the work of Paulo Freire produced in the English language from the 1990s onward. It has now become fashionable to complain of the existence of a Freire industry in view of the fact that studies on the Brazilian educator's ideas continue to be produced. This represents a cynical view of such writings. In my view, such a burgeoning literature continues to confirm Carlos Alberto Torres' view, cited at the outset of this book, that "we can stay with Freire or against Freire, but not without Freire" (Torres, 1982, p. 94). I feel that, as long as the studies being produced are rigorous, do justice to Freire's own ideas, provide fresh critical perspectives, and shed further light on the complex thinking of this often misunderstood figure, they are most welcome. Most of the works covered by this review make useful contributions not only to the debate concerning the relevance of Freire's ideas for contemporary times in different contexts but also to the process of exchanging views and experiences regarding creative uses and reinventions of concepts that derive from his large corpus of work.

Most of the writers included in this review chapter must have had their lives touched by Freire, and it is probably this more than anything else that compelled them to contribute to the ever-burgeoning literature on the Brazilian educator's work. I, too, have been feeling this compulsion for a long time, and this is what has led me, over the years, to write a number of papers on Freire and to revisit them and write fresh pieces with a view to producing this book. It is my sincere hope that this book will contribute, in its own way, to the ongoing rich debate on the legacy of Freire's work, a debate on which many of the authors cited in this chapter have left their mark.

NOTES

1. Morrow and Torres argue that there has been a certain degree of polarization with respect to the reception of Gramsci in Latin America. There are those who link him with a technocratic perspective. Here, the emphasis is placed on a critical appropriation of the dominant knowledge. This position brings to mind the Leninist revolutionary vanguard theory; it is regarded as standing in contrast to Freire's ideas. There are others, however, who posit connections between his ideas and those of Freire; they underscore the link between Gramsci's particular conception of civil society and that of popular education that is regarded as an important feature of the process of democratization of Brazilian society (Morrow and Torres, 2002, p. 79). This polarization stems from what has been perceived as being a situation of paradox characterizing Gramsci's work. This apparent situation led Morrow and Torres to pose the question: Are there two Gramsci's? (Morrow and Torres, 1995).

2. At the third Paulo Freire research conference, Douglas Kellner presented a paper connecting Freire's thought with that of Dewey. Also featured in the relevant session were connections between Freire's thought and that of Rousseau (Danilo Streck) and Gramsci (Peter Mayo).

3. For heuristic purposes, I am confining my overview of published English language literature on Freire to work that appeared from the 1990s onward.

4. Martin provided an account of his meeting with Freire and Betinho in connection with the video *Starting with Nina.* He does this in the context of a discussion concerning the relevance of Freire's ideas for workers' education, especially with respect to the Canadian labor movement.

5. See, for instance, the *Convergence* interview cited earlier (Viezzer, 1990) and the 1991 AERA recording (Freire, 1991).

6. The projects initiated during his tenure of office naturally continued under the direction of his successor, Mario Sergio Cortella. I would daresay that they continued to inspire reform in other municipalities in which the PT was in government.

7. This particular development is no doubt reflected in the term allotted to the public-sector schools that elected to join the project (schools were allowed the democratic right to choose either to join or stay out of the project)—"popular public." I will expand on many of the preceding ideas in subsequent chapters, notably chapters 4 and 6.

8. They provide important details regarding the nature and amount of social organizations and movements available in Brazil, to which reference will be made later in this book.

9. Needless to say, reference to the discussion concerning social movements and also state–social movement relations in São Paulo, as well as party–social movement relations, will be made in the forthcoming chapters on Freire's early and later work.

10. In the São Paulo case, they would fear the freedom to team up with others, work across traditional disciplines, research the community, and explore generative themes.

11. The book also becomes significant in an age when we are witnessing the emergence of a variety of projects connected with the concept of "learning cities" and "learning regions" in several parts of the world (see Walters et al., 2004, with respect to South Africa), including European regions participating in the European Union's Regional networks for Life-Long Learning—*R3L* pilot initiative (CEC, 2002, p. 1).

CHAPTER 3

Critical Literacy, Praxis, and Emancipatory Politics

Paulo Freire is synonymous with the concept of critical literacy. Critical literacy is to be distinguished from functional and cultural literacy. Functional literacy refers to the technical process of acquiring basic reading skills necessary for such actions as following instructions, reading signs, and filling in forms. Cultural literacy refers to the means of gaining access to a standard cultural and linguistic baggage very much along the lines advocated in the United States by the likes of E. D. Hirsch and Alan Bloom (McLaren, 1994). Critical literacy, on the other hand, refers to an emancipatory process in which one reads not only the word but also the world (Freire in Freire and Macedo, 1987, p. 49), a process whereby a person becomes empowered to unveil and decode "the ideological dimensions of texts, institutions, social practices and cultural forms such as television and film, in order to reveal their selective interests" (McLaren, 1994, p. 307). In the words of Myra Bergman Ramos, the translator of *Pedagogy of the Oppressed*,[1] it is the process whereby one can "perceive social, political and economic contradictions," which, one would argue, constitutes a prerequisite, once again according to the translator, for action to be taken "against the oppressive elements of reality" (Ramos, in Freire, 1970b, 1993, p. 35).

Two prominent critical pedagogues, Colin Lankshear and Peter McLaren, argued that this process is carried out in a context wherein the educators are striving to foster what C. Wright Mills calls a "sociological imagination" (Mills, 1959), the means whereby we are enabled to "perceive more clearly the relationship between what is going on in the world and what is happening to and with ourselves" (Lankshear and McLaren, 1993, p. 31).

Likewise, American critical pedagogue Ira Shor, who has for years been engaging with Freire's ideas, described critical literacy thus:

Critical literacy thus challenges the status quo in an effort to discover alternative paths for self and social development. This kind of literacy—words rethinking worlds, self dissenting in society—connects the political and the personal, the public and the private, the global and the local, the economic and the pedagogical, for rethinking our lives and for promoting justice in place of inequity. (Shor, 1997, p. 1)

It is a process, therefore, that leads one to view pedagogical practices in relation to the question of power. Pedagogical practice is viewed as a political act. This has constantly been a very important maxim in Freire's work as writer, educational philosopher, and pedagogue; it would be considered an elementary notion by all those steeped in critical pedagogy, although I still come across persons, in my everyday interactions, even among those involved in the education field, who persist in considering education a neutral activity. Critical literacy is conceived of by the many critical educationists, inspired by Freire's work, as a form of cultural politics. In Henry Giroux's words, it is defined "as a form of cultural citizenship and politics that provides the conditions for subordinate groups to learn the knowledge and skills necessary for self and social empowerment" (Giroux, 1993a, p. 367).

The reaction to Freire's advocacy of a process of education predicated on a critical or political reading of the world has been varied, ranging from accusations of being reformist (La Belle, 1986) and populist (Paiva, 1995; Youngman, 1986) to such approving comments as those by John Elias and Sharan B. Merriam, who stated that Freire's "theory is radical in the political sense of utilizing education to bring about social, political and economic changes in society" (cited in Youngman, 1986, p. 152). There are those who regard his critical pedagogy, together with that of such other critical educationists as Henry A. Giroux and Peter McLaren, as being full of repressive myths (e.g., Ellsworth, 1989).

Despite his many detractors, Freire has for long served as a source of inspiration to many. Resort to Freire's ideas has been de rigeur for several cultural workers from different parts of the world, engaged in confronting structural and systemic oppression through their specific areas of concern, as part of the process of imagining a more socially just, more humane, and more ecologically sensitive world.

In this chapter, I will argue that Freire's pedagogical ideas stand in marked reaction to a process of education characterized by prescription. In Freire's view, such a process serves to consolidate sharply defined power relations and therefore perpetuate oppressive social forms of being. I will also argue that contained in Freire's pedagogy are the elements for a model of an alternative society, very much a society not as it is now but as it should and can be. His vision is therefore not utopian in a fanciful sense. According to Gadotti, Freire's vision is utopian "not in the sense that it can never be fulfilled. For him [Freire], utopia is not idealism" but, as Gadotti (1994, p. 64) continues to point out, quoting Freire, "it is the dialectics of the acts of denunciation and annunciation, it is the act of denouncing the dehumanizing structure. For this reason, too, utopia is also a historical commitment" (Freire, in Gadotti, 1994, p. 64).[2] Freire stated that it is impossible for him to live without dreams but first one must know whether the dream is historically realizable and whether it allows a certain amount of time and space in which to move forward toward its realization (Freire, in Betto and Freire, 1986, p. 84). In this vein, Giroux argued that Freire provides us with a "notion of concrete utopianism, which embraces a notion of social change that is historical, conditional and contextual. For Freire, utopianism consists of the seemingly outmoded idea that education, in the broad sense, consists of intervening in the world in order to change it" (Giroux, 2000, pp. 139–140).

I would argue that Freire's utopianism is similar to Giroux's notion of an "anticipatory utopia," borrowed from Ernst Bloch (1986), forged in the struggle for the creation of a healthy and radical democracy, and predicated on equity and social justice (Giroux, 2001, p. 121). It is a utopia that, again in Giroux's words, drawing from Bloch, is "characterized by a 'militant optimism,' one that foregrounds the crucial relationship between critical education and political agency on the one hand, and the concrete struggles needed, on the other hand, to give substance to the recognition that every present was incomplete" (Giroux, 2001, p. 121).[3]

In the first section of this chapter, attention will be focused on Freire's analysis of the process of ideological domination as it takes place among the oppressed, with specific reference to the context that affected the development of his pedagogical ideas. In the second section, I will provide an analytic exposition of the alternative pedagogy that Freire proposes with a view to contributing to what he calls "cultural action for freedom." The third section will consist of a discussion on the use or, hopefully, re-invention of Freirean pedagogy in a postrevolutionary context. The pedagogy would here be viewed as contributing to what Freire called "Cultural Revolution." Both "cultural action for freedom" and "cultural revolution" constitute key contexts for the development of critical literacy entailing a critical reading of the world.

EDUCATION AND PRACTICES OF DOMINATION

In *Pedagogy of the Oppressed* and other early works (see Freire, 1970a), Freire provided an analysis of oppression that is rooted in Marx's theory of consciousness. Despite the criticism, referred to in the introductory chapter, that Freire was too eclectic in his approach, drawing on a broad range of sources (see chapter 1), one cannot deny the Marxian and Marxist underpinnings of his writing and particular mode of conceptualization. Freire drew on a wide range of early writings by Marx, notably *The German Ideology, The Economic and Philosophic Manuscripts of 1844*, the *Theses on Feuerbach*, and *The Holy Family*. These early writings by Marx provide important sources of reference for some of the arguments carried forward in *Pedagogy of the Oppressed* (Freire, 1970b, 1993).

Other writings by Marx, however, feature prominently in such works as *Pedagogy in Process* (Freire, 1978), in which Freire attempted to come to grips with the social relations of production in a former Portuguese African colony (Guinea Bissau) that had just achieved its independence. In this work, and precisely in letter 11, Freire adopted Marx's notion of a polytechnic education (Castles and Wustenberg, 1979; Livingstone, 1983),[4] advocating the forging of a strong relationship between education and production (Freire, 1978). Marx had specifically developed the notion of a polytechnic education in the Geneva Resolution of 1866.

Most importantly, though, with respect to the Marxian influence on Freire, *Pedagogy of the Oppressed* is written in a dialectical style, which, as Allman (1988) pointed out, is not easily accessible to readers schooled in conventional ways of thinking, often characterized by a linear approach. She demonstrates clearly that one cannot fully appreciate Freire's work without embedding it within Karl Marx's dialectical conceptualization of oppression. The more one is familiar with Marx's "tracking down" of "inner connections" and "relations" that are conceived of as "unities of opposites," the more one begins to appreciate *Pedagogy of the Oppressed*'s Marxian underpinning (Allman, 1999, pp. 62–63).[5] This is not the only book Freire has written, but it is the most compact and consistent with regard to his dialectical conceptualization of power (Allman et al., 1998, p. 9; Mayo, 2001, p. 257). In a collective piece, the introduction to the special Freire issue of *Convergence*, Allman et al. (1998) state:

Dialectical thinkers understand the internal relations among all phenomena. In the case of human beings or groups, this is a social relation which could be harmonious but which, thus far in history, normally has been antagonistic, resulting in various social relations that Freire collectively refers to as the oppressor–oppressed relation (e.g., class relations, gender, race, colonial, etc.) The antagonism is often so great that nothing short of abolishing the dialectical relation will improve the situation. When there are no longer the two opposing groups, the possibility emerges of human beings uniting in love, with a commitment to social justice and to care for all of our social and natural world. (Allman et al., 1998, p. 10)

IDEOLOGY

Freire's works, especially the early work, are anchored in a Marxian conception of ideology based on the assumption that

The ideas of the ruling class are in every epoch the ruling ideas, i.e., the class which is therefore the ruling material force of society, is at the same time its ruling intellectual force. (Marx and Engels, 1970, p. 64)

Marx and Engels go on to argue, "The ruling ideas are nothing more than the ideal expression of the dominant material relationships, the dominant material relationships grasped as ideas; hence of the relationships which make one class the ruling one, therefore the ideas of its dominance" (p. 64). Not only does the ruling class produce the ruling ideas, in view of its control over the means of intellectual production (Marx and Engels, 1970), but the dominated classes produce ideas that do not necessarily serve their interests; these classes, which "lack the means of mental production and are immersed in production relations which they do not control," tend to "reproduce ideas" that express the dominant material relationships (Larrain, 1983, p. 24). After all, as Marx and Engels had underlined, ". . . each new class which puts itself in place of one ruling before it, is compelled, merely in order to carry through its aim, to represent its interest as the common interest of all the members of society, that is expressed in ideal form: it has to give its ideas the form of universality, and represent them as the only rational, universally valid ones" (Marx and Engels, 1970, p. 66).

Paulo Freire saw popular consciousness as being permeated by ideology. In his earlier work (Freire, 1973, p. 44), Freire posited the existence of different levels of consciousness, ranging from naïve to critical consciousness, indicating a hierarchy that exposed him to the accusation of being elitist and of being patronizing toward ordinary people (Kane, 2001, p. 50). In *Pedagogy of the Oppressed*, Freire revealed the power of ideology being reflected in the fatalism apparent in the statements of peasants living in shantytowns who explain things in terms of magic, attributing their poor plight to the will of God (Freire, 1970b, 1993, p. 164).

Like Gramsci and a host of other writers, including important exponents of Critical Theory, Freire provides a very insightful analysis of the way human beings participate in their own oppression by internalizing the image of their oppressor. As with the complexity of hegemonic arrangements, underlined by Gramsci and elaborated on by a host of others writing from a neo-Gramscian perspective, people suffer from a contradictory consciousness, being oppressors within one social hegemonic arrangement and oppressed within another.

Their ideal is to be men; but for them to be men is to be oppressors. This is their model of humanity. (Freire, 1970b, 1993, p. 45)

According to Freire, the oppressed feel attached, at a particular moment, to their oppressor as a result of which they cannot view the latter as somebody existing separately from themselves and, therefore, as somebody from whom they can gain critical distance (Freire, 1970b, 1993). He goes on to say that this does not imply that the oppressed lack awareness of the fact that they suffer oppression but that "their perception of themselves as oppressed is impaired by their submersion in the reality of oppression" (p. 45).

It is a point that Audré Lorde (1984) also made, referring to "the oppressor within" (cited in Weiler, 1991, p. 464) and which, as Giroux (1981) has shown, makes its presence felt in several everyday situations as he writes of the "violence that underpins the discourse and social relationships that male subcultures display towards the women that share their experiences" (p. 16).

The same applies to the racism that white members of the oppressed classes, possibly even from ethnic minorities, direct toward blacks or other ethnic groups (cf. Borg and Mayo, 1994), a situation exacerbated by the constant reorganization of capital across different geographical boundaries (Foley, 1994, 1999) and that continues to create labor market segmentation on racial, ethnic, and gendered lines. Violent racist, sexist, and homophobic acts are examples of the kinds of behavior that indicate the presence of the oppressor's image inside the oppressed.

By indulging in such practice, the perpetrators would be striving toward their particular ideal of the human being, an ideal that makes them want to emulate their oppressors. Freire maintained that such a distorted image of the new person prevents those who project it from gaining "consciousness of themselves as persons or as members of an oppressed class" (Freire, 1970b, 1993 p. 46).

Echoing Eric Fromm, Freire goes on to maintain that, under such conditions, freedom becomes a fearful thing for the oppressed. They would be so domesticated that any activity that entails creativity presents itself to them as a fearful journey into the unknown. He states that the oppressed

suffer from the duality that has established itself in their innermost being. They discover that without freedom they cannot exist authentically. Yet, although they desire authentic existence, they fear it. (Freire, 1970b, 1993, p. 48)

He argued that they are simultaneously both themselves and the oppressor, having internalized the latter's consciousness, as a result of which they are left with a choice: they can either be themselves as persons characterized by a wholeness of being or else be divided because, in the latter case, they would not have ejected the oppressor lying inside them (Freire, 1970b, 1993, p. 48). This, for Freire, translates into a number of related choices, including those of either acting in human solidarity or remaining in a state of alienation, making choices or following prescriptions, having a voice or remaining immersed in the culture of silence (p. 48).

Freire returned to the theme of the fear of freedom and creativity in later work, especially in the exchange with Myles Horton (Horton and Freire, 1990). As Freire argued in his 1987 book with Donaldo Macedo, creativity involves risk taking (Freire, in Freire and Macedo, 1987, p. 57), something in which the oppressed are not encouraged to indulge. They are therefore encouraged to remain passive, immersed in what Freire called the culture of silence. They are not encouraged to question things. Neither are they encouraged to engage in creative and critical thinking. On the contrary, they are conditioned to obey, prescription being one of the key features of the oppressor–oppressed relationship (Freire, 1970b, 1993, pp. 46, 47). As I have shown, the theme of prescription featured prominently among the choices available to the oppressed in deciding whether to live a divided existence or to become whole beings.

Traditional methods of education, whereby the teacher becomes the automatic dispenser of knowledge and the pupil its passive recipient, would therefore contribute toward the perpetuation of existing structures of oppression—asymmetrical and dehumanizing relations of power. They are dehumanizing both in terms of those who are denied their humanity and are therefore the negative in the relation (the relation is antagonistic toward them)[6] and those who negate it by perpetrating a dehumanizing act and perpetuating a dehumanizing situation:

Dehumanization which marks not only those whose humanity has been stolen, but also (though in a different way) those who have stolen it, is a *distortion* of the vocation of becoming more fully human. (Freire, 1970b, 1993, p. 44)

Freire sees dehumanization as the key feature of the relationship between oppressor and oppressed, a dialectical relationship characterized by a unity of opposites. This relationship characterized by negation, the negation of humanization, is reflected in a variety of social relations within capitalism, not least being the traditional relationship between teacher and taught. It is a relationship characterized by domination and submission, positional superiority and being subaltern. Freire calls this process the "banking" or "nutritionist" (borrowed from Sartre) concept of education. In so doing, he reechoes Dewey's description of conventional education as "an affair of 'telling' or being told" (closely related to the "narration sickness," which Freire decries) and a process of "pouring in" (Dewey 1964, p. 38; cf. also, Shor, 1992, p. 33).[7] The latter image is remarkably similar to Freire's view of the learners, under such conditions, being "empty receptacles to be filled" (Freire, 1970b, 1993, p. 72). Freire described "banking education" thus:

Education thus becomes an act of deposition, in which the students are the depositories and the teacher is the depositor. Instead of communicating, the teacher issues communiqués and makes deposits which the students patiently receive, memorize and repeat. (Freire, 1970b, 1993, p. 72)

Freire maintains that, in this situation, the teacher is the *subject* of the learning process, whereas the learner is mere *object*. This process of education is marked by a top-to-bottom approach, and the pedagogy applied is considered by Freire to be that of the answer rather than a pedagogy of the question that would characterize a problem posing approach to knowledge and learning (Bruss and Macedo, 1985, p. 8). Banking Education entails a pedagogical approach that can smother any creative impulse that the individual might have. Borrowing from Eugene Ionesco's play, *Rhinoceros*, Freire posited that, under such conditions of learning, the good educatee is

he [*sic*] who repeats, who refuses to think critically, who adapts to models, who finds it nice to be a rhinoceros. (Freire, 1972, p. 179)

In Freire's view, banking education reduces any sense of relationship that the educatee may have with the material to be learned. The dehumanizing condition of alienation characterizes this process. The learner is alienated from the content of his or her education in the same way that workers, under conditions of capitalism, are, in the Marxian sense, estranged from the product of their labor. This 'estrangement' facilitates the ruling class' ideological domination of the subordinated classes. It renders persons receptive to the culture and ideas of dominant groups in society. Although, in his earlier work, Freire pointed to social class as the important variable in processes of domination, he projected, in his later work, a much more multifaceted conception of power, as I shall show in the chapter that follows.

This receptivity to ideas from above is what Freire calls "cultural invasion," in which dominant ideas, which mystify the social and economic arrangements, concealing their exploitative nature, become part of a person's "common sense," in Gramsci's sense of the term. They become the taken for granted aspects of reality, which enable a human being to consent to the existing arrangements, no matter how exploitative they might be in her or his regard. In this respect, ideology, in the Marxian sense explained earlier (the negative conception of ideology), is a form of cultural invasion. Cultural invasion also occurs from without as in situations of colonialism in its various forms, including dependency and neocolonialism, the last mentioned manifest in a variety of interrelated processes, notably an increasingly mobile transnational capital and the widespread Eurocentric mode of thinking. It is the sort of situation, for instance, that leads people from the small island state where I was born, bred, and still live (Malta) to excise the strong Arab element from the country's history to emphasize its so-called European vocation (Borg and Mayo, 2002a, p. 110). It is the same process that has led the African to see himself or herself as the Black European—a black skin in white mask, as Fanon would put it. We witness situations when the colonized, both in the country of origin and in the receiving country (in the case of migrants), seek to ape the demeanor of the colonizer. They would enroll in courses in the hope of not simply learning the language of the receiving country (no harm in this) but possibly also in the hope of losing their accent. This brings to mind the case, described by Fanon, of the black person who, "arriving in France will react against the myth of the R-eating man from Martinique. He will become aware of it, and he will really go to war against it. He will practice not only rolling his R but embroidering it . . . he will lock himself into his room and read aloud for hours—desperately determined to learn *diction*" (Fanon, 1952, p. 21).

Colonialism represents one of the crudest forms of cultural invasion, as captured in the following excerpt from the work of Ngugi Wa Thiong'o:

Colonialism imposed its control of the social production of wealth through military conquest and subsequent political dictatorship. But its most important area of domination was the mental universe of the colonised, the control through culture, of how people perceived themselves and their relationship to the world. Economic and political control can never be complete or effective without mental control. To control a people's culture is to control their tools of self-definition in relationship to others. (Ngugi Wa Thiong'o, 1981, p. 16)

Freire's good friend, Julius Kambarage Nyerere, wrote about the process of cultural invasion in Africa in colonial times:

Colonial education in this country [*Tanzania*] . . . was a deliberate attempt to change those values [*the values and knowledge of Tanzanian society*] and to replace traditional knowledge from a different society. (Nyerere, 1968, p. 270)

It appears that Freire saw the traditional system of banking education, certainly favored in colonial situations as well as in all contexts of domination, as serving to facilitate the process of cultural invasion. And one might add that this cultural invasion continues to render the content of education alien to the learners. They would therefore be deprived of the consciousness necessary for them to live "with" rather than "in" the world (Freire, 1970a, pp. 27–28). Elsewhere, Freire stated that such an education enables people only to adapt to their reality rather than achieve integration with their context (Freire, 1973, p. 4). The implication, here, is that, by merely being allowed to adapt, people would lack the necessary capacity to become agents of social change. For Freire has always insisted that "Men [*sic*] can intervene in reality in order to change it" (Freire, 1973, p. 4) and, later, he all too often conceived of "history as possibility" (see his 1989 speech at Claremont Graduate University reproduced in Darder, 2002, p. x). However, in merely adapting, a task they share with other species (this is a borrowing from Marx, which constantly exposes Freire to the charge of being anthropocentric), they would remain object, rather than become subject. They would therefore present no threat to the existing social arrangements, being more prone to *"adjust"* rather than to "integrate" (Freire, 1973, p. 23) and transform. Going by Freire's views, a top-to-bottom approach to education would operate in the interest of the existing social and economic arrangements, and using his terminology, one can argue that the education provided serves to "domesticate" (knowledge is complete, possessed by the educator who transfers it to the educatee) rather than "liberate" persons (in the latter case, education is utopian, prophetic, and hopefully involves a knowable object mediating "educator and educatee as subjects in the knowing process") (Freire, 1972, p. 180).

THE ALTERNATIVE: CULTURAL ACTION FOR FREEDOM

In most Latin American countries, counterhegemonic activity in education takes place outside the formal system. This is quite understandable because, in several areas of Latin America, a very small percentage of the relevant age group receives formal education. Robert F. Arnove (1986, p. 3), for instance, stated that, in Nicaragua, only 65 percent of the relevant age group attended primary school during the final years of rule by the Somoza dynasty. The same applied to several African countries during the period in which they were colonized. In his famous treatise, "Education for Self-reliance," former Tanzanian President, Julius K. Nyerere lamented lack of schooling in Tanganyika, now part of Tanzania, prior to independence in 1961, with too few people having the necessary skills and qualifications to strengthen the administration of government and even less people being suitable to "undertake the big economic and social development work which was essential" (Nyerere, 1968, p. 270).

Furthermore, Carlos Alberto Torres, in a chapter that registers the rapid increases in school enrollment in Nicaragua, Cuba, and Grenada during revolutionary periods (Torres, 1990, pp. 95–96), states that in many parts of Latin America in the late 1980s, "drop out rates in basic education are above 50% and the average level of schooling is 4.5 years" (Torres, 1990, p. 107).

All this, together with the fact that it is difficult to carry out counterhegemonic schooling under conditions of extreme repression, has rendered the area of nonformal education the ideal setting for a process of education for liberation. Because this was the situation obtaining in those countries about which Freire was directly concerned in most of his earlier writings, and certainly his better known ones, it is only natural that he should regard nonformal education as providing a possible and strong alternative context to education for domestication. This is not to say that he had no faith in schools. His later work as Education Secretary, captured in works published in the 1990s (see the next chapter), indicates the faith he had in the potential of schools, conceived of as sites of struggle, to develop into popular public spaces. This later work also indicates his willingness to even take on board, with respect to schooling, some of the ideas and practices that emerged from popular education. As I indicated in the previous chapter, this point was not lost on Moacir Gadotti when comparing Freire's ideas with those of Illich in light of the latter's advocacy of deschooling and the development of learning webs.

Freire referred to the nonformal activity carried out within the wide spaces existing outside the system as cultural action, the vehicle whereby members of oppressed groups are made aware of the social contradictions that lock them in a position of subordination. One of his finest essays of the 1970s is that in which he conceived of the adult literacy process as cultural action for freedom (see Freire, 1970a, 1985).

Carlos A. Torres (1982, p. 83; 1993, p. 126) cited Freire (1970a, p. 51) as expressing a view to the effect that "Cultural Action is developed in opposition to the elite that controls the power." Cultural action, therefore, constitutes the means whereby the oppressed acquire consciousness of themselves as a political force.

Cultural action involving critical literacy constitutes one of the areas in which, according to Freire, a sense of agency can be developed. In contrast to some of those who posit a mechanistic theory of reproduction and orthodox, positivist Marxists who favor an evolutionary economic–determinist view of social change, Freire provided us with a conception suggesting that the existing hegemonic arrangements are not permanent but in a constant process of making and remaking. They therefore can be ruptured. Things can change, albeit in circumstances not of one's own making. Cultural action is also intended to render those who partake of it the agents of change. In this context, he refuted the views of those Marxists who espoused what he called "a liberating fatalism," whereby "it is not necessary to make any effort to bring about liberation. It will come no matter what" (Freire, 1985, p. 179).

Given that the theme regarding a notion of history that "discards a predetermined future" but that "does not deny the role that conditioning factors play in the lives of women and men" (Freire, 1998c, p. 88) is a recurring one in Freire, he shared Marx's conviction that there is a reciprocal, dialectical relationship between consciousness and the world. Once again, history is conceived of as "possibility":

The materialist doctrine that men are the products of circumstances and upbringing, and that therefore, changed men are products of other circumstances and changed upbringing, forgets that it is men who change circumstances and that it is essential to educate the educator himself [*sic*]. (Marx and Engels, 1978, p. 165)

The central concept adopted by Freire to capture the dialectical relationship between consciousness and the world, reflected in the pedagogical approach for which he became famous, is praxis. Praxis is conceived of as a process entailing action—reflection—transformative action:

But human activity consists of action and reflection: it is praxis, it is transformation of the world. (Freire, 1970b, 1993, p. 125)

Freire went on to say that the whole process involved needs to be enlightened through theory and he related the whole process of action and reflection to theory and practice (Freire, 1970b, 1993). The process of action–reflection–transformative action is not sequential but dialectical (Allman, 1999). An education based on praxis is one whereby people act on their material surroundings and reflect on them with a view to transforming them. It is praxis that lies at the heart of Paulo Freire's notion of critical literacy. Freire and other intellectuals, with whom he has conversed in talking books, conceived of different moments in their life as forms of praxis. They are viewed as moments when they gain critical distance from the context they know to perceive it in a more critical light. For instance, Freire and the Chilean Antonio Faundez (Freire and Faundez, 1989) regarded exile as a form of praxis. Freire made statements to this effect also in the exchange with Ricardo Kotscho and Frei Betto. He referred to the period of exile as one that provided a profoundly pedagogical experience, thus echoing Betto who also presented, in the same book, his four-year experience of imprisonment under the military dictatorship, first as a political prisoner and later as a common prisoner, as one that had a strong and important pedagogical dimension. Freire's period of exile is presented as a time during which he gained distance from Brazil and began to understand himself and Brazil better. It was a case of obtaining distance from what he had carried out in Brazil to prepare himself better to continue being active outside his context. Freire argued that one must seek political engagement in the "borrowed context," accepting the new context with all its cultural attributes and without making disparaging value judgments about it. Critical distance from what he had carried out in Brazil also enabled Freire to prepare himself for an eventual return to his homeland (Freire in Betto and Freire, 1986, p. 58). It was a Brazil that had to be "relearned" following the long period of exile (Freire in Gadotti, Freire, and Guimarães, 1995, p. 13). The country of origin continues to serve as the focus of praxis even following one's return from exile. Freire said, on his return, that he came back to relearn Brazil and not to teach those who remained in Brazil (people like Frei Betto who stayed in Brazil during the dictatorship) as "internal exiles" (Freire, in Betto and Freire, 1986, p. 60).

With regard to praxis, one ought to underline Freire's view that action on its own, isolated from reflection, constitutes mindless activism. Likewise, reflection on its own, divorced from action, constitutes empty theorizing. It is for this reason that Freire, in keeping with the Marxist tradition, regarded one's material surroundings as the basis for the development of one's consciousness. In the words of Marx and Engels, "Consciousness is, therefore, from the beginning a social product, and remains so as long as men [sic] exist at all" (Marx and Engels, 1970, p. 51).

Cultural action is concerned with the relationship between knowledge and one's material existence. For Freire, the starting point was always that of human beings "in the 'here and now,'" that is to say, the human beings' current situation "from which they emerge, and in which they intervene" (Freire, 1970b, 1993, p. 85).

The foregoing considerations led Freire to conclude, in the words of Youngman (1986), "that education must help people in the process of objectifying the world, critically understanding it, and acting to change it" (p. 171). In doing so, they would be engaged in negating the negation, meaning the negation, in the latter sense, of the conditions for their ongoing humanization by those who are dehumanizing themselves through their partaking of the process of dehumanizing others (see Allman, 2001, p. 41).

The much-celebrated Metodo Paulo Freire constitutes an attempt to pedagogically address the foregoing considerations concerning humanization and power. It involves a process of conscientização (Freire, 1976) or conscientization through the teaching of literacy. And the process of conscientization is central to the process of critical literacy itself. The term is strongly associated with Freire, even though he is on record as having said that he should not be credited with it (Zachariah, 1986, p. 36). It is a term that had been employed by Brazilian radicals in the 1960s (p. 28), and Freire singled out Dom Helder Camara, then Bishop of Recife, as the individual who helped render it popular, enabling its use to become widespread in English (p. 36). It is also a term that Freire stopped using after 1974. He felt that it had been used in a rather loose manner, as a result of which its actual significance began to be undermined (Freire, 1993, p. 110).

Paulo was not using the word conscientização anymore (conscientização did not exist as a Portuguese word. D. Helder Câmara used it, but it was Paulo who filled it with such meaning). This was because of the criticism he had received from those who understood it to be an idealistic concept. However, lately, he used to tell me he was going to use it again, because he found it to be very rich: it indicates movement, the beginning of an action, preparation of the action that must follow.

In no way did it indicate a sense of "spontaneity" or "voluntarism." Neither did it imply that unchecked action or idealism were among its ingredients. In short, he did not intend it to convey a sense lacking in or separated from true political praxis, the praxis that reaches for theory, and goes back to it, illuminating it. (Nita Freire, in Borg and Mayo, 2000a, p. 110)

This led Freire to clarify the concept in various places (Freire, 1993, p. 111).

As soon as I heard it, I realized the profundity of its meaning since I was fully convinced that education, as an exercise in freedom, is an act of knowing, a critical approach to reality. (Freire, in Zachariah, 1986, p. 36)

In an interview with Carlos Alberto Torres, he described conscientization as "the deepening of the coming of consciousness" and argued that "There can be no conscientization without coming first into consciousness . . . " (Freire, 1993, p. 110). Coming into consciousness referred to the process of taking distance from objects, all part of the process of engaging in critical literacy. In reference to the experience of exile, we have seen how the process of gaining distance is central to the pedagogy of praxis involved. Conscientização was often associated with class knowledge and practice, as indicated by Torres (1990, p. 8), who went on to argue: "It appears as part of the 'subjective conditions' of the process of social transformation." Later, conscientização began to be associated with the subjugated knowledge of a broader range of social groups. In short, conscientização began to be associated with the subaltern in their wider and variegated contexts.

The approach adopted by Freire in his early work among adults involved a preliminary phase during which the educators were to spend time in the community in question gaining access to the people's universe of knowledge, including their vocabulary and speech patterns. They had to engage in "an arduous search for generative words" at the level of "syllabic richness" and high "experiential involvement" (Goulet, 1973, p. 11). This was to be followed by an initial codification of these words into visual images and other cultural products that would enable those who are submerged in the culture from which these elements emerged to gain critical distance from them. This was to be followed by a decodification process. Through the promptings of the coordinator and by means of dialogue and coinvestigation, the participants were to be encouraged to unveil, with the rest of the cultural circle, aspects of their own reality so that they could begin to perceive them differently and in a more critical light. A new codification was to follow whereby the participants were to become subjects of their own history (adapted from Goulet's summary, Goulet, 1973, p. 11). Of course, one is not expected by Freire to make a fetish (Aronowitz, 1993) out of this approach. What is more important is the philosophy of learning that underlies this approach, a philosophy based on a concept of praxis that continually has to be reinvented in view of ever-changing situations and contexts.

Of primary concern is the set of political principles involved in this approach, including that of rendering the culture of the learner the basis and initial stage of his or her learning (educators often research the participants' surrounding community in tandem with the participants themselves), the collective dimension of learning, the concept of dialogue, and of course, learning through praxis. Because the process throughout is a dialogical one through which the educator learns from the educatees in the same way that the latter learn from her or him, the roles of educator and learner become almost interchangeable. In what has become a classic formulation, Freire wrote in terms of "teacher–student" and "students–teachers." The teacher was thus conceived of as a person who, when engaging in dialogue with the students, is also being taught by them while the students are also teaching while being taught (Freire, 1970b, 1993, p. 80). In later work, Freire argued that

Liberatory education is fundamentally a situation where the teacher and the students *both* have to be learners, *both* have to be cognitive subjects, in spite of their being different. This for me is the first test of liberating education, for teachers and students both to be critical agents in the act of knowing. (Freire, in Shor and Freire, 1987, p. 33)

Freire considered both educators and educatees as subjects in a humanizing relationship marked by solidarity. The learner's reality constitutes an integral part of the subject matter that, therefore, becomes a mediator between the two subjects in question (i.e., educator and educatee). In his conversation with Ira Shor, Freire made an even bolder statement regarding the educator–educatee relationship. He stated that the dialogical process of education represents "the sealing together of the teacher and the students in the joint act of knowing and re-knowing the object" (Shor and Freire, 1987, p. 100). As Ira Shor argued, in the kind of dialogical education proposed by Freire, anything that the educator already knows is relearned when studied again with the educatees, a point confirmed by Freire in the same conversation (Shor and Freire, 1987). Freire (1985) stressed the need for reciprocal learning, arguing, with reference to peasants as learners, that

I have continually insisted that we must learn from peasants because I see them as learners at a particular moment in my educational practice. We can learn a great deal from the very students we teach. (p. 177)

The task of the educator is to learn the culture and community in which the learner is immersed, and this explains the first stage of the codification/decodification process described in detail by Freire in his early work. The educator would therefore move across the boundaries of his or her location to understand and act in solidarity with the learners, no longer perceived as "Other." The learners also assume the mantle of educators enabling the educator and other colearners in the group to cross the boundaries of their location.[8]

One may argue, therefore, that both educators and educatees are agents in this process. "Education must begin with the solution of the teacher–student contradiction, by reconciling the poles of the contradiction so that both are simultaneously teachers and students" (Freire, 1970b, 1993, p. 72). This constitutes an attempt to overcome the dialectical contradiction of opposites—teacher and taught are "the unity of opposites"— that is a feature of traditional education (Allman, 1994, p. 153).

One will have noticed my emphasis on the word *attempt*. I do not think that this process will ever be completely overcome, especially given Freire's insistence that educator and educatee are not on an equal footing in the educational process involved. While exhorting educators to learn from learners, Freire states that:

Obviously, we also have to underscore that while we recognize that we have to learn from our students . . . this does not mean that teachers and students are the same . . . there is a difference between the educator and the student. (Freire, 1985, p. 177)

For one thing, as a host of writers in critical pedagogy have shown, it would be amiss to celebrate student voices uncritically because they are never innocent (Aronowitz and Giroux, 1991, pp. 130–131). They contain various manifestations of the Oppressor consciousness that ought to be challenged. Dialogue, as conceived of by Freire, also involves educators allowing themselves to be challenged and to also constantly undergo self-reflection and scrutiny to confront the Oppressor consciousness within.

The *directive* nature of the educational process is affirmed (see, for instance, the discussion with Moacir Gadotti and Sergio Guimarães published in Brazil in 1989—Freire, in Gadotti, Freire, and Guimarães, 1995, p. 50). Guarding against the perceived danger of a laissez-faire pedagogy, resulting from a misconception of his particular notion of dialogue, Freire emphasized this directivity in the conversation with Ira Shor and elsewhere: "At the moment the teacher begins the dialogue, he or she knows a great deal, first in terms of knowledge and second in terms of the horizon that he or she wants to get to. The starting point is what the teacher knows about the object and where the teacher wants to go with it" (Freire, in Shor and Freire, 1987, p. 103).

Freire made it clear that he believed that the educators' pedagogical action is guided by a particular political vision and theoretical understanding. Freire, after all, considered education to be a political act, there being no such thing as a neutral education, with educators having to answer the question "for whom and on whose behalf they are working" (Freire, 1985, p. 180). In an exchange with academics and students at the University of Bologna, on the occasion of the conferment of an Honoris Causa doctoral degree in 1989, he stated that the learning experience entails a process of research and curiosity with all the elements involved— teacher, student, knowing object, methods, techniques—providing direction (Freire, in Fabbri and Gomes, 1995, p. 96). He argued that it is for this reason that every form of educational practice is directive but not necessarily manipulative and that every educational practice cannot be neutral; a directive practice cannot be neutral—no one is neutral when facing an objective to be reached (Freire, in Fabbri and Gomes, 1995). I will indicate in the following chapter that in his later works, Freire continued to underline the point about the directive and interventionist nature of education, in view of the misconceptions about his pedagogical ideas, which continue to abound. In the earlier conversation with Ira Shor, he argued that the goal of the educator, when teaching, is bound up with the political project that she or he bears in mind:

Dialogue does not exist in a political vacuum. It is not a "free space" where you say what you want. Dialogue takes place inside some program and content. These conditioning factors create tension in achieving goals that we set for dialogic education. To achieve the goals of transformation, dialogue implies responsibility, directiveness, determination, discipline, objectives. (Freire, in Shor and Freire, 1987, p. 102)

Teachers therefore have a directive role; they need to exercise their authority, an authority derived from their competence as pedagogues. Freire however made an important distinction between *authority* and *authoritarianism.* It is imperative that the authority derived from one's pedagogical competence does not degenerate into authoritarianism: ". . . the democratic teacher never, never transforms authority into authoritarianism" (Freire, in Shor and Freire, 1987, p. 91).[9] This authoritarianism would render the difference that exists between educator and educatee "antagonistic" (Freire, in Gadotti, Freire, and Guimarães, 1995, p. 50). The educator exercises what one of Freire's great disciples, Ira Shor, called "democratic authority" (Shor, 1992, pp. 156–158).[10] Dwelling on this insight within the context of teacher–student interactions in the classroom, Shor stated,

The teacher leads and directs the curriculum, but does so democratically with the participation of the students, balancing the need for structure with the need for openness. The teacher brings lesson plans, learning methods, personal experience, and academic knowledge to class but negotiates the curriculum with the students and begins with their language, themes, and understandings. To be democratic implies orienting subject matter to student culture—their interests, needs, speech, and perceptions—while creating negotiable openness in class where the students' input jointly creates the learning process. (Shor, 1992, p. 16)

Freire's revolutionary approach also entails that the educator does not possess or own the object to be known. In this respect, this educator differs from his or her reactionary counterpart who owns this object and transfers it onto the educatee. The reactionary educator "walks" with the object in hand. The revolutionary educator does not consider himself or herself as the possessor of the object of knowing. Though not being on a par with the educatee with respect to prior access to this object of knowledge, the educator engages in a process of collective unveiling of this object of knowing together with another "knowing subject" or "knowing subjects"—the educatee or educatees (Freire, in Gadotti, Freire, and Guimarães, 1995, pp. 42–43). Once again, this process allows possibilities for conflicts to emerge and be expressed, conflicts that, however, can be overcome because they occur among people who are different but who engage in a learning relationship that is not antagonistic (Freire in Gadotti, Freire, and Guimarães, 1995, p. 14).

As he explained in an audiotape, Freire (1974) felt that, in the case of the reactionary educator, the knowledge this person possesses, that is often captured in the lesson plan, is regarded by the educator as being complete. In the case of the revolutionary educator, the knowledge is perceived as something dynamic, an object of further investigation and unveiling that necessitates the participation of coknowing subjects—the educatees. The process of knowing involved, with respect to the object of knowledge, is considered by both educator and educatee as incomplete. In this respect, Paula Allman wrote,

Freire argues that this is a very different form of education. It begins with teachers having a different theory or concept of knowledge, which arises from and then exists in unity with a transformed relation to knowledge. And I can testify to the fact that when you take what he is saying seriously and try to apply it, you will experience the difference. It is a revolutionary–transformational–difference that acts as a catalyst for even more profound transformations. These . . . involve every participant in the learning group struggling to transform simultaneously the relation between teacher and students and each person's relation to knowledge. And, in so doing, they dialectically reunite the processes of teaching and learning within themselves. (Allman, 2001, p. 174)

Freire has even advocated tact and prudence when engaging in a dialogical approach, conceding that people who have been conditioned by many years of exposure to banking education do not immediately shrug aside the legacy of this experience to embrace dialogue. They often resist attempts at dialogue, perhaps even misconstruing a dialogical approach for lack of competence on the teacher's part. And of course, Freire would concede that some instruction is necessary at times. It is for this reason that he once stated that an educator can alternate between traditional and progressive teaching. It is as though he seems to be saying that, in such difficult circumstances, dialogue should be introduced only gradually (see Horton and Freire, 1990, p. 160). Elements of the old pedagogy can coexist with the new, provided the overall climate is one that fosters democratic relations.

The view that one should, however, strive to enable the learners' ideas to, as much as possible, constitute the basis of their learning is also reinforced through Freire's advocacy of a process whereby meaningful texts are created out of the learners' conversations; these texts would enable the learners to speak both the word and the world. In this respect, the texts would be different from the traditional primers, which Freire regards as culturally alien and as promoting the "ideology of accommodation" (Freire, 1985, p. 9). He regarded these primers as being alien to the peasant's reality and full of inane phrases, such as, "The wing is of the bird" or "Did Ada give her finger to Urubu?" and so forth. He goes on to say that primers are "illustrated with cute little houses, heart warming, and well decorated, with smiling couples, fair of face . . . " (Freire, 1985, p. 9). This is what he regarded as the "ideology of accommodation."

Given the strong relationship between knowledge and the learner's existential situation in Freire's method, one assumes that the participant has a repository to draw on. What lies in this repository is one's life experience. The participant is therefore encouraged to draw on this experience to arrive at new knowledge, at a new awareness. In drawing on this experience, one is able to relate to the codified material. The educator enables this process to occur not by "depositing" knowledge but by engaging the learner's critical faculties. Rather than dispense knowledge, the educator poses questions, problematizes issues. In this problem-posing education, the pedagogy applied is not that of "the answer," but that of "the question" (Bruss and Macedo, 1985). It may be argued that this pedagogy is counterhegemonic in the sense that it stands in contradistinction to the prescriptive model of education favored in alienating and dehumanizing learning settings.

In adopting a democratic, dialogical approach, the circle serves as a microcosm indicating the potential that can exist within contexts characterized by democratic social relations. Furthermore, knowledge itself is democratized and is therefore not presented any longer as the preserve of a privileged minority. Furthermore, the knowledge disseminated is in itself democratic in that its starting point is the life experienced by the participants, members of a subordinated social group, and serves their interests. Finally, it is group knowledge that emerges from this experience that emphasizes the *collective* dimensions of learning and of action for social change. Freire argued that one engages in the task of becoming more fully human not on one's own (it is not an individualistic endeavor) but in solidarity with others (Freire, 1970b, 1993, pp. 85–86). Such a task, therefore, "cannot unfold in the antagonistic relations between oppressors and oppressed" (pp. 85–86). Freire argued, in this context, that, in adopting an individualistic approach to being authentically human, one would be denying others the chance of attaining the same state (i.e., being authentically human). This individualistic endeavor would entail a dehumanizing process of "having more" (pp. 85–86).

The concept of group knowledge brings to mind the work of one important social philosopher whose writing exerted an influence on Freire. This is the Hungarian philosopher–sociologist Karl Mannheim. Reference to Mannheim's work, *A Diagnosis of Our Time* and *Freedom, Power and Democratic Planning*, can be found in Freire (1973). Nevertheless, I would refer, in this context, to arguably Mannheim's best-known work, *Ideology and Utopia*, and his concept of knowledge as group knowledge because I believe it best captures the spirit of the cultural circle with its process of collective coinvestigation of knowledge:

. . . knowledge is from the very beginning a cooperative effort of group life, in which everyone unfolds his knowledge within the framework of a common fate, a common activity and the overcoming of common difficulties (in which, however, each has a different share) [*sic*]. (Mannheim, 1936, p. 29)

The foregoing is all part and parcel of what Freire calls "Cultural Action for Freedom." It is the kind of counterhegemonic activity that is intended to precede and help create the climate for social change. The question that arises is: To what extent can this process of education truly serve as a means of liberation? Can this form of education engender social and political transformation? Freire has dealt with countries in which, for many years, the kind of popular education in which he was engaged and on which he exerted an influence was considered by the Right to be subversive and was therefore targeted for repression. Freire knew this only too well. The reader needs no reminding that his plans for the spread of adult literacy in Brazil were brought to an abrupt end in 1964 following the military coup.

Indeed, in many parts of Latin America, especially during periods of civil war, teaching was considered to be a subversive activity, and popular educators often paid for their commitment to the cause of educating others with their life, a situation described several times throughout Freire's work, including his later work, which provides biographical flashbacks to earlier periods in his life. These accounts can be found in his exchange with Horton (the American educator from the Highlander folk high school was an observer in Nicaragua for the elections, which took place soon after the overthrow of the dictatorship and the FSLN's seizure of power) and of course in *Pedagogy of Hope* and *Letters to Cristina*. It is dwelt on at length in the book with Betto (Betto and Freire, 1986) in view of the fact that both Freire and the lay Dominican friar had suffered repression at the hands of the military regime. Betto talked at length, in this book, about his experiences as an educator–learner in prison, including his efforts to preserve his sanity, marked by intellectual resilience, during a month of solitary confinement (Betto, in Betto and Freire, 1986, p. 53). In circumstances characterized by repression, as was the case with many of the contexts with which Freire was involved, there were limits to the effectiveness of Freire's approach as a vehicle for political change. And yet zones within countries that were liberated by guerillas offered spaces in which new social relations could be prefigured and popular education could be carried out. Prerevolutionary situations allow one the chance to engage in counterhegemonic activities, as Carlos Torres and Daniel Schugurensky argued with respect to Nicaragua (see also Arnove, 1986, pp. 7–9) and other places:

This autonomy is mostly enjoyed in nonformal education, and it is more evident in pre-revolutionary processes. Examples of this assertion can be found in the educational work carried out by the revolutionary guerrilla movements in Cuba and Nicaragua, by the Jesuits of the Universidad Centroamericana in Nicaragua, or by the repatriated intellectuals of MACE and The New Jewel newspaper in Grenada. (Torres, 1990, p. 99)

It has been argued that popular education of the type promoted by Paulo Freire was carried out by Jesuits from the University of Central America in the period that preceded the 1979 Sandinista revolution in Nicaragua. Of course, as always, education is not an independent variable, whatever the context. It would seem to have potential to contribute to social change when occurring within the context of a larger movement or alliance of movements. Freire constantly expressed the view that education should not be romanticized and attributed powers well beyond its reach (Freire in Shor and Freire, 1987, p. 37). This led him to consistently believe in the potential of social movements to generate forms of solidarity and cooperation among teachers and other cultural workers.

Freire insisted that "a radical and critical education has to focus on what is taking place today in various social movements and labor unions" (Freire in Freire and Macedo, 1987, p. 61). In the same passage, Freire referred to feminist movements, peace movements, and other such movements as generating in their practices "a pedagogy of resistance" (p. 6). The same point is made in the published conversation with Ira Shor:

But there is another place for the existence and the development of liberating education which is precisely in the intimacy of social movements. For example, the
women's liberation movement, the housewives' movement against the cost of living, all these grassroots movements will have emerged into a very strong political
task by the end of this century. In the intimacy of these movements we have
aspects of liberating education, sometimes we don't perceive. (Freire, in Shor and
Freire, 1987, p. 38)

   Later, in his transcribed conversation with the exiled Chilean intellectual Antonio Faundez, with whom he worked at the World Council of
Churches in Geneva, Freire pointed to the role that movements can play in
the struggle for social change, hinting in the process at the role that the
church played in the struggle for liberation in Brazil and other parts of
Latin America:

I can say without fear of being mistaken that in the seventies in Brazil and elsewhere we began to see clearly the growing development and importance of these
social movements, some of them linked with the church and some not: the struggle of environmentalists in Europe, Japan and the United States, resulting in their
direct intervention in recent elections in France and Germany; the struggle of organized women, of blacks, of homosexuals, all of them emerging as a force and
expression of power. (Freire and Faundez, 1989, p. 66)

   There is therefore evidence in Freire's work, particularly in his later talking books, that he supported the view that regards Cultural Action for Freedom as being more effective when carried out within the context of a social
movement or movements. Freire is on record as having argued in a book
published in its Portuguese version, in 1989, that these movements super-
seded and threw into relief the restrictive and traditional nature of parties
of the right and left, which, he argued at the time, were not to reach the end
of the century unless they focused on social issues (Freire, in Gadotti, Freire,
and Guimarães, 1995, p. 39). In Latin America, for many years, one came
across a strong social movement embracing a theology of liberation.
   As indicated in the section on Gadotti's (1994) book in the previous
chapter, Freire was a man of faith who regarded the church as a site of
struggle. It had what he perceived to be its progressive and anticipatory
utopian elements as well as its reactionary ones. He extolled the virtues of
the Prophetic Church, with its basis in Liberation Theology, and attributed
false consciousness to the "traditionalist," "colonialist," and "missionary"
church that he described as a "necrophiliac winner of souls" with its
"emphasis on sin, hell-fire and eternal damnation" (Freire, 1985, p. 131).
   It is against this radical religious backdrop that a significant part of
Freire's work for a critical literacy and an emancipatory politics has to be
seen. The similarities between his emancipatory views, affirming an
option for striving on the side of the oppressed, and the 1968 education

document produced by the Latin American Bishops in Medellin, Colombia, referred to in the Introduction to this book, are remarkable: "Our thinking about this panorama seeks to promote one view of education that agrees with an integral development of our Continent. This education is called education for liberation; that is, education which permits the learner to be the subject of his [sic] own development" (cited in Torres, 1993, p. 122). According to the tenets of Liberation Theology,

In this world of oppressors and oppressed, the reconciling mission of the church is to stand with Our Lord on the side of the Oppressed and to travel with him in this hard, long and narrow road leading to liberation. (cited in Hartung and Ohlinger, 1972, p. 21)

Some of the lines could easily have been lifted from Freire's writings. It must have been this relationship that has led certain sectors of the church in Latin America, especially in the Christian Base Communities, to espouse many of Freire's pedagogical principles. As the earlier citation from Torres (1990) indicated, Jesuits from the University of Central America (U.C.A.) used Freire's pedagogy when engaging in the kind of consciousness-raising activities that preceded the Somoza overthrow in Nicaragua (Arnove, 1986; Carnoy and Torres, 1987). Cardenal and Miller (1982) stated, also with regard to Nicaragua, how a church-sponsored program in the early 1970s inspired the subsequent Freire-inspired pedagogy used in the 1980 literacy campaign (pp. 209–210). The church can therefore serve as a protective umbrella for change-oriented critical literacy or popular education programs, although such killings as those of a priest in Recife during the Brazilian dictatorship, Archbishop Romero, and later, the Jesuits in El Salvador, indicate that there are limits to the extent to which regimes would tolerate such active struggles against poverty and oppression by members of the church. Although religion can serve as a source of legitimization for regimes that justify their actions on the grounds that they are keeping communism at bay, there are always limits to the extent to which the church can protect a progressive movement for social change centering around it. This qualification should not, however, lead us to underestimate the role of people belonging to specific factions within the church in supporting initiatives for social change in Brazil and the rest of Latin America. Certain figures and movements connected to the church have often been instrumental, directly and indirectly, in the preparation of the leadership for these initiatives. One such figure is, once again, Frei Betto, who has this to say about the relationship between the church and social movements:

. . . to ask what is the relation between the Church and these movements, is the same as asking where does the water end and the grape juice begin in the wine.

Everything is so mixed in Brazilian history: I myself helped to prepare many of these leaders by means of the Church. It is difficult to find a popular leader today in Brazil who did not enter into his militancy through the door of a popular pastoral. The Church is the great seedbed for popular leaders in Brazil. It is difficult for people locked in European Cartesianism to understand this. (Betto, 1999, p. 45)

It might still be argued, however, that it would seem absurd to believe that, irrespective of whether it does or does not take place within a social movement, cultural action can directly engender political action destined to bring about social change. In the cases of Guinea Bissau and Nicaragua, military action on the part of a guerrilla movement helped bring about the desired change. Such considerations should not obscure Freirean popular education's potential to be prefigurative in developing the right cultural climate that would support eventual radical changes. The best revolutionary changes are not those that occur from above in the form of what Gramsci would call a passive revolution, which, alas, is all too often the case, but those that are rooted in popular consciousness. As I argued elsewhere (Mayo, 1999a), Freire's pedagogy does not guarantee that people will engage in action for social transformation once they become conscientized and begin to critically read the world. This is not to say, however, that such pedagogical action cannot contribute to generating the right climate for change.

It can be argued, therefore, that Freire's pedagogy works best in a situation when there is a cultural receptivity to this kind of work and when it is carried out within a larger movement or alliance of movements. Freire never lost faith in the transformative potential of progressive social movements, and in later years, he would express his enthusiasm for the emerging new movements for the democratization of Brazilian society, as the next chapter will show. I will also show that he took his thinking somewhat further by also discussing the role of political parties in this context.

The foregoing considerations center around Freire's concept of cultural action. In Freire's early work, however, he drew a distinction between pre- and postrevolution or independence situations, using *cultural action* for the former and *cultural revolution* for the latter. It is to a consideration of issues related to Freire's notion of cultural revolution that this chapter now turns.

CULTURAL REVOLUTION

Quite a substantial part of Freire's work published in English from the early 1970s to the late 1980s deals with situations that, I suppose, Freire would consider appropriate to fall under the rubric of Cultural Revolution because the countries involved had just emerged from a long struggle for independence from Portugal. *Pedagogy in Process: The Letters to Guinea Bissau* (Freire, 1978) and a series of articles, including a piece in the *Harvard*

Educational Review, titled "The People Speak Their Word: Learning to Read and Write in São Tome & Principe" (Freire, 1981), are examples of writings dealing with situations marked by cultural revolution, in Freire's sense of the word. One can also mention, in this context, books published in the late 1980s, notably *Literacy: Reading the Word and the World,* which contains a postscript on the Guinea Bissau experience, and *Learning to Question,* which has a very animated exchange between Freire and fellow exile Antonio Faundez on the Guinea Bissau experience.

One other country with which Freire had some connection, albeit a peripheral one, is Tanzania. Here the concern was once again with a country's postindependence situation because this particular African country, under the leadership of Mwalimu Nyerere, sought to embark on a process of development inspired by its president's left-wing and anticolonial philosophy. It has been reported that Nyerere and Freire admired each other's writings and that, on his visit to Nyerere's home on the outskirts of Dar es Salaam in 1971, Freire proposed the setting up of a center based on the Tanzanian president's ideas and his own (Hall, 1998, p. 98). It could be argued that Freire might have had an indirect influence on the ideas that inspired some of the projects, including the literacy campaign, carried out in Tanzania during this period. The similarity between Nyerere's ideas and Freire's are uncanny. Witness these two quotations from the then Tanzanian leader:

The importance of adult education, both for our country and for every individual, cannot be over-emphasised. We are poor and backward, and too many of us just accept our present conditions as "the will of God," and feel that we can do nothing about them. In many cases, therefore, the first objective of adult education must be to shake ourselves out of a resignation to the kind of life Tanzanian people have lived for centuries past. (Nyerere, 1979b, p. 33)

. . . every adult knows something about the subject he is interested in, even if he is not aware that he knows it. He may indeed know something which his teacher does not know. For example, the villagers will know what time of the year malaria is worse and what group of people—by age or residence or workplace— are most badly affected [*sic*]. (Nyerere, 1979a, p. 53)

The first excerpt immediately recalls the well-known excerpt from Freire, cited earlier, concerning the peasant's tendency to provide magical explanations or a false conception of God, arguing that one ought to accept God's will (Freire, 1970b, 1993, p. 164). The second invites parallels with Freire's constant emphasis on listening, a concept that continues to feature in all his works, including his later ones (see chapter 4) and on building on the knowledge that the learners possess. This was a key element in Freire's conception of authentic dialogue.

Tanzania under the rule of Nyerere seemed to offer one of the most appropriate contexts for cultural revolution, especially in view of the unmistakably anticolonial tenor of the writings of the country's leader, writings that reflected the philosophy that was to underpin the country's policies in its immediate postindependence years. Given the relative poverty of the country, which could not afford secondary education for all and which faced the huge task of seeking to establish universal primary education by 1977, nonformal education seemed to be the most logical avenue to provide education for Tanzanians on a large scale because, as stated in the country's first Five Year Development Plan, "the nation cannot wait until the children have become educated for development to begin" (Unsicker, 1986, p. 231).

The nonformal education option seems to have been favored in contexts considered by Freire to have been ripe for cultural revolution. It was favored probably for the very same reason mentioned in Tanzania's first development plan. Furthermore, revolutionary governments such as those in Guinea Bissau and Nicaragua, where Freire was involved as a consultant, wanted to keep the revolutionary momentum going by providing access to the organized state-sponsored education that people lacked under the previous regime and that they craved. This explains the conventional revolutionary custom of following up on a successful armed revolution with a mass literacy crusade. It is common knowledge that both the Nicaraguan and Guinea Bissau governments, namely the FSLN and PAIGC governments, respectively, obliged in this regard and engaged Freire as consultant for this purpose. The literacy crusade seems to have been a characteristic of cultural revolution during the immediate change in rule. In previous work (Mayo, 1999a), I have argued how the need for annunciation and denunciation, as propounded by Freire, continues to be relevant, even in the post-political change situation because the struggle for greater democracy and humanization, and therefore revolution, is, on Freire's own insistence, an ongoing process with no final point of arrival. Ongoing annunciation and denunciation become all the more necessary, given that there are several factors that induce the revolutionary leadership to become authoritarian (see the section on silencing the opposition in Arnove, 1994, pp. 25–44), not least of which being the destabilizing effect of possible counterinsurrectional forces, backed by foreign intelligence, waging a war against the revolutionary government. Furthermore, there is often the danger that the revolutionary movement fails to reinvent power once it has seized it. For Freire, the challenge is not to merely seize power but to reinvent it in a process involving the active participation of the popular masses (Freire in Gadotti, Freire, and Guimarães, 1995, p. 44), a point also raised in the exchanges with Antonio Faundez (Freire and Faundez, 1989) and with scholars in Mexico (Escobar, Fernandez, and Guevara-Niebla, 1994, p. 41). According to Frei Betto, these are, after all, the very same popular masses whose discourse provided the point of departure for the revolutionary movements that had staged a successful revolution in Latin America (Betto, in Betto and Freire, 1986, p. 41).

Freire's ideas have also been distorted in the past through the overzealousness of revolutionary governments wanting to implement programs or campaigns in a short period of time and through teaching carried out by inexperienced educators, often schoolchildren, whose so-called dialogical approach amounts to hardly anything better than the mechanistic process of virtually administering a questionnaire. There was the case of Nicaragua, where "many instructors, in fact, were only one step ahead of their student neighbors and friends" (Arnove, 1994, p. 22). In this regard, and with reference to a different and later context, Nelly Stromquist (1997) indicated how, despite the 15-day period reserved for the training of educators in the MOVA-SP program, focusing on consciousness-raising (she pointed out that this is a longer period of preparation than that undergone by the average literacy educator), these educators require great support and stronger preparation through a program lasting a considerable period of time. She concluded that emancipatory education requires a great amount of preparation on the educators' part (Stromquist, 1997). These considerations serve to underscore even further the unsuitability of inexperienced and newly literate individuals for this type of work, as indicated by some accounts of the Nicaragua experience. So much has been written on these matters that one needs not rehearse more of the literature concerned.

There is one other issue, however, that undermines the kind of approach to popular education promoted by Freire that deserves to be highlighted further, given the pertinence of this situation to most countries in this day and age. Popular education can suffer from the contradictions and conflicts that characterize societies in transition, undergoing sweeping changes in a short and often prescribed period of time.

In societies going through this process of change, conflict arises not only between opposing political forces but also within the party itself, and one would also notice contradictions between the educational sector and other social sectors (Arnove, 1994, pp. 40–41). The imperatives of technocratic rationality and economic viability often run counter to the kind of pedagogical principles that Freire and other educators espouse. Examples from this literature include the chapter by Carnoy and Torres (1990) regarding Nicaragua and the relations between the formal and nonformal systems there. Perhaps the more revealing example derives from Tanzania and refers to the time Freire spent there in connection with the Tanzanian literacy campaign. Michela Von Freyhold (1982) stated, with respect to this campaign, that the ideas espoused and promoted by Paulo Freire were not observed, despite, one might add, their influence on the thinking of the country's president. She wrote: "After a visit by Paulo Freire to Tanzania there were some discussions on whether it would be advisable to make the primers more 'problem posing' and open. In the end this suggestion was turned down. The planners argued that 'If we allow the peasants to criticize the advice of the extension agent, we undermine his authority.' [sic] Nor should there be any discussion of the choice of crops: 'If peasants begin to discuss whether they want to grow cotton or not they might decide against it, and if they produce no cotton where are we going to get our foreign exchange from?' " (Von Freyhold, cited in Unsicker, 1986, pp. 241–242). This is an eloquent statement on the way the imperatives of economic viability take precedence over the demands for a liberating education, even when the political rhetoric of the government in question suggests support for the latter kind of educational effort. What renders this situation more interesting, from a Freirean perspective, is that it supports the kind of position regarding the extension agent that Freire himself wrote against in one of his earliest works, specifically the piece on extension or communication (Freire, 1973). The problem with arguments favoring the type of technical rationality promoted in the preceding statement is that they accommodate the kind of neocolonial cultural transfer that has become a feature of the structural adjustment programs being promoted in Third World countries in this day and age.

The issue regarding colonialism warrants some consideration, given that this was one of the issues with which Freire grappled in many of his writings in the 1970s and 1980s. It would be relevant to remark, with respect to the situation of newly independent countries visited by Freire in the 1970s, that the attainment of independence or the successful staging of a revolution does not change popular attitudes and misconceptions. Years of domination naturally leave their imprint on the minds of the oppressed. Colonialism, for instance, does not disappear with the attainment of independence. It is firmly entrenched in the minds of several people as a form of ideology, therefore heavily influencing certain social constructions of reality. Freire quoted Cape Verde's president, Aristides Pereira, as having said,

We made our liberation and we drove out the colonizers. Now we need to decolonize our minds. (Freire, 1985, p. 187)

Freire went on to state that, unless the mind is decolonized, the people's thinking would be in conflict with the new context that would be evolving as a result of the struggle for freedom. Critical literacy activities, through which one is encouraged to read the ideological dimensions of texts (and I am using *texts* here in the wider poststructuralist sense), should serve as a means for subaltern voices to emerge from the culture of silence. In colonial situations, this also involves the emergence and affirmation of the indigenous cultures (the use of the plural is deliberate, lest one resorts to essentialist, totalizing discourses regarding "the native culture," "the national identity," etc.). This raises issues concerning the politics of language involved in such a process.

Freire argues that not all that pertains to the colonial experience is irrelevant. He referred to knowledge of the colonizer's language, in the case of the former Portuguese colonies, as capable of proving beneficial in a postcolonial situation. This statement makes sense, particularly in relation to situations when the language of the colonizer is of international importance, knowledge of which constitutes an economic asset. Take the situation of those former British colonies that are developing microstates, my native country being one of them. I have argued elsewhere (Mayo, 1994) that their major economic preoccupation is "the active preservation or, better still, the enhancement of their status and desirability as rentier states" (Baldacchino, 1993, p. 43). I have also argued, citing Baldacchino (1993, p. 40), that this rentier status entails a situation in which revenue is obtained from such services as tourism, transshipment, bunkering, the provision of yacht berths, and so on. I argued that this and the need to guard against the danger of insularity necessitate the use of a language of international currency.

In certain countries, where different languages are used by different tribes, the colonizer's language serves as lingua franca. However, if praxis is to serve as the cornerstone for the establishment of new and more democratic social relations, it would seem that the emphasis should be placed on indigenous cultures. Furthermore, wherever there is a national indigenous medium of expression, then this ought to be used. As Freire (1985) maintained, with reference to Guinea Bissau's revolutionary leader, Amilcar Cabral, "Language is one of culture's most immediate, authentic and concrete expressions" (Freire, 1978, p. 184). This recalls Marx and Engels' statement in *The German Ideology:* "Language is as old as consciousness, language *is* practical consciousness . . ."(Marx and Engels, 1970, p. 51).

Freire provided reflections on the literacy experiences in Guinea Bissau, the target of much criticism concerning the contextualization of Freire's work and the cause of probably the only tension evident in his talking books in English (a point I shall also take up in chapter 4), the talking book with Antonio Faundez (cf. Freire and Faundez, 1989). Toward the end of the work, Faundez engaged in a direct critique of Freire's *Pedagogy in Process.* Freire's reaction was prompt and emotional. What we are confronted with, here, is not the image of a detached writer. On the contrary, in one of only a few instances in his published English language works, Freire comes across as a person highly sensitive to criticism—a feature that, nevertheless, reveals aspects of his humanity. In this particular section, the conversation flows quite naturally and is, of course, full of tension.

Freire insisted that the "so-called failure" of his work in the former Portuguese colony "was not due to the 'Freire Method' "; the failure occurred because Portuguese was used "as the only vehicle of instruction" throughout the campaign (Freire in Freire and Macedo, 1987, p. 114). This must have made him more convinced that the use of a national or more congenial language (e.g., Creole) should constitute a feature of both the formal and nonformal systems of education. Freire advocated the use of Creole in Cape Verde, Guinea Bissau, and São Tome and Principe:

These countries need to creolize in phases, starting with the first years of primary school through the high school, so that people everywhere would feel free to express themselves in their native language without fear and without perceiving any elitist restriction. Indeed they will come to terms with themselves to the degree that they speak their own language, not the colonizer's language. (Freire, 1985, p. 183)

He also argued, "Language is not only an instrument of communication, but also a structure of thinking for the national being" (Freire, 1985, p. 4). It is for this very reason that Freire shuddered at the prospect of his children having to study the history of Brazil in, say, English:

You can see what a violation of the structure of thinking this would be: a foreign subject (such as English) imposed upon the learner for studying another subject. (Freire, 1985, p. 184)

Freire made this statement with reference to the fact that Cape Verdeans adopted Portuguese as the official language for technical, scientific, and political thinking (Freire, 1985). Many other former colonies adopt the language of the colonizers for such purposes. Freire may have perhaps been worried by the possible danger that emphasis on such a language would render it a form of "cultural capital," to adopt Bourdieu's terms. As a result, it would be regarded as one of the vehicles whereby the educational system would reproduce the kind of class differences associated with the previous order. Freire provided statements to this effect with reference to postindependence education in Guinea Bissau. He wrote,

In my letter to Mario Cabral, I said that the exclusive use of Portuguese in education would result in a strange experience characterized by Portuguese as a superstructure that would trigger an exacerbation of class divisions, and this in a society that was supposed to be re-creating itself by breaking down social classes. (Freire, in Freire and Macedo, 1987, pp. 110–111)

In the same letter, Freire touched on the issue of cultural reproduction in Guinea Bissau. He stated that, because Portuguese is used as the mediating force in the education of youngsters and because students are selected for further education on the basis of their knowledge of the colonizer's language, "only the children of the elite would be able to advance educationally, thus reproducing an elite dominant class" (Freire, in Freire and Macedo, 1987, p. 111).

One may feel inclined to think that an educational process characterized by excessive use of a foreign language would stand in stark contrast to the one advocated by Freire, namely an educational process closely connected at its starting point, with the material needs and surroundings of the learners—in short, education through praxis. Of course, the issue involved is a complex one, the more so when, in a specific country, a dominant indigenous or foreign literacy and other suppressed local literacies exist (cf. Barton, 1994; Street, 1994). Freire's use of the Portuguese language in the Nord-este of Brazil can, in this regard, be considered to be problematic, given the existence in that region of other subaltern, indigenous literacies.

To what extent does this serve to undermine the notion of praxis that is the central element in Freire's critical literacy process? Freire addressed the situation of the indigenous populations of Latin America. In a dialogue, "Rethinking Literacy," he told Donaldo Macedo, "Any literacy project for these populations necessarily would have to go through the reading of the word in their native language" (Freire and Macedo, 1987, p. 57). The Sandinista government in Nicaragua sought to address this issue by carrying out, following the end of the National Literacy Cruzada, on August 23, 1980, a literacy follow-up campaign on the Atlantic strip of the Central American state (Arnove, 1986, pp. 25–26). The campaign was in the three major indigenous languages, namely English, Miskito, and Sumo (Arnove, 1986).

Freire himself highlighted the sensitivity of Fernando (the Nicaraguan Cruzada's Coordinator) and Ernesto Cardenal to this issue and their insistence that "the [Miskitos'] language would have to be a fundamental element in the literacy process" (Freire and Macedo, 1987, p. 57). Whether one should use a local and restricted, as opposed to a national popular, linguistic medium can be the subject of much debate. I would argue that the choice should fall on the larger language if the program is to be truly empowering. Otherwise, the learners would remain on the periphery of political life. The use of a language for national popular unity would therefore be necessary, the point that Freire seems to be making with respect to his insistence that Creole should have been used in Guinea Bissau.

And what of the dominant standard language? Freire argued, in the conversation with Ira Shor, that although the standard language contains the ruling ideology, knowledge of this language should not be denied to learners from subordinated social groups because it would enable them to survive in the power struggle. In developing microstates such as Malta, for instance, although teaching in Maltese would make the educational process more meaningful to a larger section of the population (English does not resonate with everyone's cultural capital), knowledge of the dominant foreign language (English) would still be important if the learners are not to remain on the periphery of economic life. It is imperative for Freire, however, that a critical literacy process incorporating the teaching of the dominant language would be characterized by a situation in which this language is taught in a problematizing manner. Freire stated that, while teaching this language, the teacher should discuss its political ingredients with the students:

While the traditionalist teaches the rules of the famous English (laughs) he or she increases the students' domination by elitist ideology which is inserted into these rules. The liberatory teacher teaches standard usage in order for them to survive while discussing with them all the ideological ingredients of this unhappy task. (Freire, in Shor and Freire, 1987, pp. 71–72)

Freire was here referring to the situation concerning the standard language and its subaltern class variants. The same situation applies to contexts in which the standard, elite language is that of the colonizer, whereas indigenous languages are spoken by the subordinated groups. The issue concerning choice of language is key in a process of critical literacy characterized by learning through praxis. In specific contexts marked by a process of cultural revolution, knowledge acquisition through praxis would entail, according to Freire, a strong relationship between education and production.

This point was emphasized in *Pedagogy in Process: The Letters to Guinea Bissau*. It marked a notable development in his pedagogical theory. Faced with the task of providing advice for the development of education in a country with an impoverished economy, lacking an indigenous bourgeoisie, and seeking to recover from the ravages of a war of liberation, Freire made the social relations of production the focus of his attention and his suggestions to the revolutionary government. While reemphasizing the point that the organization of the programmatic content of education is "an eminently political act" (Freire, 1978, p. 102), Freire wrote extensively, in Letter 11, on the unmistakably Marxian tenet that there should be no dichotomy between productive labor and education. In this respect, Freire advocated the avoidance of full-time students and the combination of study time with working hours "in intimate relationship with the peasants" (Torres, 1982, p. 88).

He argued that educational institutions should not be "distinguished, essentially, from the factory or from the productive activity in the agricultural field" (p. 105). This notion immediately calls to mind a series of socialist and Marxist suggestions or initiatives in the field of education, including, once again, Marx's notion of a polytechnic education as propounded in the Geneva Resolution of 1866, the system in China under Mao that involved a 2–4–2–4 (two months working–four months studying–two months working–four months studying) process (Chu, 1980, p. 79), and Nyerere's conception of school farms as an important feature of Education for Self-Reliance: "every school should also be a farm; that the school community should consist of people who are both teachers and farmers, and pupils and farmers" (Nyerere, 1968, p. 283). The fusion of learning and producing is best captured by Mao, who is also remembered for his advocacy of a fusion between manual and mental activity in reaction to the long-standing Confucian notion that the two should be separated:

Whoever wants to know a thing has no way of doing so except by coming into contact with it, that is by living (practising) in its environment. (Mao, cited in Chu, 1980, p. 79)

Freire is explicit on the relationship between education and productive labor:

In this sense, the new man and the new woman toward which this society aspires cannot be created except by participation in productive labor that serves the common good. It is this labor that is the source of knowledge about this new creation, through which it unfolds and to which it refers. (Freire, 1978, p. 105)

Freire stated that, in such a situation, the unit themes to be applied in the course of the program of critical literacy should be derived from the people's world of action, or more precisely, their area of productive labor. He provided examples of themes centering around the word *rice*, namely production of rice, geography of rice, history of rice, and health and rice (Freire, 1978, p. 117).

One can assume that a process of critical literacy interrelated with production, a process he also sought to promote in Chile during his work with peasants in connection with the *asentiamiento*,[11] was also intended by Freire to help produce the organic intellectual. The term is here being used in the Gramscian sense and refers to the agent who would help shape the cultural basis for consent to a way of life diametrically opposed to that experienced during Guinea Bissau's colonial period—a period lasting 500 years. In this work, Freire referred to Amilcar Cabral's affirmation that "the middle class intellectual needed the courage to commit class suicide before being reborn as a revolutionary worker, able to contribute to the struggle for liberation" (Freire, 1978, p. 116). Freire took up this idea, although at times he seemed to prefer the term *conversion,* with its Christian overtones, a choice that is conditioned, on his own admission, by his specific religious formation (Freire, in Gadotti, Freire, and Guimarães, 1995, p. 53).

I have argued elsewhere (Mayo, 1999a) that class suicide or conversion is very difficult to carry out. Many factors can separate the intellectual from the working or peasant class participants with whom he or she is working. There is the issue of habitus with which to contend. Habitus is considered by Bourdieu and Passeron to entail "irreversible" processes of learning that affect "the level of reception and degree of assimilation of the messages produced and diffused by the culture industry, and, more generally, of any intellectual or semi-intellectual message" (Bourdieu and Passeron, 1990, pp. 43–44). Other factors that come into play include one's educational background, the nature of one's everyday work, and possibly even one's acquired coherent and systematic view of the world. Cabral's notion of class suicide became a recurring theme in Freire's work of the late 1970s and early 1980s.

Amilcar Cabral was one of the few traditionally prepared intellectuals in a country that, during its colonial years, had an extremely elitist system of education. Suffice to mention one statistic: during 500 years of colonial rule, Guinea Bissau produced only 14 university graduates (Freire, 1978). Although acknowledging the importance of middle-class intellectuals committing class suicide, Freire (1978), echoing Gramsci, was convinced that, at the end of the day, "it is easier to create a new type of intellectual—forged in the unity between practice and theory, manual and intellectual work—than to reeducate an elitist intellectual" (p. 104).

One might add that, because of its infinitely greater flexibility, nonformal education characterized by praxis, geared toward engendering critical literacy, is more likely than the university to produce such an intellectual. These intellectuals, promoters of critical literacy, would be expected by Freire to further this cultural revolution and, in so doing, contribute toward the consolidation of the new political and social order. *Pedagogy in Process,* therefore, provides an example of Freire's approach being developed in the context of a situation when a radical political change has taken place. It provides an indication regarding how Freire's approach can be taken up to suit a specific country's needs. The situation in some other part of the world can be so different from that of Guinea Bissau, one of "the poorest of the poor" nations, that it necessitates an even more different use of Freire's approach. After all, Freire was fully aware of the social and political constraints that can prevent a process, successful in one context, from being developed in another. The basic philosophy as to what constitutes critical literacy applies in all cases. And it is this element, the political philosophical basis, that constitutes Freire's major contribution.

To reduce Freire's work simply to a method, devoid of its radical political thrust (Macedo, 1994), is tantamount to adulterating his work (cf. Escobar et al., 1994, pp. 45–46; Kidd and Kumar, 1981). His philosophy applies to work within a revolutionary setting and to work within a social movement seeking transformation in an industrialized society. It applies to the situation in the favelas of Brazil or among the campesinos of different parts of Latin America. It also applies to the situation in the U.S. ghettos, in poor quarters such as La Kalsa in Palermo, Sicily (cf. Dolci, 1966, pp. 124–126), and among the homeless in the metropolitan centers of Europe and North America, to name but a few examples attesting to the presence of the Third World within the First World. This notwithstanding, we must once more heed Freire's warning: "Experiments cannot be transplanted; they must be reinvented" (Freire, 1978, p. 9).

NOTES

1. The quote is inserted in a footnote in Freire's Preface to *Pedagogy of the Oppressed.*

2. Source: *A mensagem de Paulo Freire: teoria e prática da libertação* (The message of Paulo Freire: Theory and Practice of Liberation), Porto: Nova Critica, 1977.

3. Quite insightful is Giroux's chapter 5, "Something's Missing from Utopianism to a Politics of Educated Hope" in Giroux (2001).

4. I am indebted to Livingstone for this point.

5. For a thorough exposition of dialectical thinking, see Allman (2001, pp. 39–48).

6. See Allman (2001, p. 41) for an explanation of what Marx calls the "negation of the negation" in *Capital,* Vol. 1.

7. Interestingly enough, Dewey asks: Why is it that education by "pouring in" and as an affair of "telling" is widely condemned in theory, and yet is still entrenched in practice?

8. On this issue, see Giroux, 1992.

9. On this, see also Freire, in Horton and Freire, 1990, p. 181.

10. See the chapters "Critical Dialogue versus Teacher Talk: Classroom Discourse and Social Inequality" (chap. 4) and the aptly titled "Democratic Authority: Resistance, Subject Matter, and the Learning Process" (chap. 6) in Shor (1992) for an elaboration on this topic.

11. The *asentamiento* refers to the period of settlement of peasants, who had been salaried workers on the large latifundia, that preceded the one in which lands were assigned to them (Freire, 1970a, p. 23).

CHAPTER 4

"Remaining on the Same Side of the River": Neo-Liberalism, Party, Movements, and the Struggle for Greater Coherence

> He was concerned with the number of persons who let themselves be deceived by neo-liberal slogans and so become submissive and apathetic when confronted with their former dreams. Paulo used a metaphor for this situation: "They have gone to the other side of the river!"
>
> Ana Maria (Nita) Araújo Freire (Nita Freire, in Borg and Mayo, 2000b, p. 109)

INTRODUCTION

The last 10 years of Paulo Freire's life were indeed ones in which the Brazilian educator was very active in many ways. It was during this period that he served as Education Secretary in São Paulo for a short while. He also produced a sizable amount of written work, not all of which has been translated into English, taught at the Pontifical Catholic University (PUC) in São Paulo, and gave important talks in Brazil and abroad, especially at conferences held in his honor and/or inspired by his thought. The Institute marking Freire's 70th birthday, convened by Ira Shor in New York (it was held in the fall of 1991), which attracted a large number of scholars and activists primarily from all over North America, is a fine example of this type of conference. A Pedagogy/Theatre of the Oppressed conference began to be organized in the United States, originally by the University of Nebraska at Omaha, although it has subsequently been organized in various sites throughout the United States. Paulo Freire attended one of these meetings, held at Omaha, a year before he passed away. He delivered talks and shared a symposium on the final day with Augusto Boal, well known for his Theatre of the Oppressed, and the U.S.-based Canadian critical pedagogue, Peter McLaren. This event was held in March 1996. There would also be important sessions on Freire's work held at such prestigious meetings as the Annual Meeting of the American Educational Research Association (AERA). Paulo Freire shared a panel with Carlos Alberto Torres, Moacir Gadotti, and Michael Apple (discussant) at the 1991 meeting held in Chicago. These are just three examples of events held in the United States at which Freire was present, but there were many others that were held, during this period, in various parts of the world (see de Figueredo-Cowen and Gastaldo, 1995 regarding the 1993 seminar with Freire in London),[1] particularly in his own native Brazil. Freire therefore had to combine what seems to have been a very demanding writing schedule (this chapter will dwell mainly on works produced in the 1990s) with travel commitments, in the course of which he gave talks. Some of these talks were recorded, transcribed, and edited to become part of his oeuvre. It ought to be said, at the very outset, that the English language books from the 1990s onward are characterized by too much repetition (one gains the impression that, latterly, Freire produced one book too many).

FACTORS INFLUENCING FREIRE'S LATER WORK

The fatalism brought about by neoliberalism, referred to in the quote from the interview with Nita Freire (Borg and Mayo, 2000b), is one of several factors that influenced Paulo Freire's later output. There were, of course, other important factors that influenced his later work. These include, as indicated in the introductory chapter, his involvement as founding member of the *Partido dos Trabalhadores* (PT—Workers' Party) in Brazil:

That was the first time I became affiliated with a political party with card, name, and address. Everything legal. Everything right. The reason was that, for the first time in this country, a political party was born from down up. (Freire, 1993, p. 57)[2]

We have seen that there was also his work as Education Secretary in São Paulo after the Party won the municipal elections there.

To accept this invitation [*by Mayor Erundina*—author's insertion] was to be coherent with everything I have ever said and done; it was the only way to go. (Freire, 1993, p. 58)

One other factor influencing Freire's later work was the strong impact of important social movements in Brazil, especially the *Movimento dos Tra-*

balhadores Rurais Sem Terra (MST).[3] Frei Betto stated with respect to the emergence of new and progressive movements in Brazil:

The most expressive movement today is the *Movimento dos Sem Terra* (MST)—the Movement of Landless Peasants. One should also not disregard the PT—the Workers' Party—which had many mayors, besides congressmen and congresswomen, senators and some governors. One should neither disregard the importance of CUT—Central Única dos Trabalhadores (Unique Trade Unions Central Organization) and the "Central de Movimentos Populares" (Popular Movements Central Organization). But MST is the most representative because it addresses a very urgent and important question: Land Reform. (Betto, 1999)[4]

The MST is arguably one of the two most vibrant movements in Latin America. The other movement is the *Frente Zapatista* in Chiapas, which engages in a struggle on behalf of the "wretched of the earth," the indigenous peasant communities in this area of Mexico and which officially brought this struggle to the world's attention with the capture of San Cristobal de Las Casas on January 1, 1994; this date marked the coming-into-effect of NAFTA, an agreement that has been denounced, in certain quarters, for inexorably condemning these southern peasants to starvation (Cacucci, 1998, pp. 5–11).[5]

The MST, for its part, has three aims in mind: land, land reform, and a just society (Kane, 2001, p. 92). Adopting the slogan "Occupy, Resist, and Produce," it nowadays constitutes one of the world's largest grassroots organizations (Young, 2003, p. 46) and can trace its origins to the spontaneous land occupations by groups of peasants that occurred all over Brazil following the end of military rule (Kane, 2001, p. 92). Following a period of isolation and subsequent organizational efforts by the Pastoral Land Commission, these peasant groups finally united in 1984 to form a movement that currently comprises around 300,000 families (Kane, 2001, p. 92). To date, more than 250,000 families have secured 15 million acres of land titles (Young, 2003, p. 46).

The Movement allies political activism and mobilization with important cultural work, including highly inspiring music and poetry.[6] Marx, Freire, Gramsci, Martí, Liberation Theology, and Guevara feature prominently in the talk around values occurring within the MST's education sector (Kane, 2001, pp. 98–99), one of the many sectors, including health and food cooperatives, that the movement helped develop, with great respect for the environment, in the various settlement areas (Young, 2003, p. 47). The MST's extensive educational program includes courses carried out within the various landless peasants' encampments, the running of primary schools (by the end of the 1990s, there were around 900 such schools, catering to 85,000 children), and teacher education programs (Kane, 2000, pp. 40–43).[7]

As in the period that preceded the infamous 1964 coup, Paulo Freire's work and thinking must also have been influenced and reinvigorated by the growing movement for democratization of Brazilian society. In their fascinating and very revealing book, Maria del Pilar O'Cadiz, Pia Lindquist Wong, and Carlos Alberto Torres (1998) showed that the range of "NGOs and social or popular movements in Brazil is impressive," with research by Gadotti indicating the presence of 89 organizations promoting popular education and 91 NGOs engaged on behalf of public schooling (O'Cadiz et al., 1998, p. 43). Other research points to 1,041 NGOs, 556 of which work on behalf of popular movements, 251 organizations linked with women's movements, and 234 linked with African-Brazilian movements, apart from the presence of NGOs in connection with "ecologists, fishermen, the unemployed, religious communities, and indigenous peoples" (O'Cadiz et al., 1998, p. 43). This scenario must have continued to enhance the ever-so-strong sense of hope regarding possibilities for social transformation that has characterized Freire's pedagogical politics and attitude to life in general.

Traveling all over this immense Brazil we saw and cooperated with a very large number of social movements of different sizes and natures, but who had (and continue to have) a point in common: the hope in their people's power of transformation. They are teachers—many of them are "lay": embroiderers, sisters, workers, fishermen, peasants, etc., scattered all over the country, in favelas, camps or houses, men and women with an incredible leadership strength, bound together in small and local organizations, but with such a latent potential that it filled us, Paulo and me, with hope for better days for our people. Many others participated in a more organized way in the MST . . . the trade unions, CUT . . . and CEBs: *Christian Base Communities*. As the man of hope he always was, Paulo knew he would not remain alone. Millions of persons, excluded from the system, are struggling in this country, as they free themselves from oppression, to also liberate their oppressors. Paulo died a few days after the arrival of the MST March in Brasília. On that April day, standing in our living-room, seeing on the TV the crowds of men, women and children entering the capital in such an orderly and dignified way, full of emotion, he cried out: "That's it, Brazilian people, the country belongs to all of us! Let us build together a democratic country, just and happy!" (Nita Freire, in Borg and Mayo, 2000b, p. 109)

This extract derives from the interview that Carmel Borg and I carried out with Freire's widow, Dr. Ana Maria (Nita) Araújo Freire. Freire's marriage with her, following a period of desolation caused by the death of his beloved Elza, must also be included in any account of the factors that influenced his later output. Like Elza, Nita, a former student of Freire and daughter of Paulo's teacher, contributed to his output. An accomplished scholar and academic in her own right, she often provided important editorial work in the form of detailed and illuminating annotations. These annotations contribute to the reader's (particularly the non-Brazilian reader's) understanding of the contexts that gave rise to the ideas in question. The later period of Freire's life also included collaborative projects with international scholars and activists, especially key figures in the North American critical pedagogy movement.

The Watershed

It is very difficult and arbitrary to establish a cutoff point to indicate the later period of Paulo Freire's works. There are those who would argue that, as far as his English texts go, *The Politics of Education*, ably translated by Donaldo Macedo (Freire, 1985), and the conversational text with Ira Shor (Shor and Freire, 1987) represent a watershed. Ideas that were implicit in his early work, including his most celebrated work, were revisited and developed further in these books (see Allman et al., 1998, p. 9). One of these two books (Freire, 1985) is a compendium of old and what were then new pieces. It includes, for instance, the early "Adult Literacy Process as Cultural Action for Freedom" alongside a highly illuminating conversation with Donaldo Macedo. I have made extensive reference to these books in the previous chapter. For heuristic purposes, I shall be concentrating, in the rest of this chapter, on the work from the 1990s onward, a period marked by numerous publications authored by Paulo Freire. A number of these works were or are being published posthumously. Of course, there will be passing references to and quotes from earlier works because many of the ideas recur throughout Paulo's writings. Likewise, the previous chapter contained quotes from the 1990s works for the light they shed on themes developed and events described in the earlier work.

The 1990s

The work of the 1990s starts off with a continuation of his talking books series. The first book, edited by Brenda Bell, John Gaventa, and John Peters, is the taped conversation between Freire and Myles Horton to which reference has already been made (Horton and Freire, 1990). This is followed by the book marking the period in which Paulo Freire served as Education Secretary in São Paulo. The book, already cited in view of references to concepts characterizing Freire's earlier work, is aptly entitled *Pedagogy of the City* (Freire, 1993). It includes interviews and a fine postscript by his close collaborator, Ana Maria Saúl. His work as Education Secretary was also documented in other places, including a taped 1991 AERA session in Chicago and studies by Ana Maria Saúl, Carlos Alberto Torres, Pia Wong, Maria del Pilar O'Cadiz, and Moacir Gadotti, some already cited in this book (see Gadotti, 1994; O'Cadiz et al., 1998; Torres, 1994, 1995). These were followed by *Pedagogy of Hope* (1994) and *Letters to Cristina* (1996), which, as I had occasion to remark earlier, are largely autobiographical and provide the reader with an expanded and often detailed knowledge of the concrete contextual background regarding the development of Freire's ideas. These expositions of the context in which Freire's work was immersed bring to the fore the various personalities and movements that played or are still playing an important role in the larger struggle for the democratization of Brazilian society, as well as various aspects of Brazilian life that must have affected Freire's thinking. We learn more about the group of Brazilian exiles in Chile and their Chilean counterparts who engaged in discussions that were central to the development of *Pedagogy of the Oppressed* (Freire, 1994, p. 62). We learn of Paulo's childhood dreams and nightmares, about the stark reality of oppression, and not just the pain of exile but also the brutality and bestiality of torture. We learn of the publication of such key works as *Brasil Nunca Mais* (Brazil Never Again), produced after Argentina's *Nunca Mas,* which had been published in the mid-1980s by Conadep, the *Comisión Nacional sobre la Desaparición de Personas* (literal translation: National Commission concerning Disappeared Persons), led by one of Argentina's most important public intellectuals, writer Ernesto Sabato.[8] *Brasil Nunca Mais* provides a strong reminder of the coercive, apart from the ideological/consensual, basis of power. We learn of the courage of radical ecclesiastics, including, once again, the inspirational Paulo Evaristo Arns, incidentally the person who, following the *abertura,* visited Freire in Geneva to convince him to return to his homeland.[9] *Brasil Nunca Mais* was prepared under the auspices of Cardinal Arns.[10] This is an account of the horrors of torture by the military regime, details of which are provided by Nita Freire in an extensive footnote in *Letters to Cristina* (Freire, 1996). We also hear about the courageous activism of other key figures, such as the Nobel prize nominee Betinho (Herbert Jose de Soúza), mentioned earlier, who died the same year as Paulo (see Martin, 1998). He started a very important social movement in Brazil, the Movement of Citizens' Action against Hunger and Misery and for Life (Araújo Freire, in Freire, 1996, p. 247). To these one can add, once again, Frei Betto. These figures and many others convey to us, once more, the sense of a large movement for democratization in Brazil, of which Paulo Freire was just one, albeit key, representative.

Around the same time that *Pedagogy of Hope* saw the light, SUNY Press published a book-length exchange between Paulo Freire and a group of scholars from UNAM, the National Autonomous University of Mexico (Escobar et al., 1994). This is a most interesting work focusing on a variety of topics, including, as the title suggests, the role of institutions of higher education. A related issue is that concerning the role of intellectuals operating as cultural workers in both the academic and public spheres. In between these two 1994 books and *Letters to Cristina,* we saw the publication of such books as *Education and Social Change in Latin America* (edited by Carlos Alberto Torres, 1995) or booklets such as *Paulo Freire at the Insti-*

tute (de Figueiredo-Cowen and Gastaldo, 1995), the latter including pieces (interviews, talks, responses to discussants) by Freire. Significant papers such as the exchanges with Carlos Alberto Torres and Donaldo Macedo in McLaren and Lankshear (1994) and McLaren and Leonard (1993), respectively, and exchanges with Macedo in the *Harvard Educational Review* (Freire and Macedo, 1995) and in Steiner et al. (Freire and Macedo, 2000) were also produced. I would also refer, for good measure, to the already cited interview with Carlos Alberto Torres in a book dealing with biographies of leading, predominantly North American, academics (Torres, 1998b). Around the time of his death, we saw the publication of *Pedagogy of the Heart*. Later, *Teachers as Cultural Workers: Letters to Those Who Dare Teach* (Freire, 1998c) and *Pedagogy of Freedom* (Freire, 1998a) were published. The latter is the English version of the much-acclaimed *Pedagogia da Autonomia: Saberes necessários à prática educativa*.

WHAT IS NEW IN FREIRE'S LATER WORKS?

I would argue that, in his later work, Freire stressed and elaborated on points that were already present in his early work. In a collaborative piece from the *Convergence* special issue on Freire (Allman et al., 1998), it was argued that "these positions were also revised in the light of the new experiences of oppression and emancipation to which he was exposed in the later years of a highly eventful life as educator, activist, consultant to revolutionary governments (Guinea Bissau, Nicaragua, Grenada) and ultimately educational policy maker and administrator. His life was lived across different borders and different geographical contexts" (p. 9). Very few, if any, of his later works have that "unity of dialectical thought and style" (Allman et al., 1998, p. 10) that remains the distinctive feature of *Pedagogy of the Oppressed*. This having been said, it would be amiss to attempt to do justice to Freire's work and ideas by referring only to this celebrated piece. Like most critical intellectuals, Freire was a person in process, constantly in search of greater coherence.

He has offered us ideas and conceptual tools that constantly warrant further elaboration, in view of the new experiences and challenges encountered across different borders. These experiences and challenges shed new light on Freire's concepts, providing them with more nuances. Some elements that are considered to be central to the Freirean concept of authentic dialogue and discussed in the previous chapter, are revisited and given expanded treatment in later works. Take the basic concept of Listening. To engage in dialogue, educators must stop suffering from "narration sickness" (Freire, 1970b, 1993, p. 71) and become "listeners." We would assume that this is basic to a Freirean conception of teaching. For how can one engage in genuine dialogue without being able to listen, to resist the urge to speak (as Freire puts it)? Otherwise, one would be simply talking past the other. And yet, I would still find refreshing Freire's and Nita's illuminating reflections on the notion of listening in *Pedagogy of Freedom* and *Convergence* (Araújo Freire, 1998, pp. 4–5), respectively:

Listening is an activity that obviously goes beyond mere hearing. To listen, in the context of our discussion here, is a permanent attitude on the part of the subject who is listening, of being open to the word of the other, to the gesture of the other, to the differences of the other. This does not mean, of course, that listening demands that the listener be "reduced" to the other, the speaker. This would not be listening. It would be self-annihilation. (Freire, 1998a, p. 107)

Works such as *Pedagogy of Freedom* abound with reflections on some of those concepts or themes that recur throughout Paulo Freire's work, including Methodological Rigor, Praxis, Respect for what students know, Risk, Autonomy and Dignity, and Agency. Agency is, once again, stressed in the notion of "history as possibility" (Freire, 1993, p. 65; 1998c, p. 88) and that we are *conditioned* (Freire, 1998a, p. 54) but not *determined* beings. One finds new meanings, experiences new sensations, and discovers new sources of inspiration each time one rereads a piece of good poetry. Likewise, one discovers new sensations, new meanings, and fresh sources of inspiration when being led by Freire himself and Nita to revisit some of the basic concepts in the Freirean pedagogical approach.

One cannot help being struck by the emotional impact of the following evocative account by Nita, again focusing on the basic concept of Listening. Like Paulo, Nita captures the tactility of the experience involved, fusing reason with emotion. And here we experience this only in translation!

Paulo's act of touching while looking at people made the act of touching, an act so natural in our Brazilian culture, more than body to body contact. Touching with his hand and with his look, Paulo somehow connected his whole being, his reason and emotion, to the whole being of another . . . His ability to listen, not just to hear the other person, but that way of listening mentioned in the *Pedagogy of Autonomy* [*Pedagogy of Freedom*—author's insertion]—also noticeable in his look signaled the moment when he accepted and gathered within himself what he was hearing from the other. . . . In Paulo, to touch, to look and to listen become moments of *me and you in dialogue* about something which he and the other person wanted to know. (Araújo Freire, 1998, pp. 4–5)

Similar basic concepts are resorted to, elaborated on, and refined not just by Paulo and Nita but also by many cultural workers and researchers who draw on Freire when grappling with a variety of phenomena. Praxis and reading the word and the world remain central concepts in Freire's work. They remain at the heart of his pedagogical philosophy. The theme of exile as a form of praxis, which, as I indicated in chapter 3, was broached in the exchanges with Faundez (Freire and

Faundez, 1989) and Betto (Betto and Freire, 1986), is a recurring one in his later works (see Freire, 1997a, pp. 67–72). It is used, once again, in the sense of a period of a temporary absence that enabled Freire and others to gain critical distance from their native land, to view it in a critical light. This can lead to transformative action. It would be appropriate to reiterate the point that this entailed Freire's *relearning* his own native country following his return to Brazil, an important and recurring theme in his later work. Later works provide different ways of making creative use of these concepts, often allying them to concepts elaborated on by other theorists. As I shall indicate later on in this chapter, Freire took up his much-favored notion of education through critical literacy and praxis in the context of his efforts to help reform public schooling in São Paulo. This notion was adopted by others within the context of redemptive memory (see McLaren and Da Silva, 1993; Mayo, 1999a, pp. 147–151).

In this context, the codification is the means to recuperate collective histories. After all, the collective process of praxis involved within a cultural circle entails a critical engagement with historically accumulated concepts and practices (Mayo, 1999a, p. 147).[11] And the same applies to many others who, like Freire, resort to these concepts to *reinvent* them within such areas as cultural studies, community theatre, feminist and antiracist pedagogy, anticolonial or postcolonial pedagogy (in a variety of different sites), gay/lesbian studies, critical multicultural pedagogy, and even such unlikely areas as museum education (this involves the quest to transform traditionally colonizing spaces into decolonizing ones), the last mentioned being an area that I shall tackle in the book's final chapter. The list is by no means exhaustive.

Furthermore, the explications and reformulations of positions already present in his early work were probably rendered necessary because of the constant misappropriations of his ideas. Misconceptions concerning Freire abound, the sort of misconceptions that irked Paulo Freire and, as indicated in the previous chapter, led him, after 1987, to stop using such terms as *conscientização* (Freire, 1993, p. 110; Freire, in Escobar et al., 1994, p. 46).

The assumed nondirectiveness of a genuinely democratic education is one misconception that Freire continued to refute in his later work. I have shown how this refutation was already present in work of the 1980s, *The Politics of Education* (1985), the conversational book with Ira Shor, *Pedagogy for Liberation: Dialogues on Transforming Education* (1987), and the dialogical book with Gadotti and Guimarães (originally published in 1989 and subsequently produced in Italian translation as Gadotti, Freire, and Guimarães, 1995) being cases in point. This remains a recurring theme in the later works (see, for instance, Freire, in Freire and Macedo, 1995, p. 394). In an interview with Carlos Alberto Torres, Freire stated,

There is no education without objectives, without ends. It is precisely this that by making it directive, one prevents its neutrality of the neutrality of the educator. (Freire, 1993, p. 116)

What later works do is explicate this position further, also in view of many criticisms leveled at Freire's work, often based on a misconception of his position in this regard. Recall my earlier reference (chapter 2) to Frank Youngman's critique of Freire's pedagogy that is analyzed within the context of its potential suitability or otherwise for a socialist pedagogy. In my view, Youngman seemed bent on lopping off the feet that would not fit his procrustean bed (a set of abstracted concepts for a Marxist education). He maintained that Freire is "ambivalent about saying outright that educators can have a theoretical understanding superior to that of the learners" (Youngman, 1986, p. 179). Freire might not have said this outright in his early work, but this is certainly implied in his contention that education is not neutral and that educators–activists must ask themselves on whose side are they when they teach or act. Furthermore, the books I cited, in which Freire stated explicitly that educator and learner are not on an equal footing (Freire, 1985; Shor and Freire, 1987), were published around the same time that Youngman's work came out. These writings seem to have been overlooked in a number of studies on Freire. In this respect, I would refer back to Paul V. Taylor's formulation based on the common misconception that Freirean pedagogy claims to be nondirective and involves a "dialogue among equals" (Taylor, 1993, p. 129) or my criticism of Elias along similar lines (Elias, 1994, p. 116). Alas, important misconceptions concerning the nature of Freirean pedagogy abound, even in book-length single studies on Freire.

Teachers are presented by Paulo Freire as people who are engaged in work that necessitates the delicate balancing between freedom and authority, to which an entire section is devoted in *Pedagogy of Freedom*. And this brings me to an important theme in Freire's later work—a point that, in my view, was taken up in his early work but was rendered more pronounced in his later ones. The issue of authority and freedom is broached time and again in Freire's later works (see, for example, Freire, 1998a, pp. 95–99; 1998c, p. 88). Indeed, such repetition is necessary. Witness Diana Coben's (1998) insistence on a fundamental contradiction in Freire's work in which dialogue and democratic social relations are preached, whereas it is always the teacher who "holds the cards" (p. 186).

In my view, the alternative to the teacher holding the cards would be laissez-faire pedagogy. In Freire's words, ". . . in avoiding directivity they [*educators*] need to prevent losing themselves in the lack of clear limits that often leads to a laissez faire approach" (Freire, 1993, p. 117). As I have argued elsewhere, this particular approach constitutes pedagogical treachery of the worst kind that often results in the violence meted out to learners by members of an in-group in possession of the required cultural capital; these in-group members are allowed to abuse a pseudodialogical process (Mayo, in McLaren and Mayo, 1999, p. 402). Because it connotes a laissez-faire approach, the term *facilitator* was dropped from the Freirean lexicon—it was probably used not by Freire but by commentators. *Teacher* is the term used by Freire. This comes across quite strongly in his series of letters to those "who dare teach" (Freire, 1998c). As I have shown in the previous chapter, Freire had been arguing, at least since his book with Shor, for an authentically dialogical process in which the teacher has authority, deriving from his or her competence, and commands respect, also because of this competence "Teachers maintain a certain level of authority through the depth and breath of knowledge of the subject matter that they teach" (Freire, in Freire and Macedo, 1995, p. 378). This, however, does not degenerate into authoritarianism (Freire, in Shor and Freire, 1987, p. 91; Freire in Horton and Freire, 1990, p. 181; Freire, 1994, p. 79).

Freire argued that progressive educators must figure out "what do they need to do to diminish the distance between what they say and what they do so as not to allow directivity to turn into authoritarianism or manipulation" (Freire, 1993, p. 117). He later argued, in the same vein, that, to avoid manipulation and authoritarianism, the educator must ensure that her or his "directivity" does not interfere with the "creative, formulative, investigative capacity of the educand . . . " (Freire, 1994, p. 79). On this point, Stanley Aronowitz forcefully and eloquently stated that ". . . the educator's task is to encourage human agency, not mold it in the manner of Pygmalion" (Aronowitz, 1998, p. 10). The position regarding authority and freedom has uncanny similarities with that expressed by Gramsci in his piece on the Unitarian School, where the Sardinian calls for a balance to be struck between the kind of authority promoted by the old classical school (without the excess of its degeneration into authoritarian education) and the freedom proposed by proponents of the Rousseau school. The latter school, for Gramsci, had to develop from its romantic phase, predicated on unbridled freedom for the learner, based on her or his spontaneity, and move into the classical phase, classical in the sense of striking a balance. This is the balance between freedom and authority (see Gadotti, 1996, p. 53).

Teachers are presented as people who need to be competent, who teach when necessary, and who require opportunities for ongoing teacher formation. With respect to the last point, Freire stated: "One cannot think of changing the face of the schools; one cannot think of helping the schools become serious, rigorous, competent, and happy, without thinking about the permanent preparation of teachers. For us [*the Education Secretariat*—author's insertion], the continuous preparation of teachers will take place whenever we can, preponderantly, through reflection on practice" (Freire, 1993, p. 34). This explains the emphasis placed, in the development of the popular public school in São Paulo, on the *Grupos de Formação,* continuing professional development groups involving "teachers, pedagogic coordinators and school directors" (O'Cadiz et al., 1998, p. 72). In addition to the need for ongoing teacher formation, Freire also placed the emphasis, in his later work, on teachers' professional recognition that includes the provision of adequate pay: Freire is on record as having proposed, as Education Secretary, the kind of minimum pay rise for teachers that would have enabled São Paulo to have "the highest minimum salary" for this specific occupational group (Freire, 1993, p. 80). With respect to teachers' working conditions and salaries, Paulo Freire wrote,

It is urgent that we drum up more support in this country for public schools that are popular, effective, democratic, and happy and whose teachers are well paid, well trained and in constant development. Never again should teachers' salaries be astronomically lower than those of the presidents and directors of government corporations, as they are today. . . . It is not acceptable on the eve of the new millennium that we continue to experience the alarming quantitative and qualitative deficits that currently exist in our education. We cannot enter the new millennium with thousands of so-called lay teachers, even in the poor areas of the country, sometimes making less than the minimum wage. They are heroic people, giving, loving, intelligent people, but people treated with contempt by national oligarchies. (Freire, 1998c, p. 35)

This brings us to one important contribution that Freire's later work has made. And the book I would single out here is that from which the preceding quote has been taken: *Teachers as Cultural Workers: Letters to Those Who Dare Teach* (1998c). This is one of the finest books in English from Freire's later output. It is a pity that, at the time of writing, the book is available only in hardcover. A paperback version would render the book more accessible and therefore an important source for prospective teachers undergoing preservice preparation as well as teachers currently in service. What this book places on the agenda is that there is no contradiction between a Freirean approach to an authentically dialogical education and the quest for professional recognition. By professional, Freire is not referring to the excesses of the ideology of professionalism (Larson, 1977), based on the trait model of professionals (Runté, 1995) that often results in the following arrogant posture: I know what's best for you. Freire is using *profession* in the sense of people who are competent, both in terms of the subject matter taught and in terms of pedagogical disposition, and who engage in very important work that demands respect and adequate remuneration. He obviously has in mind the plight of teachers in the Brazilian public school system. Freire worked hard as Education Secretary to improve the working conditions of teachers in São Paulo. This included not only adequate financial remuneration but the right for them to engage their critical capacity, rather than have their competence undermined through the imposition by a "half a dozen self-proclaimed specialists" of content-oriented "packages" and manuals or guides that describe how to use these packages (Freire, 1998b, p. 67).

Freire regarded such an imposition of teacher-proof material as indicative of an authoritarian disregard for "the critical capacity of teachers, their knowledge or their practice" (Freire, 1998b, p. 67) and an authoritarian attempt "to instill in teachers a fear of freedom" (Freire, 1998c, p. 9). In contrast, Freire not only advocated but also helped develop policies, with his Secretariat's team and other stakeholders in education, that enabled teachers to work collaboratively across disciplines to create an interdisciplinary curriculum (O'Cadiz et al., 1998, p. 93). The content derived from across the various subjects was to be linked to the pupils' sociocultural realities and the material was to be obtained from various sources of knowledge and not from a single-subject textbook or some prepackaged teacher-proof material (O'Cadiz et al., 1998). Freire advocated and helped devise an active and a dynamic role for teachers and students, in keeping with his general educational philosophy.

For Freire, teachers were not to be regarded as coddling aunts or mothers—*professora sim, tia não*, the original Portuguese title for *Teachers as Cultural Workers* (Freire, 1998c), which, when translated, reads: teacher yes, aunt no. This position, regarding teachers not being coddling aunts, can sound problematic in that it somehow smacks of a *machista* devaluation of what has often been termed a feminized profession (see Fischman, 1999, pp. 557–558). Equally problematic is his reference to the fact that teaching proves attractive to women during the short period of their working life prior to marriage (Freire, 1998c, p. 36). Unfortunately, Freire raised this issue without any engagement on his part in a critique of the *normalizing discourse* regarding women's role in the family, generated by and supporting the existing patriarchal structures of economic oppression. This is, after all, a discourse that continues to limit women's involvement in the public domain because it continues to channel them, for the greater part of their working life, into the domestic sphere. In this so-called post-Fordist period, the domestic sphere also constitutes an important site for casualized work. It is therefore a normalizing discourse that limits women's chances of embarking on a career rather than simply a job.

This having been said, one must appreciate the main reason that motivated Freire's writing of this book, which was meant as an attack on what was then an emerging ideology in Brazil intended to deprofessionalize teachers by suggesting that they be called "aunties" by the children in their care (Freire, 1995b, p. 17). The implicit message was: "How can you go on strike if you are aunties and the children are your nephews and nieces?" (Freire, 1995b, p. 17). This argument was reminiscent of the one made in England, many years ago, with regard to the idea of teaching being the noble and dignified profession, one of the means for the state to control teachers and curb their potential militancy (see Ozga and Lawn, 1981, p. 91). Freire stated that when he wrote *Teachers as Cultural Workers* he "aimed at criticizing the de-professionalization of the teacher" (Freire, 1995b, p. 17).

On the subject of teachers, one of the themes that recurs throughout Freire's later work is the need for teachers to extend their work outside the sphere of the classroom, adult education setting, cultural circle, or university and to connect with what goes on in the public sphere.[12] In his exchange with scholars from UNAM in Mexico, Freire stated,

In reality, when you work toward convincing the students, your effort is in relation to a political victory that takes place outside of the university. Your act of convincing seeks to obtain support for your greater dream, not simply to be a good professor. If you accept that your teachings do not go beyond the walls, in my opinion you are making a mistake, that of elitism. You will be a Marxist who only knows Marx through books and who restricts Marxism to the classroom, outside of which he [*sic*] claims to be only an academic. This is denying Marx and denying education itself. (Freire, in Escobar et al., 1994, p. 37)[13]

It was important for Freire to engage with the system and not shy away from it for fear of co-optation:

The ideal is to fight against the system taking the two fronts, the one internal to the schooling system and the one external to the schooling system. Of course, we have much space outside the schooling system, much more space to work, to make decisions, to choose. We have more space outside the system, but we also can create the space inside of the subsystem or the schooling system in order to occupy the space. (Freire, in Horton and Freire, 1990, p. 203)

In a conception denoting strong Gramscian overtones, the system, for Freire, was not monolithic. On the contrary, it offered spaces for counter-hegemony, for "swimming against the tide" (see Freire, in Escobar et al., 1994, pp. 31–32). Teachers and other social actors who see themselves as transformative intellectuals and cultural workers should, to use a popular Freire phrase, "be tactically inside and strategically outside" the system. Here the theme of social movements is given prominence (a recurring theme in most of, if not all, his books from the mid-1980s onward), attesting to Freire's recognition of the role of social movements as agents of change.

We have seen how the emergence of MST in Brazil and other movements elsewhere, including Europe, captured Freire's imagination and how he himself was part of, and indeed contributed to, a movement, the Liberation Theology movement, which strove for an important process of change, of radicalization, within the church, an important institution in Latin America and beyond. He and his team at the Education Secretariat in São Paulo saw themselves as giving rise to the emergence of a curriculum reform movement. MOVA-SP, the focus of Nelly Penalosa Stromquist's study (Stromquist, 1997), has also been described as a "federation of movements" (O'Cadiz et al., 1998, p. 57):

The remarkable distinction which sets the PT's reform agenda apart from other major school reform and improvement efforts is the dual political-pedagogic focus of the administration's efforts and its attempts to create a reform process defined as a political/educational movement. (pp. 74–75)

Freire strove to bring social movements and state agencies together in São Paulo when Education Secretary there (see chapter 3 in O'Cadiz et al., 1998). Ironically, O'Cadiz, Wong, and Torres quoted Moacir Gadotti as saying that "being tactically inside and strategically outside" the system, the phrase used earlier in relation to Freire's exhortation for teachers to work within the system, was the attitude adopted by social movements with respect to their relationship with the Education Secretariat in São Paulo; they were wary of the State's nature in this city, even, if in this particular case, the State was being represented by a progressive municipal administration (O'Cadiz et al., 1998, p. 44). This attitude did not deter the municipal government from striving to forge such a collaborative partnership. With regard to MOVA-São Paulo,

The initial idea that the municipal government collaborate with existing social movements in fomenting an organized literacy movement within the city was announced by the Secretariat in October 1989 when Freire first took office as Secretary of Education. . . . Consequently, MOVA's structure grew out of an agreement between the democratic popular administration and a number of social movements in São Paulo concerned with issues such as land tenure, housing, health and education. (O'Cadiz et al., 1998, p. 54)[14]

Of course, the idea of educators working within the contexts of social movements has gained prominence in the literature on transformative education, most particularly in the area of adult education (for a critical review of this, see Foley, 1999, pp. 135–138). Here, the discussion centers around a very non-Gramscian use of the concept of civil society. Freire's exploration of the links between movements and the State (Freire, 1993) featured in his later writings as did the theme concerning the potential relationship between social movements and party, a position no doubt influenced by his role as one of the founding members of the PT. The latter is quite interesting, given the criticism often leveled at social movement theorists, namely that they tend to ignore the role of the party. For instance, authors such as John Holst (2001, p. 112) have argued that social movements activists writing on the relevance of Antonio Gramsci's ideas for adult education tend to ignore the central role that Gramsci attributed to the party in the process of social transformation. In view of this criticism, Freire's ideas concerning the relationship between party and movements are quite interesting and suggest a link with Gramsci's conception of the historical bloc involving an alliance between the party and mass organizations.

In a position that echoes Raymond Williams, Freire argued that the party for change, committed to the subaltern, should allow itself to learn from and be transformed through contact with progressive social movements. It had "to reconnect with the general interest" (McIlroy, 1993, p. 277), as John McIlroy put it, with reference to Raymond Williams's ideas in this regard. Williams was here referring to not only the party but also all organizations traditionally associated with the working class.

One important proviso Freire made in this respect is that the party should do this "without trying to take them over." Movements, Freire seems to be saying, cannot be subsumed by parties, otherwise they lose their identity and forfeit their specific way of exerting pressure for change. The same applies to relations between municipal state and movements, a situation that movement activists must have dreaded, hence their attitude of being tactically inside and strategically outside, or, to use a one-time popular British expression, being in and against the state (London and Edinburgh Weekend Return Group, 1979). In terms of the links between party and movements, and with specific reference to the possible links between the PT and such movements as MST, Paulo Freire had this to say:

Today, if the Workers' Party approaches the popular movements from which it was born, without trying to take them over, the party will grow; if it turns away from the popular movements, in my opinion, the party will wear down. Besides, those movements need to make their struggle politically viable. (Freire, in Escobar et al., 1994, p. 40)

The concept of party, therefore, features prominently in Paulo Freire's thinking concerning the idea of a broad coalition of forces for social change, the kind of coalition called for both at the national and international levels. The much-augured international type of coalition or, more appropriately, convergence of forces has often been referred to as "globalization from below" (Marshall, 1997, pp. 60–61). It is the kind of convergence that the British sociologist Glenn Rikowski (2001) sees as being a feature of the antiglobalization movement, which made its presence felt in such places as Seattle, Nice, Prague, and elsewhere:

The significance of organised labour working together with social movements, environmental activists and other radical groups on a scale previously unknown invokes an anti-capitalism of real substance and significant scale. (p. 16)

Freire's later work and biographical elements help to elucidate themes that have always been connected with his work. The major contribution here is that of rendering the concepts more concrete. The theme of connecting with the lifeworlds of the learners, the "concrete knowledge of the reality" of the community in question (Freire, 1998a, p. 122) as the basis for genuine democratic teaching, is a recurring one. "Educands' concrete localization is the point of departure for the knowledge they create of the world" (Freire, 1994, p. 85). Once again, it is the starting point, however, and not the be-all and end-all of the pedagogical encounter (see Freire, 1994, p. 84). In remaining there and not moving beyond (through coinvestigation of the object of inquiry), one would be engaging in "basism," the romanticization (or "mythification") of the vernacular. We must start, however, by connecting with the learners' "concrete context" (Freire, 1998c, p. 78), including the child's dreams (in the case of young learners) or possibly nightmares (Freire repeated, throughout at least three of his last books, the response of a child from the slums who stated: I do not have dreams, only nightmares). To ignore this is "elitism" (Freire, 1994, p. 84). This theme applies to the kind of adult literacy work described and discussed in his earlier work. In his later work, this point applies to the issue of using generative themes within the context of the popular public school. These generative themes are conceived of, in the words of O'Cadiz, Wong, and Torres, as "the building blocks for the construction of a locally relevant curriculum" (O'Cadiz et al., 1998, p. 85). However, as the three authors rightly point out, it is only an "initial" step in engaging students and teachers in a critical reading of their world (O'Cadiz et al. 1998, p. 87). The preceding qualification concerning the need to avoid *basismo* applies.

Connecting with the lifeworlds of the learners as the initial stage in the educational process is part of an attempt to link the school to the popular classes and therefore to render it an institution that is no longer alien to these classes, a concern shared by the PT's Secretaria Municipal de Educacão (SMED) in Porto Alegre with respect to the Citizen School (Gandin and Apple, 2002, p. 110). Freire conceived of the Popular Public school in São Paulo as an institution that does not program people for failure but, on the contrary, to use Freire's own words, programs them to learn (Freire, 1998b, p. 96). The popular schools are conceived of in such a way that the popular classes develop a sense of ownership of these public spaces. The schools are very much conceived of as community public spaces. This is a theme to which I will return in the final chapter with specific reference to my own country. The pedagogy provided is intended to be not a pedagogy *for* the popular classes, or the oppressed, but a pedagogy *of* the popular classes and the oppressed, one that is developed *with* them (see Freire, in Gadotti, Freire, and Guimarães, 1995, p. 26). This has been the leitmotif of Freire's entire body of writings on pedagogy. It is the salient feature of the kind of popular education with which he is associated. His later writings render this the key feature of his conception of the school—the popular public school.

Arguably, the greatest contribution of Freire's later works lies precisely in the demonstration of this ability to introduce concepts connected with popular education to the municipal state school system (see Freire, 1991, 1993, 1997a, pp. 59–63; Saúl, 1995). The democratic, popular public school is very much a community school that is not the exclusive domain of teachers and educational administrators but that is open to many other people with a stake in education, including parents and other guardians, community representatives, students, janitors, cooks, and so on. And it would be appropriate to reiterate the point by Freire made in the introductory chapter: all those who are in contact with children in schools were to be formed as educators, including the cooks and janitors (see Freire, 1991). Parental participation was also another important factor in the development of the school (Saúl, 1993, p. 158), a theme that recalls Freire's earliest work in the northeast of Brazil, where working with parents became a feature of his work for SESI (Social Service of Industry) in Recife (see Freire, in Betto and Freire, 1986, p. 22; Freire, 1994, pp. 18–22; 1996, p. 90).

This was all in keeping with the recognition that "the school also belonged to the popular classes" (Freire, 1998b, p. 69), even though these classes were traditionally alienated from these schools that were found by the Freire-led Secretariat to be in a terrible state when it assumed office. The overall scenario, concerning children who would attend such schools, rendered the task of reform most daunting: 8 million children of school age failing to spend a single day at school with 6 million of those who enter being expelled (the term *dropout* is a misnomer for Freire) after the first or second year, and all this in a city that, at the time of the interview, had about 13 million inhabitants with 800,000 to 1,000,000 children living on the streets (Freire, in Morgagni, 1995, p. 87).

Freire and colleagues indicated that members of the popular classes waged violence on the school, with break-ins, for the purpose of looting, having been frequent. School directors were often attacked. School vandalism was a serious occurrence also in other parts of Brazil, including Porto Alegre, where it was brought to an end by educational reforms, carried out by the PT municipal government (Gandin and Apple, 2002, p. 110), which were similar to those of the Freire Secretariat in São Paulo. The perpetration of violent acts against the school often resulted in the institution setting up barriers and adopting tougher security measures that continued to isolate it further from the community it intended to serve, rendering it a veritable fortress, the antithesis of the much-desired notion of the school as a community learning center (see Gadotti, Freire, and Guimarães, 1995, pp. 58–60). Freire quotes an ex-prisoner who stated on TV that, although everyone discussed the violence that he and others committed, nobody discussed the violence they suffered (Freire, in Gadotti, Freire, and Guimarães, 1995, p. 59), the reference here being to the symbolic violence perpetrated by institutions such as schools on the working class. Freire went on to state that, according to him, it is necessary to research the motives for the violence being perpetrated against schools and also research the school's significance for the community, given that the latter reacts violently toward it (Freire, in Gadotti, Freire, and Guimarães, 1995).

It is against this terrible scenario that Paulo Freire and his team took on the onerous task of reforming the public school sector in São Paulo with a view to turning public schools into places that appeal and belong to the popular classes, rather than places that are perceived as being antagonistic toward these same classes. Those educators who are involved worldwide in democratizing public schools and education in general would do well to read Freire's works on the subject of changing the face of the schools (Freire, 1993, pp. 21, 129; 1998b, p. 95). This process might have been interrupted in São Paulo following the PT's loss of government there (the PT was returned to power in this city in the fall of 2000), but as I had occasion to indicate earlier, the spirit of these reforms and of Freire's educational philosophy is captured in at least one other city in Brazil, Porto Alegre in Rio Grande do Sul. This city is well known for the widespread experiments in deliberative participatory democracy that the PT introduced, particularly a Freire-inspired democratic approach to education, via the Citizen School, and the Participatory Budget experience (Gandin and Apple, 2002). Daniel Schugurensky's writings and presentations on the latter initiative by a PT municipal government seem to suggest strong affinities with the kind of philosophy that guided Freire and his team's efforts in democratizing education in São Paulo. With respect to the Participatory Budget (Gandin and Apple, 2002; Schugurensky, 2002a, 2002b), Schugurensky stated that although many "local planners, city officials, community organizers and participants do not perceive the pedagogical potential of participatory democracy," a number of "active participants" in the Porto Alegre project "understand the Participatory Budget as an educational space," often referring to it as a "citizenship school" (Schugurensky, 2002b, p. 72). He went on to say, with respect to the Participatory Budget, "By engaging actively in deliberation and decision making processes, individuals and communities learn and adopt basic democratic competences and values" (p. 72). It is this that, in my view, Freire and his colleagues sought to achieve by attempting to change the face of the public school and develop it into a veritable learning community for the popular classes.

The ideas connected with the São Paulo reforms remained influential, certainly in other parts of Brazil. This renders such books as *Pedagogy of the*

City and *Pedagogy of Hope* of great importance to cultural workers, policy makers, and educational administrators who work toward the democratization of the public educational system. If one looks at the printed literature (in English) connected with the Porto Alegre experience in the democratization of schooling, one can immediately detect the Freirean influence. The spirit of his São Paulo reforms runs through this municipal project (City Secretariat of Education of Porto Alegre, 1999).

Pedagogy of the City (Freire, 1993) and *Education and Democracy* (O'Cadiz et al., 1998) strike me as being two publications worth recommending for any educational policy or educational administration program in schools or faculties of education. Of course, this raises the question regarding spaces available for such reforms within the context of the hegemonic neoliberal state whose funding policies are closely monitored by the IMF and the World Bank. It would be interesting to follow the spread of these ideas and initiatives throughout the various municipalities and states in which the PT was successful during the fall 2000 elections and the entire country, now that the PT won the last presidential elections. Once again, the ideas emerging from São Paulo were not intended to serve as a blueprint for other schools to emulate. Each school had to find its own way of responding to the needs of its surrounding community, and it is for this reason that Freire emphasized the notion of school autonomy that does not, however, relieve the state of its responsibilities in providing adequate funding for a quality education. Gadotti and Freire stated that they have learned that there is no single model capable of rendering courageous the educational action carried out within the school; they argue that each school is the product of its own contradictions and that it is for this reason that they argue in favor of school autonomy as a strategy for enhancing the quality of the educational experience the school provides (Freire and Gadotti, 1995, p. 6).

What emerges clearly from these writings on Freire's work as Education Secretary is the image of a person striving to make up for lost time, caused by his period of exile, by attempting to stamp his mark on his homeland. Of course, by the time he took up this position, he had been enriched by an array of experiences, including the many experiences to which he was exposed during exile. One would point, once again, in this context, to his involvement with workers' education circles in Italy and Switzerland, especially his work with Spanish migrants in the latter country (see Freire, 1994). One must also mention the immediate postcolonial experiences in Portugal's former African colonies (see Freire, 1978; Freire and Faundez, 1989; Freire and Macedo, 1987). This notwithstanding, exile, for Freire, entailed a cruel severing from his Brazilian roots during the best years of his life, "when he was at the peak of his activist energies, intimately linked to a society roused for transformation" (Shor, 1998, p. 78).

This brings the age factor into consideration. Of course, Freire raised the issue of "returning old" in *Pedagogy of the Heart* (Freire, 1997a, p. 72), affirming how his return was a form of reinvigoration: "I was returning hopeful, motivated to relearn Brazil, to participate in the struggle for democracy . . . " (Freire, 1997a, p. 72). Given the lost years, he had to feel young to be able to make the most, in terms of activism, of his remaining years. The more recent works are full of accounts of this later activism that was jolted by the loss of his beloved Elza in the fall of 1986 and possibly reinvigorated through his 10 years of marriage to Nita. These are described as 10 years of love and passion and are captured by Nita Freire in *Nita e Paulo: Cronicas di Amor*, subsequently released in English in a translation by Donaldo Macedo. The sense of making up for one's lost years is what runs through these later works that project the image of Freire as a role model for people in their Third Age: "As I write this at seventy five, I continue to feel young, declining—not for vanity or fear of disclosing my age—the privilege senior citizens are entitled to, for example, at airports. . . . People are old or young much more as a function of how they think of the world, the availability they have for curiously giving themselves to knowledge" (Freire, 1997a, p. 72).

Love and humility continue to remain recurring themes in his later work. He constantly exhorted teachers to engage in their work with humility, tolerance, and love (see Freire, 1995b, pp. 19–21, 1998a, pp. 65, 1998c, pp. 39–41). Love was always a key feature of his work, as I indicated in the introductory chapter. It reflects several key elements in the genesis of Freire's work, not least its Christian overtones. I have indicated its revolutionary overtones strongly associated with the words of Ernesto "Che" Guevara. It was also emphasized by the MST as one of the ingredients for the education of children occurring within its own encampments: "those who do not love life cannot teach how to live" (Kane, 2001, p. 99). Love was also, for Freire, one of the emotional elements that drives a person forward in any humanizing activity. In the introductory chapter we have seen how, for Freire, there could be no teaching and other humanizing activity without love (Freire, in McLaren, 1997a, p. 37). The concept of love becomes arguably even stronger in his later work. Strongly connected with love is the value of humility, another recurring theme in his later work and in his earlier writings. For all their competence and authority, teachers must be humble to relearn that which they think they already know from others and to connect, through learning ("there is no teaching without learning"—Freire, 1998a, pp. 29–48), with their learner's lifeworlds.

Tolerance, another recurring word in both his early and later works, strikes me as being a trifle condescending when used in English, and I would much prefer the term *solidarity* in this context. Solidarity became an important issue in Freire's writings in the late 1980s and 1990s, which stress the need for persons to gain greater coherence throughout life (see Freire, 1998a, p. 58). The quest for life and for living critically became an ongoing quest for greater *coherence* as a human being—an elaboration on

his earlier modernist contention that a person's ontological vocation is
that of becoming fully human. Gaining coherence, for Freire, entailed
gaining greater awareness of one's unfinishedness (Freire, 1998a, pp. 51,
66) and one's multiple and layered identities (Freire, 1997b). These identities are often contradictory, rendering a person oppressed in one context
and an oppressor in another, in the latter case being a manifestation of the
oppressor within, a very important theme in Freire's most celebrated
work. This makes nonsense of the criticism, often leveled at Freire in U.S.
circles, that he failed to recognize that one can be oppressed in one situation and an oppressor in another and that he posits a binary opposition
between oppressor and oppressed. If anything, the relations between
oppressor and oppressed have always been presented by Freire as *dialectical* rather than as binary opposites (see Allman, 1999, pp. 88–89, for an insightful exposition in this regard).

Gaining greater coherence entails getting to know and engaging in
solidarity with, as well as learning from, the other. This theme becomes
all the more pertinent, given the quest among democratic educators–
cultural workers, to press for a revolutionary, critical form of multiculturalism (see McLaren, 1997b). The theme of gaining coherence is a
recurring one in Freire's later work, especially in a brilliant piece that
constitutes a response to a number of commentators on his work (Freire,
1997b). It reflects a recognition, on Freire's part, that forms of domestication can emerge from an ostensibly emancipatory practice. The contradictions arising from our multiple and layered subjectivities render this
a constant possibility. Rather than indulging in a nihilistic renunciation
of attempts at an empowering pedagogical practice, Freire saw this as
one of the strengths of critical pedagogy. Being based on praxis, on the
recognition of our unfinishedness as human beings and as pedagogues
and on the constant need to engage in annunciation and denunciation,
genuine critical pedagogy involves the ongoing struggle of reflecting on
oneself, on the social collectivity involved, and on the pedagogical practice. This is done with a view to transformative action—action intended
to enable one to confront one's contradictions to become less unfinished/
incomplete, less incoherent. This emerges from the piece by Freire in
Mentoring the Mentor, but it was always present in his work. It is implied
in Freire's exhortation, in *Pedagogy of the Oppressed,* to recognize the
presence of and to confront the oppressor within (the oppressor consciousness—the internalization of the oppressor's image). In this work,
Freire had argued that, through a problem-posing approach to education, human beings are conceived of as persons engaged in a "process of
becoming"; they are unfinished persons engaged in and with an "unfinished reality" (Freire, 1970b, 1993, p. 84). Being central to his notion of
history as possibility, the notion of incompleteness remains a central
theme in his work and features in practically all his later works, which

include at least one essay, available in English translation, focusing on the topic (Freire, 1998b, pp. 73–79).

The response to commentators in *Mentoring the Mentor* is a piece that throws into sharp focus Freire's later concerns with forms of oppression that are related not only to class issues but also to issues concerning race and gender. As he stated time and again in his later works, one cannot explain anything under the sun in terms of the class struggle. At the same time, he has often argued that *Perestroika* did not have the power to suppress the existence of social class (Freire, 1991). With respect to his discussions on race, gender, and other forms of identity, Freire's contact with the North American critical pedagogical milieu strikes me as having been instrumental. I reiterate the point, made in the introductory chapter and in chapter 2, that collaborators like Donaldo Macedo and the contributors to the *Mentoring the Mentor* volume pressed him hard on these issues, as have such writers as Kathleen Weiler (1991), through her criticisms of Freire's writings, and the largely sympathetic bell hooks (hooks, 1993). This point deserves some further treatment with special reference to Freire's later work, beginning from the early 1990s.

One ought to refer here to his discussions on machismo (Freire, 1994, 1996; Freire and Macedo, 1993, 1995) and racism (see Freire and Macedo, 2000). In the latter case, Freire and Macedo condemned the scientism that is often a hallmark of Eurocentric regimes of truth. In the other conversation, he broached the issue of gender. Having said this, I winced at his statement, in the 1993 dialogue with Macedo, "I am too a woman" (Freire, in Freire and Macedo, 1993, p. 175), concerning solidarity with women. I feel that there is a limit to which we men can be at one with women in their struggles, not being able to feel the pain of this specific form of oppression (Mayo, 1999a, p. 115). This notwithstanding, Freire sought to address the totalizing gender discourse of his earlier works, thus responding positively to the numerous American feminists who took up issue with him on this matter. As stated in the Introduction, one of the major criticisms leveled at Freire's work, a point that I had discussed in a chapter on the limitations of Freire's work (chapter 5) in my previous book-length study on Freire (Mayo, 1999a), is that for all the references to issues concerning the oppression of women in his work, and his assertion that class constituted the major focus of his early work, there is no sustained analysis of these forms of oppression. With regard to race, I consider it odd that a book-length conversation with Myles Horton, a person strongly identified with a center that had strong connections with the civil rights movement (Adams, 1972; Horton and Freire, 1990; Peters and Bell, 1987), did not lead to a sustained discussion on race.

A talking book in English between Freire and a woman or a black person would have been much appreciated. bell hooks expressed her desire to engage in such a book with Freire (hooks, 1993, 1994a) but, for some reason or other, this never materialized. It would seem to me that the work of the 1990s called out for this type of book. Talking books with persons totally committed to and immersed in the struggles involved in each type of oppression (one must constantly engage issues arising from the strong intersections that exist between the various oppressions) would have helped indicate the relevance and limitations of his ideas for the struggles involved. The tensions likely to arise from these discussions could have helped stretch Freire's ideas with respect to these issues and could have possibly rendered his work, coauthored with significant other educators, even more insightful, instructive, and powerful in its analysis of the different forms of oppression. It would be worth reiterating the point attributed to Darder (2002), in my review of her book in chapter 2, namely that, in a genuine conception of dialogue, motivated by a love for humanity and a deep sense of solidarity with others, conflicts are not to be avoided but to be confronted. This should be a feature of the dialectical approach so strongly advocated by Freire. Conflict is often absent from many of the talking books in English, involving exchanges between Freire and another educator, where, for the most part, the two figures involved are ever so agreeable toward each other. The 1989 book with Antonio Faundez, specifically the debate on the Guinea Bissau experience, referred to in the previous chapter, provides one of the few instances in Freire's English language talking books when such conflict occurs, once again within the context of a relationship between two people who are different but not antagonistic.

It ought to be remarked, however, that a number of the talking books, in English, of the late 1980s (one of which was published in 1990) raised several issues, but perhaps their very format often prevented sustained discussions on specific and intriguing issues from taking place. There seems to have been a tendency, in a number of talking books (certainly not all), for the authors to broach numerous topics and, as a consequence, few of these topics could be developed in sufficient depth. The authors tended to move freely from one topic to another.[15] These books have their merit, but perhaps they could have been complemented by a different kind of talking book, one with a sharper focus. Perhaps a conversational book between Freire and someone directly suffering from a specific form of oppression (racism, homophobia, sexism) and deeply committed to the struggle involved (e.g., antiracist education) would have guaranteed the necessary focused and sustained discussion because the authors would have rendered the issue in question the book's main topic.

What renders a sustained discussion on, say, race/ethnicity issues most relevant is the fact that they cannot be extricated from the broader issue of colonialism, a recurring theme in Freire's works. His early work, including his most famous book and most particularly Education as the Practice of Freedom (Freire, 1973), is rooted in the history of the Brazilian colonial experience, whereas the Guinea Bissau, Cape Verde, and São Tome and Principe writings (see Freire, 1978; Freire and Faundez, 1989; Freire and Macedo, 1987) reflect a concern with a national, postcolonial educational strategy for decolonizing the mind. In his later work, the issue of colonialism is addressed in many ways. One gathers that Freire used the term *colonial* in the broader Foucauldian sense of *colonized subject*. One obvious example here is his reference to the oppression of women, through sexist discourse and enfleshment in "concrete practices," as colonial (Freire, 1994, p. 67). He also dealt, in his work, with the legacy of colonial structures and thinking in countries that went through long historical periods of foreign colonial occupation or domination. For instance, he regarded the policies affecting the establishment of priorities with regard to salaries in Brazil as a colonial hangover (Freire, 1998c, p. 37). The theme of colonialism was also developed in a manner that is in keeping with the situation of most countries worldwide—neocolonialism in its most predatory form (McLaren, 1995). For Freire, the struggle for decolonization had to be an ongoing one. Analyzing Freire's work in relation to that of Ernesto "Che" Guevara, Peter McLaren underlined:

Freire acknowledges that decolonization is a project that knows no endpoint, no final closure. It is a lifetime struggle that requires counterintuitive insight, honesty, compassion, and a willingness to brush one's personal history against the grain of "naive consciousness" or commonsense understanding. After engaging the legacy of revolutionary struggles of the oppressed that has been bequeathed to us by Freire, it remains impossible to conceive of pedagogical practice evacuated of social critique. Freire has left stratified deposits of pedagogical insight upon which the future development of progressive education can and must be built. There is still reason to hope for a cooperative pedagogical venture among those who support a Freirean, class-based, pedagogical struggle, feminist pedagogy, or a pedagogy informed by queer theory and politics, that may lead to a revival of serious educational thinking in which the category of liberation may continue to have and to make meaning. (McLaren, 2000, p. 170)

It is fitting, therefore, to conclude this chapter the way it started. In confronting the fatalism of neoliberalism, Freire had embarked on his latest attempt to confront the most recent form assumed by colonialism. For colonialism is a constant feature of the capitalist mode of production that is characterized by restructuring, the search for new markets, and the constant drawing of more and more of the world's population into capitalist relations of production. Colonialism takes on different forms, and the one it is assuming at present is predicated on neoliberalism with its concomitant ideology of the marketplace.

The "fatalism of neo-liberalism" (Araújo Freire, 1997, p. 10) is an important theme in Freire's later English language books. He spoke of the nihilism of what he called reactionary postmodernity, a nihilism that denies people the chance to dream of a better world. The kind of nefarious and insidious thinking that becomes the subject of his attack is what he termed the ideological negation of ideology: "the ideology of ideological death"[16] (Freire, 1998c, p. 14). Freire's thinking in this regard, predicated on the sense of agency and the constant unmasking of ideologies through a process involving *denúncia* and *anúncio,* strikes me as being in keeping with what Frei Betto anticipated to be "a world movement to rescue utopias" (Betto, 1999, p. 45). In Betto's words:

This is exactly it: it is an ideology that preaches the death of ideology. I think this is all nonsense, because human beings need dreams, need utopia and there is no ideology, no system that can stop this force. Dostoyevski was right when he said: "The most powerful weapon of a human being is his [*sic*] conscience" and this nobody can destroy. I think it ridiculous when they preach that there is no ideology any more, in order to be able to state that the only ideology is the neo-liberal one. I think that it is a matter of time before we witness the eruption of a world movement to rescue utopias. (Betto, 1999, p. 45)

Of course, in these later works, Freire seems to be expressing his immediate reactions to an ideology that is fatalistic and contradictory. These reactions are sporadic and were yet to be developed into a coherent and systematic work, precisely the kind of work he was contemplating at the time of his death. Freire expressed his anger at this ideology in *Letters to Cristina,* where he argued:

We therefore don't have to continue to propose a pedagogy of the oppressed that unveils the reasons behind the facts or that provokes the oppressed to take up critical knowledge and transformative action. We no longer need a pedagogy that questions technical training or is indispensable to the development of a professional comprehension of how and why society functions. What we need to do now, according to this astute ideology, is focus on production without any preoccupation about what we are producing, who it benefits, or who it hurts. (Freire, 1996, p. 84)

And yet, as I have argued elsewhere (Mayo, 1999a, p. 5), the scenario of general impoverishment, often bordering on destitution, in various parts of the world, especially those under the sway of structural adjustment programs, with an ever-widening gap between north and south and the constant rape of the earth for profit, necessitates that we remain preoccupied with *how* (an addition to Freire's phrase) and "what we are producing, who it benefits, or who it hurts" (Freire, 1996, p. 84). We need a pedagogy concerned not only with the preceding but which, in response, enables us to imagine and strive collectively toward the realization of a world that can and ought to be different, a world governed by life-centered rather than market-driven values (see Miles, 1996, 1998, p. 256).

The quest for such a pedagogy by Freire, the anticolonial or postcolonial pedagogue par excellence, is in keeping with his long search for the refinement of pedagogical approaches that confront colonialism in its different forms (see Giroux, 1993b, 1996). Freire was exploring the ingredients for what would have been his next major and timely book project, a project that was, however, not meant to be.

He was obstinate about writing about neo-liberalism with another member of the PT . . . from the State of Minas Gerais. He never tired of condemning the proclaimed fatalism, with which the neo-liberals justify the historical route they themselves have traced to attain their objectives, as an inexorable force against which there is nothing to be done. They say that this is the natural course of human socioeconomic and political evolution and there is no way and even no reason for changing it. He said: "Fatalism is only understood by power and by the dominant classes when it interests them. If there is hunger, unemployment, lack of housing, health and schools, they proclaim that this is a universal trend and so be it! But when the stock market falls in a country far away and we have to tighten up our belts, or if a private national bank has internal problems due to the inability of it's directors or owners, the State immediately intervenes to 'save them.' In this case, the 'natural,' 'inexorable,' is simply put aside." He wanted to clarify and denounce this more complete and perverse form of capitalism, because he felt it was his duty as an educator. (Nita Freire, in Borg and Mayo, 2000b, pp. 108–109)

One wonders whether his new work would have extended beyond the anthropocentric framework that characterizes much of his output and that of many other authors whose work he inspired. The point concerning Freire's anthropocentrism was raised also by Stanley Aronowitz (1998, p. 11) especially with respect to Freire's very debatable distinctions between animals and humans concerning critical acumen. In confronting neoliberalism by positing life-centered values in contrast to market-driven ones, we require a radicalism that extends beyond the realm of social relations, to embrace the larger domain of human–earth relationships.

This very evident anthropocentrism marks one of the limitations of Freire's vision for social transformation. There is need for the *Eco* prefix to be placed in the title of any of the radical *isms* we embrace, as in *Ecofeminism* (see Mies and Shiva, 1993). The *Eco* prefix is not simply an add on but an integral feature of the struggle involved. With regard to human–earth relationships, we can draw sustenance from the works of people like Metchild Hart (1992) and Maria Mies and Vandana Shiva (1993). Among the most recent works, I would cite that by Edmund O'Sullivan (1999; O'Sullivan, Morrell, and O'Connor, 2002), which draws a lot on the writing of Thomas J. Berry. I would also cite the work of Brian Milani (2002), who focuses on green community development with an analysis grounded in political economy, green politics, an awareness of the impact of capitalism on the culture industry, and an assessment of the potential and limitations of social movements. One other important work to be cited, in this context, is that by Francisco Gutierrez and Cruz Prado (2000), the term *Ecopedagogia* being used in this case. It is also heartening to note that the Instituto Paulo Freire (IPF) in São Paulo, officially founded on September 1, 1992, has a program in Ecopedagogy, contributing to the promotion of the construction of a *planetary citizenship*. The IPF is working assiduously within the context of the *Earth Charter (Carta da Terra)*, a charter that recalls the Universal Declaration of Human Rights (IPF, 2000, pp. 11–12). It is likewise heartening to note that ecological issues featured prominently among the generative themes within the interdisciplinary curriculum developed in some of the popular public schools as part of the reform introduced by the Education Secretariat in São Paulo under the direction of Education Secretary Paulo Freire (see O'Cadiz et al., 1998, pp. 152, 201).

Edmund O'Sullivan forcefully expressed the point, concerning the anthropocentric nature of much critical pedagogy, in his highly inspiring book:

Probably one of the most prominent omissions in the critical pedagogical approaches to education at this juncture of its formulations is its lack of attention to ecological issues. My major criticism of a critical perspective is their preeminent emphasis on inter-human problems frequently to the detriment of the relations of humans to the wider biotic community and the natural world. The general direction of critical perspectives is toward anthropocentrism. The criticism of anthropocentrism is by no means a reason for dismissal of the vital concerns that critical perspectives pose for contemporary education. These issues must be taken forward and fused into wider biocentric concerns. (O'Sullivan, 1999, pp. 63–64)

This requires our building on and going beyond the struggle commenced by Freire. What is required is a process of transformative learning on the lines of what Freire has called unity in diversity He used it to account for social difference and as part of a search for elements unifying the various subaltern groups in their struggle against oppression. The concept of diversity would, however, assume the broader meaning conveyed by O'Sullivan when projecting his educational vision for the twenty-first century, what he calls an "ecozoic vision" characterized by our connectedness to the ecosystem that sustains us, as opposed to the current state, which he describes as being characterized by the technical–industrial values of Western-Eurocentric culture. One might perhaps speak of the need for unity in biodiversity in this context.

All told, Freire has provided us with a huge corpus of literature containing ideas that can inspire people committed to the fostering of greater social justice. It is now left to others to make creative use of his theoretical and biographical legacy with a view to making sense of the contexts in which they operate, both the immediately surrounding context and the broader one. This is the challenge I attempt to take up in the final two chapters, with the one immediately following focusing on the Mediterranean region that constitutes the larger surrounding context for my work. My exploration of Freire's relevance to this context remains tentative.

NOTES

1. The seminar, held at the Institute of Education, University of London, centered around the topic: the educational theory of Paulo Freire.

2. In our taped interview with him, Plinio Sampaio lamented the fact that the PT did not avail itself of Freire's presence in its ranks to develop an educational program for its rank and file. Freire would have been the ideal person to help develop this program.

3. Literal translation: Movement of Rural Workers without Land. The abbreviated title is *Movimento dos Sem Terra* (MST—Movement of Landless Peasants).

4. Needless to say, this interview, carried out in April 1998, could not anticipate the string of victories obtained by the PT in the 2000 municipal and state elections and Lula's presidential victory in 2002.

5. One book that dwells on Freire, Guevara, and the Zapatistas is McLaren (2000). McLaren dwells at length on the struggles in Chiapas in this book and constantly makes reference to this struggle in other work (see McLaren in Borg, Mayo, and Sultana, 1997). For a brief but very insightful discussion on Mexico, NAFTA, and the Zapatistas, see Chomsky (1999), chapter 10.

6. See, for instance, the following compact disks: *Terra* by Chico Buarque, MST, 1997; *Arte em Movimento* (19 pieces of music and a poem), interpreted by Ires Escobar, Marcos Monteiro, Ze Pinto, Ze Claudio and Protasio Prates, *Movimento dos Trabalhadores Rurais Sem Terra*.

7. For another account of educational work within the MST, particularly work in mathematics carried out by Gelsa Knijnik, see the last chapter of Coben, 1998. Chapter 4, "Popular Education and the Landless Movement in Brazil," of Liam Kane's excellent and revealing book on popular education and social change in Latin America (Kane, 2001), which is based on his earlier stand-alone piece (Kane, 2000), is a must read for those seeking a well-informed and lucid introduction to the work of the MST. Gelsa Knijnik wrote a review of this chapter, which is also included in Kane's book, at the end of chapter 4.

8. I am indebted, for this information, to my good friend, Daniel Schugurensky, from the Department of Adult Education and Counseling Psychology at the Ontario Institute for Studies in Education/University of Toronto.

9. Carmel Borg and I are indebted to Cardinal Arns for this information—private conversation, in the presence of Frei Joao Xerri, in the Sacristy of São Paulo Cathedral, April 1998. The point was confirmed to me by Nita Freire at the Pedagogy/Theatre of the Oppressed Conference, New York, June 1999.

10. I am indebted to Lilia Azevedo for confirming and clarifying facts surrounding this document and other matters referred to in this paper. I am also indebted to Frei Joao Xerri because I picked up lots of information, referred to in this paper, from him.

11. I am indebted for this point to David W. Livingstone, from the Department of Sociology and Equity Studies in Education at the Ontario Institute for Studies in Education/University of Toronto.

12. Freire himself speaks of his own experience, in this regard, following his return to Brazil. He was not content to simply teach at PUC and at the UNICAMP and engaged with a number of social organizations (Freire, in Betto and Freire, 1986, p. 86).

13. Earlier, Freire had stressed this aspect of his own work in the exchanges with Betto and Kotscho (Freire, in Betto and Freire, 1986, p. 86).

14. The literacy experiences of the participating grassroots groups differed greatly. Stromquist (1997) argued that these groups underwent a program of intensive training, focusing on consciousness-raising approaches, which lasted a fortnight. This exceeds the amount of time the average literacy teacher spends in training. Stromquist (1997) argued that the educators needed greater support to be effective in their literacy work and concluded that emancipatory education necessitates a great amount of preparation on the educators' part.

15. Of course, ample space is accorded, in the 1994 book with the UNAM scholars (Escobar et al., 1994), to the related issues of intellectuals, the public sphere, and universities. There are sustained discussions on rigor and liberating education in the earlier, late 1980s conversational book with Ira Shor (Shor and Freire, 1987). There is also a sustained discussion on race issues in the Freire–Macedo (2000) conversation cited earlier on, but then this was a single chapter, in an edited book (Steiner et al., 2000), which focused exclusively on this issue.

16. Throughout his work, Freire uses the term *ideology* in two different ways, at times with reference to Marx's negative concept of ideology and at times with reference to a system of ideas. One can detect the different uses from this chapter in which reference is made to Freire's dual usage of the concept.

CHAPTER 5

Reinventing Freire in a Southern Context: The Mediterranean

One of the greatest challenges Freire has posed to those who subscribe to his pedagogical approach and draw sustenance from his theoretical insights is not to use him as an instrument of cultural invasion but to *reinvent* him in the context(s) in which they are operating. For Freire's pedagogical approach privileges *context:* "Reading the text must be preceded by the reading of the context. In the last analysis reading texts is a dialectical exercise which leads us permanently to the reading of the original context" (Freire, 1995c, p. 62). His pedagogical approach is therefore based on the negation of a one shoe fits all strategy, which has been a feature of the dominant neoliberal, neocolonial, and technical rational discourse in education:

I couldn't possibly give you recipes that basically fall into providing a kind of certainty of teacher-proof curriculum or ways of teaching in a Black ghetto in the United States, or ways of teaching in the new communities of color in Europe, or ways of teaching in ethnic neighborhoods anywhere else. It would be dishonest of me to do that without knowing the context. Thus I have to be reinvented and re-created according to the demands—pedagogical and political demands—of the specific situation. (Freire, 1997b, p. 309)

The three Paulo Freire forums that have been organized by the Instituto Paulo Freire (IPF) thus far (São Paulo, 1998; Bologna, 2000 and Los Angeles, 2002) have provided us with opportunities to witness the reinvention of Paulo Freire's ideas and pedagogical approach in a variety of settings, including local, national, and regional settings. Quite revealing was the second forum that took place at the University of Bologna in

2000 and that included a plenary session, in which I participated, on the use of Freire's ideas in different contexts (Telleri, 2002). Included among these contexts were continents and regions. This particular panel provided me with a unique opportunity to reflect and write on the relevance of Paulo Freire's ideas for the countries of the Mediterranean region, that area which has provided the larger regional backdrop to my formation as a person, citizen, educator and writer. I come from this part of the world that has constituted the focus of enquiry for a network of scholars specializing in a variety of areas including education and more specifically comparative education. Various initiatives are taking place in the area of comparative education with a special regional focus on the Mediterranean.[1] I therefore consider it most opportune to examine the relevance of Paulo Freire's ideas to the specific southern regional context that is the Mediterranean, hoping also to show some of the ways Freire can be reinvented, not only within the specificities of micro-contexts such as schools and other learning settings, admirably captured in works by Shor (1987), Kirkwood and Kirkwood (1987), and most recently Darder (2002), but also in a regional context which does not normally feature prominently in the all pervasive Anglo-North American-Australian literature on Freire.

It ought to be affirmed, at the very outset, that the Mediterranean is a *construct*.[2] Depending on their location in the North–South axis, different people construct it differently. There are those, especially in the North of Europe, and also elsewhere, who define the Mediterranean in a manner that reflects a colonial and Eurocentric conception of the world. Pride of place is often given, within this conceptualization, to those traditions that lie at the heart of Western civilization, notably the Greco-Roman tradition. I used the word "elsewhere" in that one often finds this conception also among colonized subjects. For, as Fanon wrote:

The colonialist bourgeoisie, in its narcissistic dialogue, expounded by the members of its universities, had in fact deeply implanted in the minds of the colonized intellectual that the essential qualities remain eternal in spite of all the blunders men [sic] may make: the essential qualities of the West, of course. The native intellectual accepted the cogency of these ideas, and deep down in his brain you could always find a vigilant sentinel ready to defend the Greek-Latin pedestal. (Fanon, 1963, p. 46)

This process of cultural invasion leads one to think of the Mediterranean only in terms of those centers in the region that are directly associated with the Greek–Latin tradition. In this respect, the Rome-based Croat scholar Predrag Matvejevic wrote, "We need to get rid of this European habit of speaking about the Mediterranean and think only of its northern shore: the Mediterranean has another shore, that of Africa and the Maghreb"(Matvejevic, 1997, p. 119).[3]

There are, in fact, those who construct the Mediterranean differently, projecting it as a region having all the characteristics of what can be broadly called the "South." According to this conception, one appreciates the region's richness and cultural diversity, as well as the many voices and identities that constitute it. One can consider many of these voices and identities marginalized, typical of southern voices and identities. In the Eurocentric centers of cultural and intellectual production, these voices and identities are constructed as forms of *alterity*, and they are often exoticized, if not demonized, being very much subaltern voices engendering, in Foucauldian terms, a subjugated body of knowledge. And yet, as I shall attempt to show, this body has in the past contributed significantly to the development of the dominant Western Eurocentric tradition.

With respect to its Latin Arc, in other words, the Southern European side of the Mediterranean, one can speak of the presence of the Third World in the so-called First World. I am speaking here of uneven levels of regional development in a single country (e.g., northern Italy vis-à-vis the *Mezzogiorno*, a situation discussed by Antonio Gramsci in his notes on Italian history, in the *Quaderni*, and his unfinished piece, "Alcuni temi sulla questione meridionale").[4] This context invited parallels with the process of uneven regional development in Freire's Brazil, a point registered in works comparing Gramsci's views with those of Freire (see Mayo, 1999a) and works foregrounding the influence of Gramsci's thinking on popular education in Brazil (Ireland, 1987). Gramsci's Italy and Freire's Brazil have for years been characterized by a state of internal dependency or, to use Gramsci's term, internal colonialism. I stated, in the introductory chapter, that the national indigenous bourgeoisie, located in the southeast area of Brazil, has historically been engaged in an alliance with the rural landowning oligarchy in the northeast. It is partly through this alliance that the bourgeoisie established its control over the rest of the country. In Ireland's words "the expansion of industry in the South east of Brazil was premised both politically and economically, upon the stagnation of the North-east"(Ireland, 1987, p. 12). Gramsci's analysis of the Southern Question underlined the means whereby the industrial bourgeoisie in the north of Italy exercised economic and political control over the rest of the Italian peninsula. They engaged in an alliance with the landowners in the south (Ireland, 1987, p. 9), a situation for which Gramsci held the southern intelligentsia to be partly responsible (Nairn, 1982, p. 174). Pasquale Verdicchio stated, "Almost seventy years since Gramsci's essay, many of the problematics regarding the relationship of the South to the North remain unresolved" (Verdicchio, 1995, p. 6). It ought to be said that these uneven levels of development are part and parcel of the capitalist mode of production.

This vision of the Mediterranean is linked to a larger vision of the south. In my view, this conception of the Mediterranean as an example of the south renders Paulo Freire's voice, a voice that belongs to and speaks to the concerns of the south, very relevant to countries in this region. It ought to be said, however, once we are discussing Freire in this context, that the region has produced a number of progressive educators. Italy, for example, has produced such progressive educators as Lorenzo Milani (Burtchaell, 1988; Fallaci, 1993; Pecorini, 1996; Scuola di Barbiana, 1996), Danilo Dolci (Dolci, 1966) and Antonio Gramsci. Besides being a very important figure in the Italian political scene and a significant social theorist, Gramsci was very much involved in adult education, an engagement that started during his youth. Martin Buber, a very important influence on Paulo Freire and whose concept of dialogue in such works as *I and Thou* invites parallels with Freire's work, emigrated to Palestine in 1938 where, among other things, he was an adult-education organizer. Even a small Mediterranean island such as Malta has produced its fair share of people who have made their contribution to teaching against the grain in specific historical contexts, namely Gorg Preca (Sultana, 1995) and Manwel Dimech (Zammit Marmara', 1997a, 1997b). One of our challenges here is to discover other educators from the Mediterranean and pay tribute to them, underlining their contributions to educational and social development in the various contexts in which they were engaged. Referring specifically to adult education, Ettore Gelpi once asked " . . . are adult educators incapable of discovering other 'Paulo Freires' in the southern part of the world and quoting them in their articles?" (Gelpi, 1999, p. 263).

The contributions of several progressive, counterhegemonic or anticolonial educational figures from both sides of the Mediterranean need to be explored. There is likely to be a number of such figures, especially given the tendency to discover educational contributions in the work of historical figures whose best years were dedicated to the cause of liberating their country and people from oppression. Most revolutionary governments promote the image of folk and national heroes to place their own revolution within a particular historical context. Sandino and Zapata are classic examples, and we have seen entire movements rally around them, emphasizing a continuity between these figures' struggles and that of the revolutionary movement in question. The words of these figures, some written and some attributed to them and spread by word of mouth, are taken up for their alleged pedagogical insights and constitute the basis for entire pedagogical theories. In Freire's Latin America, these figures form part of a radical or revolutionary pedagogical tradition, becoming important sources of reference even with respect to the work of somebody such as Freire.

Can the same apply to similar figures from Mediterranean countries? Should we, for instance, consider the Libyan, Omar Al Mukhtar,[5] an educator, in the same way that Augusto Cesar Sandino (Tunnerman, 1983) and Ernesto "Che" Guevara (McLaren, 2000) are considered educators?

When conceiving of education in its widest context, as Freire himself would urge us to do, he himself deriving inspiration from the likes of Che, Mao, Lenin,[6] and others, then there is always the possibility of regarding as educators people who would not prima facie appear to be so (interestingly enough, accounts refer to Al-Mukhtar as a Quranic teacher by profession turned guerilla). The sources from which these educators can be found are many. For instance, should those who engage in itinerant community theatre be considered educators, given the importance attached to communal drama in the literature on emancipatory education? Ramon Flecha (1992), a Basque scholar who has made a contribution to critical pedagogy and Freirean scholarship (Macedo, 1998, p. xv), cites Federico Garcia Lorca and his theatrical company, *La Barraca,* as exemplars of progressive community education in Spain (Flecha, 1992, p. 191).

The long and short of this paranthesis is to recognize the presence of indigenous educators, some of whom can easily be regarded as progressive, counterhegemonic or anticolonial when viewed within the context of their geographical and historical location, before attempting to demonstrate the relevance to the region of someone who shares the same kind of southern voice but who hails from a different regional context. One ought to remark, however, that, in Freire's case, the regional context has strong diasporic connections with the Mediterranean.

Paulo Freire established contacts with Mediterranean countries, especially Southern European countries such as Italy and Spain. One should add, here, Portugal given, as I indicated in the introductory chapter, this country's cultural affinities with the Mediterranean context despite its geographical location on the Atlantic strip. Freire came into contact with these countries mainly during his period of exile from Brazil, during the time that he worked for the World Council of Churches in Geneva. In his book, *Pedagogy of Hope,* Freire (1994) refers to his experiences with groups of Spanish and Italian labor leaders (the Italian leaders were engaged in securing the 150 hours[7] right to paid educational leave) (Freire, 1994, p. 121). He would meet the Italian labor leaders in either Geneva or Italy and the Spaniards solely in Geneva because *Pedagogy of the Oppressed* was usually the topic of discussion during these meetings, and the book had been banned in Portugal and Spain. Freire stated "Franco's Spain, like Salazar's Portugal had shut us both out. *Pedagogy* and me" (Freire, 1994, p. 122).

His ideas, of course, were eventually given great importance in Spain and Portugal, especially in the context of the process of democratization that occurred immediately after the fall of fascism in the countries of the Iberian peninsula (Flecha, 1990, 1992; Lima, 1992; Lind and Johnston, 1986). Despite Freire's contention that *Pedagogy of the Oppressed* and its author were shut out by the Franco regime, Ramon Flecha stated that the Brazilian's ideas had an impact even prior to Spain's turn to democratic rule:

Paulo Freire is the most significant writer in the development of adult education in Spain from the late sixties up to the coming of democracy. Adult educators found in his theory principally four elements:

- *Political:* an orientation for an adult education allied with worker and popular movements in fighting the dictatorship.
- *Sociological:* an analysis of how . . . [banking] . . . education reproduces society and how a liberating one can transform the structure.
- *Psychological:* the consideration of adult learners as people with an important background of non-academic culture and social life experiences.
- *Pedagogical:* some resources to build an education-learning process adapted to adulthood. It was valuable mainly in literacy activities. (Flecha, 1992, pp. 192–193)

As always, there would be tensions involved, even when using ideas from Freire in the context of ostensibly liberatory experiences, as we saw in chapter 3 with respect to Tanzania. Following the overthrow of the Caetano regime in Portugal through the so-called revolution of the carnations, Portugal witnessed a profusion of popular education activities (Melo, 1985). The situation then was one that would have been congenial for the flourishing of Freire-inspired popular education, also given the strong cultural and political ties that exist between the Portuguese and Brazilian contexts (Mayo, 1999a). In the words of Alberto Melo:

The programmes were to promote what the people had in abundance . . . popular culture, the people's own store of knowledge . . . in short, their own living culture. (Melo, 1985, pp. 42–43)

These goals immediately bring Freire to mind, even though Melo did not mention the Brazilian educator in his piece on the Portuguese experience in adult education after 1974 (Melo, 1985). Agneta Lind and Anton Johnston, in their report on adult literacy for SIDA, made reference to a Freire-inspired state-sponsored program taking place in Portugal following the revolution and the transition to civilian rule. They referred to Portugal, however, as one of two examples (Peru provides the other example) of situations when national directors are suspended because of the state-sponsored program's "political implications of action or potential action against the government" (Lind and Johnston, 1986, p. 61). According to Lind and Johnston (1986), who cite another source published in Sweden, the Portuguese situation occurred in 1976. These situations highlight the danger that, in sponsoring Freire-inspired programs, the state would be perceived to be providing the people with a weapon that can eventually be wielded against it. This episode should not, however, minimize the fact that Freire is an important source of influence in this part of the world, and his name is often cited alongside that of other courageous educators from the region, such as, in the case of Portugal, Luiza Cortesão. Centers named after and inspired by Paulo Freire abound, such as the Paulo Freire Institutes in Oporto, Valencia (CreC, namely Centre de Recursos I Educació Continua), Malta (a Jesuit-run community learning center in a specific locality), and the *Centro de Investigacão Paulo Freire,* University of Evora, Portugal.

One can draw a lot of inspiration from Freire as we confront the many pedagogical and social challenges facing people in the Mediterranean region. In many Mediterranean countries, we come across the scars left by northern colonialism. One of the main challenges is to develop an educational process that "de-colonizes the mind," to use a phrase rendered popular by people such as Frantz Fanon and John Ngugi Wa Thong'o. We have seen that, in an interview with Donaldo Macedo, Freire attributed this phrase also to the former Cape Verde president Aristides Perreira (Freire, 1985).

I have stressed in the previous chapter that Paulo Freire represents a postcolonial voice (Borg and Mayo, 2002a; Giroux, 1993b; Hickling-Hudson, 1999). Recall that his early well-known works, such as *Pedagogy of the Oppressed, Cultural Action for Freedom,* and "Education as the Practice of Freedom" (Freire, 1973) attach much importance to the Brazilian colonial experience. The texts by Freire concerning educational development in Portugal's former African colonies (Guinea Bissau, Cape Verde, São Tome e Principe, Mozambique, etc.) focus on the need to develop a national post-colonial strategy to decolonize the mind. We discover, in Freire, a continuous confrontation with the reality of colonialism, a recurring feature of a capitalism constantly engaged in exploring new markets and drawing more of the world's population into capitalist social relations of production. Freire's ideas, and those of other authors, such as Frantz Fanon, Albert Memmi, Julius Nyerere, Walter Rodney, Edward Said, Samir Amin, and Nawal El Saadawi, enable us to understand, or to deepen our understanding of, the legacy of northern colonialism that constitutes a feature of the reality of many countries in the south, including the Mediterranean. Recall also that, in his latest writings and speeches, Freire confronted colonialism in its latest form. He confronted neocolonialism, the intensification of globalization, and the concomitant ideology of neoliberalism. Quite revealing, in this respect, is the quote, cited in the previous chapter, wherein Nita Freire stated that her husband intended to write a book on the fatalism of neoliberalism (Araújo Freire, 1997, p. 10).

GLOBALIZATION

Like all regions of the world, the Mediterranean is under the sway of the phenomenon commonly referred to as globalization, a process that, strictly speaking, has always been a feature of the capitalist mode of production characterized by periodical economic reorganization and an ongoing quest for the exploration of new markets. In fact, it is most appropriate, in the present historical conjuncture, to repeat the term I used earlier: the *intensification* of globalization. This intensification is brought about through developments in the field of information technology. This process "not only blurs national boundaries but also shifts solidarities within and outside the national state" (Torres, 1998a, p. 71). It is a period marked by mobility. Mobility is a characteristic of globalization's inner and outer circuits (Torres, 1998a, p. 92). We can speak of mobility in terms of the threat of the flight of capital in a scenario where the process of production is characterized by dispersal and cybernetic control (outer circuit) and mobility of workers within and beyond the region (inner circuit). Migration is an important feature of the Mediterranean. As underlined at the 1997 Civil Forum EuroMed:

Immigration represents the emerging aspect, probably the most evident, of the wide process which characterizes more and more the whole planet—globalization. Migrations represent more than a phenomenon, a historical certainty that can be found today, though with different features, in all countries and, in particular, in the most developed [*sic. read: industrially developed*]. Migration phenomena are becoming more and more important within the Mediterranean basin. (Fondazione Laboratorio Mediterraneo, 1997, p. 551)

For centuries, according to Braudel, exchange was a prominent feature of life in and around the Mediterranean basin. In this day and age, however, the exchange takes on a different form. In terms of mobility of people, occurring "on a scale never seen before in history" (El Saadawi, 1997, p. 122), it would be amiss to consider the exchange one that occurs on a level playing field. It can also be argued, with respect to the movement of people from the Southern Mediterranean to the Northern Mediterranean and beyond, that the specter of the violent colonial process the old continent initiated has come back with a vengeance to haunt it (Borg and Mayo, 2002b, p. 45). What abets this process are the requirements of the economies in highly industrialized countries concerning certain types of labor and the consideration that these requirements cannot or should not (to minimize labor costs) be satisfied by the internal labor market, despite the high levels of unemployment experienced within these countries (Apitzsch, 1995, p. 68). This brings into focus the issue concerning the so-called guest workers. This issue is touched on by Freire in *Pedagogy of Hope.* He speaks of his work in Geneva when he came in contact, through meetings and projects, with guest workers from Italy, Spain, Portugal, Greece, Turkey, and Arab countries. In short, he came across people from a region of the South (the Mediterranean) seeking a new life in the thriving central European environments. As Verdicchio (1995, p. 11) so eloquently argued, with respect to his country of origin, the Southern Question extends beyond Italy through the presence elsewhere of the Southern Italian migrant diaspora. One can apply this consideration to the Mediterranean at large to indicate how the Southern Question of the Mediterranean extends beyond this region through the presence elsewhere of the Southern Mediterranean diaspora. If one can take liberties with a statement by Verdicchio, one can say that the emigrant from the south that is the Mediterranean is a "de-contextualized expression of the contradictory process" of state formation in the country of origin. One of the challenges for critical pedagogical work with migrants to emerge from this formulation is that of enabling the migrants to read not only the world they now inhabit as immigrants but also the world they left. As Freire discovered, with respect to Brazil, the period of migration (exile in his case) presented an opportunity for a critical distancing from the world one once knew to relearn it (a favorite Freire term with respect to Brazil) in a more critical vein. The same would apply to critical educators, engaged in Northern Mediterranean countries, working with migrants from the Mediterranean's southern shores.

Migrant guest workers in Switzerland enabled Freire, on his own admission, to begin to come "in contact with the harsh realities of one the most serious traumas of the 'Third World in the First': the reality of the so-called guest workers . . . and their experience of racial, class and sexual discrimination" (Freire, 1994, p. 122). Freire went on to indicate the fear of the oppressor as one of the challenges to be faced in this context in view of the fact that the opportunity to work, irrespective of how exploitative the conditions are, becomes the primary concern, which takes precedence over the concern for political mobilization to confront the exploitation induced by this process of mobility of labor power across national boundaries. This mobility involves, in most cases, a severance from one's roots in view of the process of uneven levels of development that is characteristic of the capitalist mode of production. Confronting the fear of oppression remains a key challenge here for progressive educators working with migrants; it is a key challenge for progressive educators working in the countries that many of these emigrants left.

The other theme that emerges from Freire's writing on the issue, with respect to a critical pedagogy confronting neoliberalism in an age characterized by increasing labor market segmentation on ethnic grounds, is that of class solidarity. There is an important role for labor unions here, and a process of workers' education based on interethnic class solidarity is one of the challenges facing labor unions in many countries of the region currently becoming increasingly multiethnic through the influx of immigrants from the region's southern shores and elsewhere:

a Spanish worker, enraged and almost in physical pain, protested a lack of class solidarity on the part of his French colleagues. "Lots of 'em come up and kick our butt," he said with irritation, "if we're not looking!"

Behavior like this could reinforce today's neo-liberal discourse, according to which the social classes are vanishing. They no longer exist, we hear. (Freire, 1994, p. 122)

Of course the foregoing points apply to most regions in the world and not just the Mediterranean. What renders the whole process significant in the context of this region is, once again, the fact that the receiving countries are the same countries that once witnessed mass waves of emigration. These countries have experienced the shift from being exporters to importers of labor power. This is not the place to engage in a discussion concerning the way the prejudice and racism experienced by settlers from North Africa and elsewhere differs from that experienced in the past by emigrants from today's receiving Mediterranean countries. Nevertheless, in combating xenophobia and racism in this context, one would do well to recall the plight of people from the receiving country when settling abroad or in a more industrially developed region of the same country.

Drama can serve as a powerful pedagogical tool, in this regard, to foster greater interethnic solidarity and understanding. One can draw inspiration from a dramatic representation to which participants at a 1998 conference on education in the Mediterranean held in Sestri Levante, Liguria, Italy, were exposed. It was carried out by a troupe of players from Genoa, the *Laboratorio Interculturale Comune di Genova,* and involved a juxtaposition of situations concerning the harsh realities of migration, both past and present. The plight of Italians migrating to the United States, Argentina, and elsewhere, and of Italians from the south moving into the country's northern regions, was juxtaposed against that of Africans (including Arab) and Eastern Europeans, with their personal narratives, moving into Italy. The scenes were poignant and quite revealing, based on a dialectical movement between past (a kind of redemptive remembrance) and present in the hope of a transformed and healthy multiethnic democracy—that which is not yet. It is the sort of redemptive memory writers like Peter McLaren and Tomaz Tadeuz da Silva (McLaren and Da Silva, 1993) propose for a process of critical learning based on Freire's ideas, a process in which once again the codified reality, that is, the focus of co-investigation between educator and educatee, is regarded as one that would normally comprise a number of historically accumulated concepts.

UNEQUAL MULTIETHNIC RELATIONS: COLONIALISM TRANSPOSED

Solidarity among ethnic groups along the lines suggested earlier would serve to challenge the entire structure of the society that exists within the recipient country, a structure that is intensely colonial. Colonialism, it ought to be stressed, is a characteristic not only of the migrant's country of origin but also of the receiving country. Colonial relations between countries are transposed to the country of settlement, with certain cultures being regarded as the norm, because of their relation to the dominant group (e.g., the WASPs in North America), and others being regarded as *subaltern*. The subaltern cultures are the cultures of those that are perceived to constitute the ethnic *alterity*, the ethnic other. As McLaren argues, with reference to the United States, postcolonial pedagogy is

a pedagogy which challenges the very categories through which the history of the colonized has been written. I am certainly talking about not simply colonial countries, but also about groups who have been colonized in this country. (McLaren, 1997b, p. 230)

With the influx, in the Northern Mediterranean, of people coming from the Southern Mediterranean, one can expect to find, in certain countries of the region, this reality quite visible for quite some time in countries such as France, Spain, and Italy. In contexts such as these, the Freirean approach to pedagogy would strike me as being relevant. It is based on the valorization of subaltern cultures, conceived of not solely in terms of class and ethnicity but also in broader terms to incorporate gender, sexuality, race/ethnicity, and other forms of identity. These subaltern cultures serve, according to the Freirean conception, as the point of departure for a genuinely democratic pedagogical process.

One of the greatest challenges in several Mediterranean countries, characterized by the presence of many diverse ethnic and racial groups, is that of ensuring a genuinely democratic process of interethnic conviviality. There is a lot of talk, in this part of the world, concerning multiculturalism. At the Sestri Levante conference (Mayo, 1999b, p. 121), no less than 60 projects, concerning multicultural education, were presented.[8]

One must bear in mind the criticism that was leveled in North America at policies concerning multiculturalism (McLaren, 1997b). This type of multicultural policy was scathingly criticized by many writers for serving as a form of containment and absorption through which the dominant group (the *mainstream* culture) is constructed as the invisible norm (the word *ethnic* is never used with reference to this group) presupposed by the existence of the ethnic other.

The architectural and demographic landscapes of Northern Mediterranean cities are undergoing significant changes. Against this scenario, we are witnessing the transformation of Mediterranean cities. Whereas the population in these cities increasingly becomes cosmopolitan, the architecture is a melange of the old coexisting with the new. The global exists alongside the local in a situation of hybridity that has led to what is currently being described as the multicultural city, where, for example, Giotto's *campanile* is juxtaposed against McDonald's twin golden arches.

In certain Southern European cities and towns, the cupolas of churches that for centuries have been perceived as bulwarks of Christendom against Islam now coexist alongside minarets. This coexistence of architectural symbols of the different monotheistic religions, which have been the subject of much conflict in the past, is becoming an important feature of the skyline of many a Southern European city.

Within this cultural hybridity, a characteristic of several Mediterranean cities, especially those in the Northern Mediterranean, one can easily encounter the tensions that have characterized the region for centuries. Xenophobia (the more accurate term, in this context, would be *islamophobia*) and racism, especially with regard to people who profess the Muslim faith, constantly rear their ugly head. They have their historical roots, among other things, in the anti-Islamic crusades that left their mark in several places in this region, becoming a feature of their so-called cultural heritage. Cultures that, for centuries, had been constructed as being antagonistic are now expected to coexist within the same geographical space. These racial tensions reflect the tension that is a feature of this region, a region that, among other things, gave rise to the three great monotheistic religions. Judging from what happened in the aftermath of September 11, 2001, these tensions are likely to escalate following the Madrid carnage that occurred at the time when the manuscript for this book, in its final copyedited version, was about to go to press in March 2004.

One of the great challenges for Freire-inspired education, in this context, would be that of allowing participants to cross their mental and cultural borders, to use Giroux's phrase. Crossing borders would, in this context, entail that one begins to understand something about the culture of others, religion included. Perhaps the most important feature of a Freire-inspired education is that of developing an educational process wherein dialogue is regarded as the means for (1) permitting the different cultures that make up our societies to become an integral feature of the educational process and (2) allowing participants to listen to others, listening in the sense used by Paulo Freire in *Pedagogy of Freedom*, which is not simply hearing and which, once again, implies one's being "open to the word of the other, to the gesture of the other, to the differences of the other without being reduced to the other" (Freire, 1998a, p. 107).

LEARNING ABOUT THE "OTHER" AND CONFRONTING THE POLITICS OF MISREPRESENTATION

The various situations of conflict that characterize this region and that can cause tension in multiethnic societies, render it indispensable that one crosses boundaries in a variety of ways. Many of the Southern European regions of the Mediterranean have traditionally been steeped in the Christian religion, mainly Catholic and also Greek Orthodox. It is imperative, in a truly multiethnic environment, that knowledge of the different religions is provided in schools and in other educational sites. One ought to mention here projects such as the one promoted by IRRSAE[9] in Puglia, Southern Italy, which focuses on the curriculum with special reference to the three great monotheistic religions that emerged from the Mediterranean (Ministero della Pubblica Istruzione, 1998, p. 5). There is always the danger, however, of providing a caricature. The complexity of the situation can easily be ignored, with the religions being represented in simplistic terms (Fondazione Laboratorio Mediterraneo, 1997, p. 51).

The study of different religions should therefore be approached with the utmost seriousness and best preparation possible, with special emphasis being placed on the teacher doing justice to the different religions involved. This applies primarily to programs in schools, in adult education centers, universities and preservice and in-service courses for teachers and those involved in the mass media. In the case of the last mentioned, this would be in keeping with the recommendations of the 1997 Civil Forum EuroMed: "Mass media are invited to present a correct image of religions or cultures resorting, where suitable, to experts on the matter" (Fondazione Laboratorio Mediterraneo 1997, p. 512). Misconceptions regarding Islam abound in the Western world. Countries of the North Mediterranean, which are recipients of immigrants from Arab countries, are no exception. One of the greatest misconceptions regarding Islam is its strong identification, in the minds of many, with the Arab world (Pallavicini, 1998) Ahmed Moatassime makes the following point— "the Arabs *in stricto sensu* are a minority—approximately a fifth—in a milliard of Muslims" (Moatassime, 2000, p. 113). In effect, the Arab world is characterized by difference also in terms of religious denomination, whereas Islam is a truly international religion. As Shaykh'Abd Wahid Pallavicini, the President of the Italian Islamic Community (CO.RE.IS), underlines, it is present not only among Arab, Persian, Turkish, and Indian people but also in all nations of the West, Africa, and the Far East (Moatassime, 2000). Islam knows no geographical, racial, or ethnic boundaries. It is common to find distortions of religions in many school texts, as Mahmoud Elsheikh so clearly points out with regard to the way Islam is presented in Italian manuals (Elsheikh, 1999, p. 35). The foregoing is indicative of the fact that, for greater conviviality and dialogue to occur between people of different ethnic background with different cultural and related knowledge traditions, an effort must be made to learn about others, to cross the boundaries of one's location, and to obtain the necessary understanding and knowledge to be able to engage in a critical reading of widely diffused texts (media images, news packages, representations in film and documentary). This is necessary for one to be able to confront and problematize the politics of misrepresentation that results from historically entrenched prejudices and deep-seated antagonistic dispositions. Freire's insistence on the rigors of teaching and learning, as opposed to a laissez-faire approach to pedagogy, becomes all the more relevant in this context. Only through such rigor would one obtain the background knowledge necessary to engage in a problem-posing approach to confronting the images of *alterity* with which we are assailed daily.

The images that can be targeted through a Freire-inspired problem-posing approach derive from a variety of sources. In many countries of the Mediterranean, we are confronted by a Eurocentric cultural heritage that reflects a colonial past, especially in former centers of colonial power such as Spain and Portugal, and as I mentioned earlier, a past marked by crusades against the Ottoman Empire. A critical education program in the Southern European regions would enable its participants to problematize the region's or country's much acclaimed cultural heritage (*culture* not being used in the anthropological sense) and its politics of representation. Exotic and often demonic (mis)representations of alterity abound throughout this cultural heritage, be it the colonized indigenous populations of the Americas or the Saracen, the latter constituting the traditional Other in relation to whom Christian Europe was constructed. The other becomes the subject of a particular kind of construction, a form of *Orientalism* in Edward Said's sense of the term. It is a demonization reminiscent of the French colonial construction, "taught in the universities for over twenty years" and based on so-called "scientific proof" (Fanon, 1963, p. 296), of the colonized in Algeria, and North Africa in general, so forcefully exposed by Frantz Fanon in his classic anticolonial volume (Fanon, 1963). What we have here is an example of the kind of racism, predicated on scientism, that Paulo Freire condemned in his conversation with Donaldo Macedo, to which reference was made in the previous chapter (Freire and Macedo, 2000). It is the means whereby racist distortions of facts are given a pseudoscientific explanation.

I would focus, as an example here, on a church with which I am familiar—St. John's Co-Cathedral in Valletta, Malta's capital city. It serves as a pedagogical site for many, be they schoolchildren, adult learners, foreign visitors, participants in foreign Elderhostel programs, and so forth. Generally regarded as one of the finest treasures of Baroque art, it was built by the Sovereign Order of St. John as its conventual church. The Order's commissioned works of art contained exoticized baroque images relating to its war against the Ottoman Empire. Borrowing from Said (1978), I would argue that the iconography expresses a strong sense of *positional superiority,* in the construction of *alterity,* by those who commission the work (see Borg and Mayo, 2001b, p. 49). It is the Saracen who is represented as the exoticized other in these works. In recent pieces of work (Borg and Mayo,

2000a, p. 83, 2001b, p. 49), Carmel Borg and I asked: "What effect can such representation of the Muslim 'Other' have on present day racial politics in Malta with regard to Arabs, in a context characterised by geographical proximity to the Arab world, the presence of an Arab (mainly Libyan) community and an evident eagerness by political and opinion leaders to assert a European identity?" We posed these questions, bearing in mind that the specific historical contexts that gave rise to these representations can easily be overlooked nowadays as these images continue to prey on popular sensibilities. Similar questions can be posed in relation to the politics of representation in other museums and archaeological sites, not only in Malta but also in various other parts of the region and, I suspect, elsewhere, as I intend to show in the chapter that follows.

Even canonical works in the receiving country are not innocent in this regard and have been severely criticized by Mahmoud Elsheikh on these grounds, being guilty of reproducing distortions generated by popular accounts in the West (Elsheikh, 1999, pp. 37–41), despite the fact that Elsheikh argues that these Western works owe much to Islam, a point registered by the Spanish scholar Miguel Asin Palacios (Elsheikh, 1999, p. 39). Indeed, many of the celebrated domains of study and the institutions that promoted them owe much to the Arab and, one should add, Iranian cultures, be it literature (and here one can also include pre-Islamic poetry), science, mathematics, medicine, or philosophy. The same applies to those hallowed centers of learning that are the universities, the oldest documented is to be found in an Arab context.[10] Referring to what he calls the "debtor's syndrome," Elsheikh stated forcefully:

the person to whom one is indebted is constantly a hated person; particularly if the creditor, as in this case, is a strange body, rejected by the collective consciousness, hated by the political, social, cultural and religious institutions. If anything, the rage against the creditor, in these circumstances, becomes an almost moral duty and a necessary condition for the survival of that society. (Elsheikh, 1999, p. 38)[11]

A similar politics of representation characterizes the realm of popular culture in the Southern European—or Northern Mediterranean—region, with the Sicilian marionette shows, involving Crusaders and the Predator (often the Saracen Other), being a case in point. In introducing immigrants to popular culture traditions in the receiving country, one ought to be wary of their contradictions. They often contains elements that constitute a denigration of aspects of the immigrants' own culture.

Cultural productions, at the popular level and at the level of so-called highbrow culture, can serve as codifications, in the Freirean sense, that permit us to engage in a critical reading of our contemporary reality. The concepts that form part of our common sense, used in Gramsci's sense of the term, can partly have their roots in our cultural and folklore traditions. Once again, they are concepts that have been accumulated over a long historical period.

PEDAGOGICAL STRATEGIES: OBJECT TO SUBJECT

Critically confronting the canon, the much-celebrated cultural heritage and popular cultural traditions, constitutes an important pedagogical strategy. There are, however, other pedagogical approaches to pursue. In projects concerning immigrants, it is imperative that the education provided is not merely a form of what the Italians would call *assistenzialismo*[12] through which a deficit model of the participant is cultivated. Piero Banna warned against this in his exposition of the immigrants project carried out in the multiethnic center Casa dei Popoli in Catania (Banna, 2000, p. 246) at the opening of a 1999 conference on education and culture in the Mediterranean held in the same Sicilian city (Pampanini, 2000). Using Freirean terms, the challenge for projects of this kind is to become not another form of banking education but the means through which the participant is conceived of and acts as subject rather than object.

The issues of social difference and multiethnicity render ever more pertinent a democratic approach to the investigation, rather than mere transmission (banking education), of knowledge in the learning setting. Ample space should be accorded to the different voices or narratives in this setting, voices or narratives that reflect the different ways by which meaning is circulated and negotiated. This is not to say that these voices—all voices for that matter—should be celebrated uncritically because each voice contains its contradictions, especially in its representation of other identities in the learning setting. One constantly comes across manifestations of the oppressor within not to mention the fear of the oppressor, as indicated by Freire, echoing Memmi and Fanon. The fear of the oppressor can lead participants from subaltern ethnic groups to hold back when expressing themselves for fear of reprisals:

In line after line of *Pedagogy of the Oppressed,* I discuss this phenomenon. Fanon and Memmi did the same, or had done it before me. I mean the fear that fills the oppressed, as individuals and as a class, and prevents them from struggling. (Freire, 1994, p. 124)

LANGUAGE AND LITERACIES

One cannot extricate the issue of social difference and multiethnicity from questions concerning literacy and language. The work of Paulo Freire strikes me as being relevant here, although one ought to reiterate that it would be a grave mistake to reduce Paulo Freire's voice to simply one that is explicitly concerned with literacy. In the Brazilian northeast,

Guinea Bissau, and Chile, the process of literacy was meant to serve, in a rural context, as simply the vehicle to enable people to read the world (Freire and Macedo, 1987). I have indicated in chapter 3 and elsewhere that Freire's writings are concerned not with providing a new method to overcome illiteracy but with providing a new social and educational philosophy:

> But the process of reading does not mean literally reading written words. Above all comes reading the world as an anticipation of reading words. We first read reality and afterwards we read the texts. (Freire, 1995c, p. 62)

As such, Freire is relevant also to contexts in which people are literate in the conventional sense of the term. However, there are countries and regions in the Mediterranean where, as with Brazil and the rest of Latin America, a literacy education can serve as the initial means to develop critical consciousness. In an editorial introduction to the first issue of the *Mediterranean Journal of Educational Studies,* Ronald Sultana (Sultana, 1996, p. ii) indicated that there are many parts of the Southern Mediterranean in which, until 1991, approximately 30 percent of the population had no access to formal elementary education. According to this article, there are many illiterates in several Maghreb and Macharek states (Sultana, 1996). There were high rates of illiteracy in these countries, with those for Morocco being 50.5 percent, Tunisia, 34.7 percent, Algeria, 43 percent, and Egypt, 48 percent (Sultana, 1996). One wonders to what extent a lack of literacy also in the first language constitutes a feature of immigrants from these areas and whether bilingualism should be accorded importance in a progressive literacy education in the receiving country. This is a form of cultural hybridity, if you will, that reflects the cultural hybridity that has always been a feature of postcolonial societies (e.g., the learning of Maltese and English in Malta or Arabic and French in Tunisia, with *code switching* between the two languages—colonizer's and colonized—occurring in many contexts).

Learning to be effectively *bilingual* is part and parcel of a postcolonial education in that it enables one to retain a strong connection with one's ethnic roots and at the same time ensures that one learns the dominant language not to remain on the periphery of political life. As far as immigrants are concerned, confronting the colonial by entrenching oneself in the traditional subaltern colonized culture often results in ghettoization. The alternative to this is, of course, assimilation. Assimilation is therefore characterized by a forsaking of one's ethnic roots and one's contribution to the bolstering of a Eurocentric colonial structure of oppression. One way of putting it, using Freirean terms, is that of internalizing the image of the oppressor, in this case the dominant colonizing ethnic group.

The ability of people to operate skillfully in their two cultures can be perceived as a source of enrichment of their ethnic culture, in that it does not remain stagnant but proves to be organic, and of the larger society in general. What we come across in this situation is the learning of the language that is closely connected to one's roots, in short, the popular first language, and at the same time the dominant language in the receiving country. Learning the latter language, as all standard languages for that matter, is, for Freire, of vital importance if one is not to remain on the periphery of political life. The reader will recall Freire's statements to this effect in the conversation with Ira Shor, to which reference was made in the discussion on language in chapter 3.

A MULTICENTRIC CURRICULUM?

The foregoing discussion concerning the relevance of Paulo Freire's idea for the Mediterranean regional context points in the direction of a critical multiethnic education. Needless to say, a critical multiethnic education, as part of a larger multicultural education predicated on the valorization of difference and identity, involves a process of democratization of the entire educational system in terms of curricula, texts, and the entire pedagogical process. The curriculum is a selection from the cultures of society, to modify a statement that derives from Raymond Williams but that has been used in the field of education by Dennis Lawton (Lawton, 1984, p. 276). It would be pertinent to ask: In whose interest is the selection being made? Whose cultural arbitrary, to use Pierre Bourdieu's term, is reflected in the curriculum? These questions would be posed in any society in terms of the social differences involved—gender, class, race/ethnicity, sexual orientation, ability, or religious affiliation. These questions will be posed with greater vehemence the more socially differentiated and *secular* a society becomes (Borg and Mayo, 2001a, p. 74).

There are those who would argue, in this context, for a multicentric education, one that allows the traditionally marginalized not simply to be included or "grafted" onto "the existing order" but, echoing bell hooks (1994b), to "move from the margins to the centre" (Dei, 1997, pp. 81, 82). The traditionally marginalized ethnic groups must become major actors in the curriculum and not simply adjuncts to a cast formed of people from the dominant ethnic groups (Dei, 1997, p. 83). In contexts such as these, the Freirean approach to pedagogy, based on the valorization of subaltern cultures, would strike me as being relevant. These subaltern cultures serve, according to the Freirean conception, as the point of departure for a genuinely democratic pedagogical process, as indicated in the previous chapter.

As far as the issue of cultural contestation is concerned, one must, of course, recognize the complexity of the region in this context. At the risk of reproducing a colonial argument, I would submit that, for all their subtle and not so subtle forms of discrimination (often institutionalized forms of discrimination), there are countries in the Mediterranean, particularly those around its northern shores, that offer greater spaces than others in this regard. It is more likely that one discovers greater opportunities for the affirmation of different cultures in settings that are characterized by a spirit of secularization than in settings wherein, for instance, a particular religious culture is hegemonic. With respect to the latter, the following immediately come to mind: Catholicism in Malta (Borg, 1995), Islam in a number of Arab countries and elsewhere, and the Greek Orthodox religion in Greece.

In nonsecularized contexts, there are severe limits to the degree of multicultural democracy, as conceived of in this chapter, which is possible. Discrimination in the form of racism, homophobia, and sexism are, of course, also features of secularized contexts, including Western contexts. It is common knowledge, however, that certain countries of the Mediterranean lag behind others with respect to the acquisition, by traditionally marginalized groups, of what would generally be regarded in other countries of the region and elsewhere as taken for granted rights. The writings of such intellectuals as Nawal El Saadawi (1997, 1999) and contributors to the periodical *Mediterraneo. Un Mare di Donne* (Mediterranean Review—a Sea of Women), among others, stress this point with respect to the situation of women.

The issue concerning spaces available for a multicentric curriculum immediately brings into focus the issue of identity, an issue that, as I indicated in the previous chapter and earlier ones (see chapter 2), was a feature of Freire's later work. This is clearly evident in the published exchanges in English with Donaldo Macedo and in such pieces as his response to comments by 16 scholars in *Mentoring the Mentor.* In this piece he addressed the issue that constantly crops up in seminars on Freire's work held in the United States. I personally obtained first hand evidence of this during a plenary session of the 1996 Pedagogy of the Oppressed/Theatre of the Oppressed conference at the University of Nebraska at Omaha; Paulo Freire, Augusto Boal, and Peter McLaren were the guest speakers in this session held at the university's Rose Theatre. The whole identity issue, particularly with regard to race and gender and the intersections between them, dominated the discussion that arose during the time allotted for interventions by members of the audience. I experienced the same situation in the parallel session in which I delivered my paper. Needless to say, one cannot hope to engage in discussions on critical pedagogy without foregrounding issues concerning identity and difference, comprising not only social difference but also the larger context of biodifference.

Identity issues strike me as being of crucial importance in any context, not just in the United States. I sought to address the issue of identity and social difference with respect to the contributions of Antonio Gramsci and Paulo Freire in my previous work (Mayo, 1999a) and more substantively in that book's chapter 5, which focused on some of the limitations in the work of these two figures when considering their relevance for contemporary projects of transformative learning.

One must guard against the danger of engaging in totalizing discourses when discussing oppression. In my view, however, we should heed Predrag Matvejevic, who joins others in warning against the excesses of identity politics: "We have become used to respecting differences but there are also differences which are ends in themselves, being very particularistic, and which destroy forms of solidarity . . . one must bear in mind the difference between the identity of being [*identita' dell'essere*] and the identity of doing [*identita' del fare*]" (Matvejevic, 1997, pp. 122–123).[13]

After all, there are no fixed identities: "Recognition of the complexities posed by the process of hybridization and the notion of multiple identities in the social and the psychological construction of the pedagogical subject should challenge any attempt to essentialize differences based on 'race,' gender, class, nationality, ethnic, religious and sexual preferences" (Torres, 1998a, p. 254). Lê Thánh Khôi demonstrates this by means of an erudite historical overview of the intermeshing of cultures throughout the Mediterranean (Lê Thánh Khôi, 2000, p. 60).[14]

It is quite common, in Europe and elsewhere to refer to immigrants from North African countries as simply "Arab" and therefore represent them as unitary subjects, thus underwriting the differences in subjectivities contained within this group—Muslim or Christian,[15] Tunisian, Libyan, Moroccan, or Algerian—not to mention also the distinction between Arab and Berber and so on. In so doing, we also tend to underwrite the intersections between their ethnicity and other subjectivities (class, gender, ability/disability).

For Matvejevic, the first type of identity he mentions (identity of being) is very strong throughout the Mediterranean, even though the situation concerning identity can be quite complex, as indicated by Ahmed Moatassime with respect to the Maghreb, where numerous contrasting and contradictory identities cross each other's paths: Berber, Arab, and francophone identities.[16]

The second kind of identity mentioned by the Croatian scholar strikes me as suggesting *agency*, involving what Carlos Alberto Torres would regard as the opening up of "areas of negotiation in the context of progressive alliances based on multiple identities and learning communities" (Torres, 1998a, p. 254). Nawal El Saadawi states that, in the present conjuncture, the tendency toward homogenizing and unifying the world into a single market is allied to a fragmentation of power at the bottom, thus constituting a postmodern version of divide and rule:

The movement towards a global culture is therefore not contradicted by this postmodern tendency towards cultural fragmentation and identity struggles. They are two faces of the same coin. To unify power, economic power at the top it is necessary to fragment power at the bottom. To maintain the global economy of the few, of the multinationals, unification must exist at the top, amongst the few, the very few. (El Saadawi, 1997, pp. 121–122)

Emphasizing the constant shifts in identities, she goes on to state that

. . . we are so engrossed in defining our identities, when they are changing all the time. Instead of stressing what is different perhaps we should spend more time discovering what is common to you and me. Or perhaps we cannot do one without the other. Our humanity is common but it takes many forms. (El Saadawi, 1997, p. 126)

This statement connects with Freire's contention, with which I concluded the previous chapter, that "It is exactly because of my growing awareness over the years concerning the specificities of oppression along the lines of language, race, gender and ethnicity that I have been defending the fundamental thesis of Unity in Diversity, so that the various oppressed groups can become more effective in their collective struggle against all forms of oppression" (Freire, 1997b, p. 310). The issue of dialogue, so central to Freire's conceptualization of pedagogy and transformative politics, becomes key in this context. In remaining within the boundaries of one's identity of being, one is contributing to a process of fragmentation. In making the effort to transcend these boundaries, one would be engaging in the sort of integrative process of transformative action that is necessary to combat oppression in its systemic global forms. Once again, using Freire's terms, it ought to be stated that dialogue cannot exist without solidarity. The challenge remains that of exploring opportunities for solidarity, with humans and other species, in the context of biodiversity.

NOTES

1. The journal *Mediterranean Journal of Educational Studies,* now in its eighth volume, is a key feature of this work in the area of comparative education research in the Mediterranean. It is the brainchild of University of Malta academic Professor Ronald G. Sultana, himself a contributor to critical pedagogy (see Sultana, 1997), who, among other things, organizes an annual research seminar focusing each year on one aspect of education in the region and directs the University of Malta's Center for Euro-Mediterranean Studies in Education.

2. This introduction on the Mediterranean is extracted from Peter Mayo, in McLaren and Mayo (1999, p. 398).

3. My literal translation from Predrag Matvejevic's address, in Italian, at the ll Civil Forum, Euromed, Naples, 1997.

4. Translated literally, this would read: Some Themes concerning the Southern Question. The work is often presented in English as simply "The Southern Question." See Gramsci (1995), edited and translated by Pasquale Verdicchio.

5. Omar Al-Mukhtar, called the "lion of the desert," is a national hero in Libya. He led a nationalist rebellion against the Italian fascist domination of Libya, for which he suffered death by public hanging at the hands of the Italian authorities in 1931 (Habib, 1979, p. 50). He was 80 at the time of his captivity and execution. The rebellion is generally referred to as a Muslim rebellion against European imperialism. A film on Al-Mukhtar was released in 1981, entitled *Lion of the Desert* and featured, among others, such actors as Anthony Quinn (in the part of Al-Mukhtar), Oliver Reed, Irene Papas, Rod Steiger, and John Gielgud.

6. During my visit to the Paulo Freire Institute in São Paulo, in April 1998, I noticed that a statue of V. I. Lenin and a crucifix lay prominently on Freire's personal desk on permanent display at the premises.

7. Freire referred to these as the "fifty hours" (Freire, 1994, p. 121). In earlier work, he referred to the "ninety hours" (Freire, in Gadotti, Freire, and Guimarães, 1995, p. 49), which led the Italian editors, Bartolomeo Bellanova and Fausto Telleri, to provide a corrective in the form of a footnote stating that reference is probably being made, in this context, to the Italian experience of the so-called 150 hours (Freire, in Gadotti, Freire, and Guimarães, 1995, p. 49).

8. Cf. "Mappa dei progetti italiani sul Mediterraneo," Commissione Nazionale sull' Educazione Interculturale, Ministero della Pubblica Istruzione, p. 6.

9. Istituto Regionale di Ricerca Sperimentazione e Aggiornamento Educativi—Regional institute for educational research, experimentation and update.

10. The university is widely believed to have originated in the Mediterranean, with Quaraouiyine University in Fez, Morocco, being established in A.D. 859, followed by Al-Azhar University in Egypt in A.D. 970, the University of Bologna in 1088 and the University of Paris in 1160 (Sultana, 1999, p. 7).

11. My translation from the Italian original.

12. Freire often uses this term, borrowing from its equivalent in Portuguese.

13. My translation from the original in Italian.

14. See also Lê Thánh Khôi (1999) on this and chapter 4 of Young (2003).

15. Shaykh 'Abd al Wahid Pallavicini (1998) "Identita' e Differenze" (Identity and Differences), paper presented at the international conference, "'Il Mare che Unisce. Scuola, Europa e Mediterraneo" (The Sea that Unites. School, Europe and the Mediterranean), Sestri Levante, Italy, October 22–24, 1998.

16. Ahmed Moatassime states that persons from the Maghreb feel that they belong to the Berber identity each time the Arab identity threatens to limit the Berber language and culture. Once the Western francophone culture poses a threat to the Arab culture, the person from the Maghreb defends the Arab identity. This person would then defend the ties with the francophone culture in the face of an anglophone invasion. Almost a literal translation from Ahmed Moatassime (2000, p. 113).

CHAPTER 6

Engaging with Practice:
A Freirean Reflection on
Different Pedagogical Sites

In this chapter, I would like to use some of the previous considerations to reflect on projects with which I have had some connection over the years, projects that strike me as lending themselves to an engagement in education of a socially transformative nature, predicated on the idea of education for social justice. I have been involved as coordinator in one of these projects, a project of parental involvement in a state primary school (a public-sector school) and as an occasional educator in another (a program of workers' education run at the University of Malta). I am also coordinating a group in connection with the national curricular reform process focusing on the idea of developing schools as community learning centers. I have also carried out research, with colleagues, concerning museums in my country (Malta) with a view to exploring ideas to render them more socially representative institutions and more democratic public sites (Borg and Mayo, 2000a; Borg, Cauchi, and Mayo, 2003). I can safely state that, throughout our analysis, Freire's ideas constituted a major source of influence. His ideas and those of others influenced our view of these institutions as public sites in which the challenge, as Peter McLaren and Ricky Lee Allen, echoing Patti Lather, have suggested, with respect to social cartography, remains that of converting the space that they offer to one that "is both decolonized and opened to the colonized" (McLaren and Allen, 1998, p. 229).

The section in this chapter dealing with museums and their educational provision is intended to demonstrate how Freire's ideas can be taken up and reinvented in different sites of practice. Indeed, the whole chapter is also intended to demonstrate the relevance of Freire's thinking for a variety of sites of practice, some immediately identified with education in its narrow sense and others associated with education in its broader context. The agencies involved, in the latter case, provide examples of what Henry Giroux terms *public pedagogy* (Giroux, 1999, p. 4).

Needless to say, only some of the considerations, raised in the earlier chapters, can be brought to bear on my analyses of and reflections on these projects, given the contextual specificities encountered within each of the learning settings in question. The context for these settings, one in which I have been active as teacher, researcher, and citizen, is that provided by a microisland state with a population of one third million and a land mass, for the whole archipelago, of 316.3 sq. km.

IN AND AGAINST THE SYSTEM

The university where I obtained my initial teacher preparation and where I have been teaching and researching is one of the oldest within the Commonwealth, originally set up as a Jesuit-run theological college in 1592. I have been working on a full-time basis at the University of Malta since the early 1990s, a period that saw several developments in the field of adult education in Malta. One of the many university agencies involved in adult education is the Workers' Participation Development Centre (WPDC). It was set up in 1981 to cater for workers' education, involving education for a genuine industrial democracy, and to provide research concerning the participatory experiences that were introduced by the then Labor government in a number of enterprises on the island.[1] The Center was also intended to help promote the setting up of worker cooperatives (Kester, 1980).

The international influences for the development of this project were many, not least being the Yugoslav system of self-management, the Mondragon experience with regard to cooperative development, and the writings on self-management by Jaroslav Vanek (1977), a Czech Professor of Economics based at Cornell University, who has specialized in "Participation and Labor Managed Systems."[2] Vanek's ideas and writings are often cited in the literature produced by researchers connected with this organization. Vanek had developed connections with the WPDC, which was instrumental in bringing him over to Malta in 1987 to act as consultant to the government on the issue of participation.[3] It seems most appropriate to mention this in the context of a book on Paulo Freire in view of the fact that Vanek considered the Brazilian's pedagogical approach relevant to his conception of self-management. Plinio Sampaio disclosed this in the taped interview he gave to Carmel Borg and me. In fact, Plinio Sampaio was instrumental in Freire's visit to the American university, where the latter delivered a couple of lectures. Sampaio, who was pursuing graduate studies at Cornell at the time,[4] helped set up a meeting between Freire and Vanek after having been requested by the latter to do so. According to Sampaio, Vanek regarded Freire's pedagogical approach as "the other side of self-management,"[5] that is to say, the kind of pedagogical approach that would suit his conception of industrial democracy through self-management.

I have followed the fortunes of the Workers' Participation Development Centre over the years, through (a) my occasional involvement in some of its projects (occasionally teaching in the Labor Studies, subsequently Industrial Relations, diploma course, participating and leading workshops in residential weekend seminars, etc.) and (b) carrying out qualitative research concerning the Center, involving a case study approach (Mayo, 1997c, 2003).[6] Many of the considerations I provide in my discussion of the WPDC derive from the voices of course participants, educators, and WPDC personnel, culled from structured and semistructured interviews, which appear in this case study. Readers intending to pursue this matter further are referred to the two pieces that comprise the case study (Mayo, 1997c, 2003), the second piece providing a more updated version of the study.

The WPDC is committed to outreach activities involving participatory experiences in different sectors of the Maltese public sphere. However, the bulk of its activities consists of projects and courses held at the university's main campus.[7] An attempt was made to attract traditionally marginalized groups to the university, indicating a commitment, on the WPDC's part, to groups that have traditionally occupied a subaltern position in the Maltese social hierarchy. The target groups during the WPDC's initial years included a large number of employees at the Malta Drydocks and people from the trade union sector. Subsequently, the target group changed with more women and people from the services sector being visible in the WPDC courses. When I taught a few sessions on workers' education in the then Labor Studies diploma course, in 1996–1997, people from the trade union sector and from labor politics were present.

As I had indicated in the published case study (Mayo, 1997c, 2003), I felt that the WPDC programs could be regarded as an attempt to democratize the University in many ways. Here is an institution, funded, for the most part, out of public taxes, being made available to those who bear the brunt of such taxes (salaried employees) in a context wherein tax evasion by nonsalaried employees is considered to be high. Furthermore, in a microstate context in which the cost per capita of facilities is high compared to that in larger countries, the university has, as a result, rendered its facilities more accessible. I refer, in particular, here to the university library, which is undoubtedly the best available in Malta. As far as the question concerning whose cultural arbitrary is reflected in the organization's program, the WPDC's courses were among the first at the university to allow the use of the Maltese language as a medium of instruction and writing. In most of the courses at university, English is the medium used for instruction and for the writing of theses, papers, and projects. English constitutes an important form of cultural capital in Malta. And yet Maltese is the national popular language, the language widely used by members of the Maltese popular classes. Participants in the course can therefore operate in the language they know best, the language that, as Freire insisted, echoing Cabral, constitutes one of their "culture's most immediate, authentic and concrete expressions" (see chapter 3). Furthermore, the Center introduced, within the university setting, two areas that have potential for transformative education. These are "labor studies," subsequently "industrial relations," and "women and development," subsequently "gender and development" (there is a diploma course in each of these areas).

The areas of "labor studies" and "women and development" had the potential of enabling educators to draw on material that can relate to the experiences of traditionally subaltern social groups, namely women and people from the working class, the two not being exclusive of each other because the domains of class and gender constantly intersect. The choice of knowledge base in this context signifies, in Freire's terms, an option in favor of traditionally subaltern groups and therefore potentially a pedagogy of the oppressed. With respect to women, however, the research has revealed the low participation of women in the main Labor Studies course, and reasons for this were provided by some of the female participants who were interviewed. They referred to the patriarchal nature of Maltese society, which allows women little opportunities to be relieved of family chores, if only for a short time, to pursue courses, as well as the fact that the content of what is tackled in the course program reflects a cultural arbitrary, which is androcentric.

The Center also helped introduce innovatory participatory pedagogical approaches to an institution where it has often been argued that teaching is, generally speaking, traditional, smacking of banking education (see Mayo, 1997c). The pedagogical approach nominally favored by the Center is one that would normally be based on considerations resulting from the language of critique that heightens awareness of the way the traditional educational system discriminates against traditionally subordinated groups by immersing them in a structured culture of silence.

As one former participant put it:

the course which the Center is holding is different [from mainstream education]. I am talking through experience. [W]hoever did attend had work experience. . . . So when we go there we share our own work experience. And we discovered, in the course I took, that several lecturers who came to deliver their lecture found it difficult at first to convey the message to us. Why? Because we would not accept, as a result of our life experience, what the person said as gospel truth. We questioned everything.[8]

Of course, it is not easy to use concepts from the more progressive traditions in adult education, and especially Freirean concepts, within the context of the very hierarchical institution that is the University of Malta. There are many contradictions to be faced. In the first place, the WPDC's courses lead to recognized academic qualifications and therefore reflect an important concern in adult education, namely the concern with certification. These courses, therefore, have to conform to uniform procedures and regulations governing all diploma courses held at the university. Some of these procedures and regulations can serve to undermine the very concept of participation that the Center intends to promote. One had to be really creative to come up with innovative approaches within the established constraints. From my own experience as coordinator of diploma courses at the same university (run by a different University agency, the Faculty of Education), I would argue that it is possible for the participants to conceive of and engage in a collective on the ground project in lieu of, for instance, writing the traditional dissertation. This has very much been the case with the diploma courses in adult education in which I have been involved as coordinator and educator. The WPDC can follow suit by organizing the participants into groups working collectively on a project of communal participation, either at the place of work or in a particular locality. This has the added advantage of underlining the collective dimension of learning, so central to the concept of transformative education conceived of by Paulo Freire and others. It is one of many ways by which one begins to confront the ideology of individualism that characterizes not only capitalist relations of production but also the kind of neo-liberal-inspired educational programs that support it, programs that project the notion of learning not as a social act, involving relational knowing subjects, but as a domain for individual appropriation where " . . . *to be is to have* and to be the class of the 'haves' " (Freire, 1970b, 1993, p. 58).

Toward the end of the project, the participants can be encouraged to write a collective evaluative report, stressing not only the outcomes but also, more significantly, the process involved. This is precisely what the participants in the diploma courses I coordinated did. It allows for collective reflectivity in which theory and reflection on experience are combined. Another constraint, faced by the WPDC, is that one would be hard-pressed to find teachers for the different course units at the WPDC who subscribe to the institution's philosophy. My case study indicates that participants were often appalled at the presence of course instructors who embraced a teaching philosophy at odds with that of the Center. The university regulations stipulate that one ought to give priority, when selecting potential course teachers, to recognized university specialists in the field. Of course, there are ways and means of getting around this to ensure greater coherence between what is preached and what is practiced, the sort of coherence Freire is at pains to emphasize in his later works (Freire, 1998c). One way of attempting to do this is by couching the title of the area in terms that presuppose a particular pedagogical orientation.

In terms of connecting with other agencies, the WPDC works in tandem with groups and agencies that reflect a variety of social interests, such as, for instance, the Commission for the Advancement of Women and the Maltese trade union movement. One of the challenges for the WPDC is to engage in broader alliances, especially with potentially transformative social agencies, and therefore to reach out to the broader domains of civil society, conceived of here in the Gramscian sense. This is the sort of alliance or partnership Freire has called for and that he sought to bring about with respect to the MOVA-SP program he helped develop in São Paulo. For as indicated earlier, potentially transformative education occurs in a variety of sites, including those that would not prima facie be regarded as educational.

WORKING OUTSIDE THE ACADEMY'S HALLOWED WALLS

The WPDC case study underlines the difficulty of trying to engage in transformative education within, or possibly in and against (see Mayo, 2003), the system. And one ought not ignore the issue of working *within* the system, as Freire himself emphasized, exhorting us to be tactically inside and strategically outside the system. Here the discussion on working inside the system and confronting the risk of co-optation, carried out with Myles Horton (Horton and Freire, 1990), immediately comes to mind (see chapter 3), as well as the point illustrated by Gadotti (1994) regarding the way Freire differed from Illich in regarding institutions, including the school, as sites of struggle (see chapter 2). All this is based on the consideration that hegemony is never complete, its arrangements being constantly renegotiated.

As Paula Allman (2001) stated, with respect to the transformative thrust of Freire-inspired pedagogy, "I cannot deny that applying a Freirean approach to critical education within the context of formal education is difficult—in fact, the most arduous and time-consuming approach that one could choose. Nevertheless, the rewards one experiences more than compensate for this and even for the various, and I presume obvious, risks one takes in adopting this approach" (p. 212).[9] It is here, in the spaces offered by institutions that are not conceived of as monolithic, that one faces the tension of trying to strive toward the progressive and socially just end of the continuum while being constantly pushed toward the other end by the bureaucratic and commodifying forces with which one has to contend daily. It remains to be seen whether there is any significance, in this context, in the shift from Labor Studies to the more encompassing

Industrial Relations in the diploma course title. Does this shift represent a broadening of the agenda conditioned by market forces, as a result of which the specific politics traditionally underlying the area of Labor Studies are diluted to also incorporate managerial concerns? Which way is the war of position going?

In addition to working within the university system, there is also the option of working beyond the academy's hallowed walls. It ought to be said that there is no coherent pattern concerning the university's engagement with projects outside its walls. In fact, this involvement occurs on an individual basis. There are those, and our Faculty of Education thankfully has a few of them, who see their role as public intellectuals, and I am here using the concept of intellectual not in its pretentious elitist sense but more in the sense of transformative intellectuals as propounded by Henry Giroux and others. This constitutes a minimal though important effort in enabling the university to contribute, in its own way, to a revitalization of the public sphere in an age when the corporatist culture holds sway as public spaces are shrinking through the onset of increasing privatization and predatory commodification (see Giroux, 2001, on this).

As I indicated in my response to an interview question by Peter McLaren (Mayo, in McLaren and Mayo, 1999, pp. 405, 406),[10] many of us working in critical pedagogy in Malta feel compelled to be involved in the public sphere. Paulo Freire constitutes a perfect model for many of us in this context. He is not simply the author of inspiring books. He is also a person whose writing derives from and consists of reflections on his own fearless engagement in the public sphere in a variety of contexts worldwide. This, of course, includes his engagement in reforming the public education sector in one of the world's largest cities. This particular engagement represented a severe test for the credibility of much of what he wrote throughout the previous 20 years or so. It occurred when Freire was well into the so-called Third Age. By then, he could easily have been forgiven for confining himself solely to the writing of books, articles, and speeches, given his earlier dangerous political pedagogical work in such countries as Brazil, for which he suffered imprisonment and exile, and Chile, where, many years after Freire had left the country, he was declared persona non grata by General Augusto Pinochet. No one would have called into question his stature as a committed and socially engaged intellectual. And yet we have seen how Freire remained ever so willing to make up for the lost years away from Brazil by engaging in a most challenging, original, and at the same time, potentially hazardous process of municipal educational reform with limited funds, with the opposing political party in power at the federal level, and in a city that, like most Brazilian cities, is characterized by tremendous social contrasts; great affluence coexists with obscene poverty. Although my colleagues and I draw inspiration from Freire, the level of our engagement in the public sphere cannot, by any stretch of the imagination, be compared to his.

One major preoccupation we face, however, is that of being relevant, of engaging in concrete attempts to try and make a difference. Now this is not to minimize, in any way, the value of committed academic work. To do so is to engage in a type of populism (or *basismo*, to use this term once again) that is dangerous and ultimately reactionary. New Right policies, intended to minimize opportunities for critical reflective thinking, placing the emphasis on what works and learning on the job, thrive on such anti-intellectualism.

PARENTAL EMPOWERMENT

I am committed, with a faculty colleague (Carmel Borg), to the coordination of a parent empowerment project in a state primary school located in a working class locality in the south of Malta. Once again, a connection with Freire's work can be established in the context of parental participation in schools (see Borg and Mayo, 2001a, p. 250) because this issue constituted a main area of concern in his efforts, as Education Secretary in São Paulo, to democratize public-sector schools in this city. Furthermore, we have seen earlier how parent education was one of Freire's first activities in education when he worked for SESI.

The coordinating team of the project in which I have been involved includes the mother of a child attending this school, and members of the School Council. The mother in question, who at the time happened to be a member of the School Council, approached us for the purpose of this project. She is a middle-class parent, one of the very few such parents in the locality to send their children to a state school. Her father was an esteemed figure in the community, and the rest of the parents look up to her. She expressed the Council's wish to develop a parental empowerment project and felt we can both make a contribution in this regard.

More than 50 parents, all women, turned up for the first meeting. The first session centered around the theme of Homework, which the parent coordinator and staff at the school identified as a topic very much on the minds of mothers/female guardians within the community. The session itself, which was coordinated by one of us, consisted of a mixture of teaching and dialogue. The women themselves identified the second topic. Every effort is made to ensure that the women participants have a direct say in the selection of the theme for coinvestigation. Only thus can one ascertain that the object of coinvestigation is one that connects with their thematic universe.

The pedagogy throughout is directive (Freire, in Shor and Freire, 1987, p. 103). One of the coordinators, or guest resource persons, anchors the discussion on the topic agreed to by the participants, interspersing the dialogue with brief expositions. The intention is to ensure that the sessions do not degenerate into examples of laissez-faire pedagogy. On the other hand, every effort is made to ensure that the authority that the guest speaker enjoys, granted to him/her by the participants as a result of their recognition of the guest's competence in the matter at issue and as a pedagogue, does not degenerate into *authoritarianism* (Freire, in Shor and Freire, 1987, p. 91; Freire, in Horton and Freire, 1990, p. 181).

The persons who consistently attend the sessions are women. The agendas are introduced by the mothers/guardians, including grandparents. They are discussed at the various meetings with the project coordinators and have led to an identification of priority areas. One of the priority areas is creative expression, given that it was felt that people from this particular area of the island tend to be very low on confidence. This led to an engagement, in the project, of another cultural worker, a faculty colleague who is a specialist in creative arts among primary school children. Given the importance of a language of international currency in a microstate context (Baldacchino, 1993; Baldacchino and Mayo, 1996; Bray, 1992; Mayo, 1994), it is not surprising that parents chose, as the other priority area, the teaching of English.

The demands of the parents, who regularly turn up for the sessions (there was a time when we had an average of 30 per session), eventually began to translate into something concrete. Detailed research on this project can be found in a paper published in the *British Journal of Sociology of Education* (Borg and Mayo, 2001a).

This was socially committed action research, a form of praxis on our part and, therefore, a reflection on our world of action, as a contribution to transformative action. An ongoing involvement in the project might enable us to eschew the traditional tendency among certain academics to engage in "studying and anthropologizing subordinated cultural groups" (Macedo, 1998, p. xxvii), being "tourists" (Macedo, 1998, p. xxvii) and "enamored and perhaps interested in the [groups] for a time" (Memmi, in Macedo, 1998, p. xxvii) and then move onto something else. Our research and reflective pieces on the project also enable us to problematize our own involvement in transformative education and hopefully remain constantly suspicious of its own limits and the limits of the action to which it can give rise. We constantly need to problematize the assumptions we make, often based on some of the most convincing research available in the area, especially regarding who we construct as oppressed in specific contexts.[11]

There are important issues that have to be faced in projects such as this. On whose terms is the partnership carried out? To what extent are the social relations involved genuinely democratic, that is to say, involving a two-way flow of ideas for action, as opposed to being hierarchical? One of the dangers is the fact that we are seen to be experts by virtue of our university background and position (see Horton, in Horton and Freire, 1990, p. 192). This can easily lead us into adopting a patronizing posture, engaging in what Michael Apple once called "The Bolshevik solution. . . . We shall bring you freedom!" (Apple, 1991).

One of the greatest challenges is that of being able to listen on the lines suggested by Paulo and Nita Freire and discussed in chapter 4 of this book. One must reiterate, even at this late stage, that this might come across as being a very simple idea. Being able to listen is, however, no mean task. A colleague of mine, Ronald Sultana, captured the idea beautifully when, writing in Maltese and in the context of a process of parental involvement in public schools, he argued for the development of a "school that listens" (Sultana, 1994, pp. 14–16). The kind of listening being advocated here is, once again, that mentioned by Paulo Freire in *Pedagogia da Autonomia* (Freire, 1998a, p. 107).

We are also under no illusion that the task ahead is plain sailing; indeed, it cannot be. Connecting with the participants' universe of knowledge and relevance is not a straightforward task. As indicated in the discussion on Cabral's class suicide (see chapter 3), *Habitus*, in the sense conveyed by the French sociologist Pierre Bourdieu, often hinders us in attempts to remove or, more realistically, mitigate class obstacles. Constant recognition of the ways in which we are differentially located with regard to those with whom we claim to work should be born in mind as we seek to occupy different spaces within the system that, though structurally oppressive, is not monolithic and therefore offers spaces in which transformative action can be engaged.

TO BE INSPIRED BY THE POPULAR PUBLIC SCHOOL? SCHOOLS AS COMMUNITY LEARNING CENTERS

One of the spaces available to me was that of getting involved, by responding to a public call for applications, in a group, appointed by the National Curriculum Council, to prepare plans for the development of Maltese schools as community learning centers. This is in keeping with one of the recommendations of the country's new National Minimum Curriculum (NMC) document.

It would be appropriate, at this stage, to provide some background information regarding this project. In 1988, a National Minimum Curriculum was established by the Malta government (the Nationalist Government, which is Christian-Democrat) covering primary, secondary, and postsecondary institutions of learning in Malta. This curriculum was criticized (see Borg, Camilleri, Mayo, and Xerri, 1995; Borg and Mayo, 2001b; Wain, 1991) for the top-to-bottom and therefore nonparticipatory manner in which it was introduced, a reflection of the centralization that has for years characterized the Maltese educational system. It was also criticized by Darmanin (1993) and Borg et al. (1995) for its politics of absence with respect to issues concerning social class, race/ethnicity, gender, religious orientation, and disability. These criticisms, and others appearing in the press and in workshops (Borg, 1991), reflected a concern for the current state of education in Malta (Borg and Mayo, 2001b, p. 67). A change of Minister led to a consultative committee on education being set up, comprising members from a broad spectrum of the Maltese educational sector. This committee produced what can safely be regarded as a very progressive report on the state of education in the country and its prospects for the future (Wain et al., 1995), a report that provides guidelines regarding the kind of changes that need to be made for greater social justice. Prominent in this committee were colleagues of mine who are well known for their contributions to critical pedagogy. In my view, the key term, among the four key principles outlined in this report (entitlement, effectiveness, equity, and economy), which indicated the report's clear option in favor of subaltern social groups, was that of equity (Borg and Mayo, 2001b, p. 68). They argue:

By equity we are not referencing "sameness," or even "equal resourcing for all." Students will bring different intellectual, cultural, social and financial resources to the school, and when we ignore these differences hoping to conjure away distinctions, by treating all students equally, we inadvertently reinforce these same differences, and create new ones along the way. (Wain et al., 1995, p. 9)

The publication of the document just referred to is considered the first step in the long process of reviewing, or rather revamping, the old national curriculum (Borg and Mayo, 2001b, p. 68). Soon after, the review began. It entailed a broad process of consultation involving social partners and the general public. Numerous formal invitations for submissions were sent out, and the public was invited to contribute through a series of activities including a press conference. On the basis of the submissions received, a draft document (Vella et al., 1998) was prepared for wide circulation (Borg and Mayo, 2001b, p. 68). "The tenor of the draft document was quite radical" (Borg and Mayo, 2001b, p. 68). The document was meant to trigger a national debate, which would culminate in the agreed on principles being contained in what would be a final set of curricular guidelines. The draft document proposed such ideas as "destreaming at the primary level, the elimination of the 11t examination and the comprehensivisation of secondary education" (Borg and Mayo, 2001b).[12] Among other things, the draft document also called for an acknowledgment of the full range of sexual identities, an open attitude toward sexuality and respect for people of different sexual identity (Borg and Mayo, 2001b, p. 69; Vella et al., 1998, p. 42). The focus throughout was on a socially inclusive educational system.

One of the proposals submitted for public consideration through this draft document is that schools be developed as community learning centers. This particular provision in the curriculum, as well as the provision on sexual identities, is among those that remained untouched when the final document (Ministry of Education, 2000) was produced in light of the reactions to the draft document. The final new NMC document states:

Schools should serve as community learning centres that also cater for the adult members of the community. This principle combines the commitment of this Curriculum to a holistic education with the recognition of the importance of lifelong education and the need for stakeholder participation in the educational process. (Ministry of Education, 2000, p. 89)

Needless to say, being primarily a social consensus document, this final NMC document reflects the long process of negotiation and compromise that occurred in reaction to the draft. The commitment toward an inclusive politics was retained, and there are elements that gesture in the direction of greater interdisciplinary approaches to knowledge although, of course, not to the extent attained by the curricular reforms carried out by the Secretariat in São Paulo and SMED in Porto Alegre where the curricular focus is on thematic complexes derived from action research carried out in the immediate surrounding local community (Gandin and Apple, 2002, p. 105). Certainly, given the Maltese context in question, the São Paulo Education Secretariat's idea of having generative themes as the basis of teaching and learning within an interdisciplinary curriculum, though laudable and justifiable with regard to the development of an approach promoting a critical reading of the world, did not feature anywhere in the proposals contained in the NMC document in Malta. Apart from the fact that knowledge of the São Paulo reforms strikes me as being quite minimal in my country, this approach would have been considered as too sudden and too drastic a change, representing a major overhaul of the system of education. It would have probably been counterproductive and suffered a response worse than that reserved for the proposal to comprehensivize the Maltese educational system. Compromises were made in the latter case. These compromises occurred possibly because of the still vivid memories, among the older and influential sectors of the population, of the sudden comprehensivization policies introduced by an overzealous Labor government in Malta in the 1970s. This might explain why, at present, a more gradual approach to changes in education seems to be favored and is being widely advocated.[13]

The preceding compromises notwithstanding, the proposal for schools to be developed as community learning centers seems to have been accepted, probably owing to the fact that much of the discussion has centered mainly on the after school (read: after conventional school hours) program. Of course, this concept also implies changes to the way education occurs among children during the conventional school hours. One wonders what the reaction would be when proposals regarding the day program start being made. Once the NMC document was released, a number of working groups, consisting of representatives of different stakeholders, were organized, each to provide policy guidelines regarding a specific aspect of the document. Probably because of my adult education background, I happened to be invited to join the group concentrating on schools as community learning centers. I naturally accepted and contributed, together with others, to the production of a set of guidelines, which were presented by the group's coordinator at a national conference on the implementation of the NMC held in June 2000, and which attracted a large number of participants—different stakeholders from different walks of life. The reports of the various working groups and the conclusion of workshops focusing on the specific themes were captured in a volume containing the conference proceedings (Giordmaina, 2000). The executive summary of the report by the working group on schools as community learning centers states that the project should initially be restricted to a few pilot schools and that

A call for project proposals from School Councils interested in implementing this initiative in their locality should be issued. Co-ordinators are to be employed by School Councils following a call for applications and interviews. An Interviewing Board should be established composed of one representative each from the School Council, the Local Council and the Monitoring Panel. The main function of the Monitoring Panel is to monitor the development of this initiative. This document outlines the main principles, broad aims, specific objectives, and the roles and responsibilities of stakeholders. It is being recommended that the interests of marginalised and potentially marginalised individuals and groups are held uppermost in any strategies and plans formulated by the School Councils through the Co-ordinator. . . . (Giordmaina, 2000, p. 355)

In 2001, a number of focus groups dealing with different aspects of the NMC were set up following a public call for applications. I applied to join the focus group on schools as community learning centers and was selected to form part of a focus group combining this area with that of parental participation in schools. It was argued that schools could not be developed as community learning centers without a certain degree of parental participation. I was subsequently elected as the group coordinator, and an action plan for the implementation of this project was drawn up with appropriate budgetary recommendations. Importance was devoted to the preparation of personnel to be involved in this project. One idea in the Action Plan, derived from Freire's experience as Education Secretary in São Paulo, is that of "Designing and Running an Induction Course in the Idea of Schools as Community Learning Centres for Non-teaching Staff of Schools participating in the Initiative."[14] They have an educational role to perform within this setting. Like the cooks and janitors in the popular public schools in the Brazilian city, they too must be prepared to serve as educators.

The more immediate task, however, apart from the need to carry out meetings with heads of schools, mayors, and local council representatives, is that of carrying out a preparatory course for those wanting to be involved as coordinators and educators in connection with this project. The preparatory course will also coincide with a call, targeting local councils and school councils, to submit proposals for their local schools to be developed collaboratively as community learning centers. Following the approval of a smaller budget than was originally proposed by the Group, three schools will now be selected to serve as pilot community learning centers. The intention is to help develop these pilot schools into models of community learning centers before involving other schools in the project.

There are several reasons that justify the development of schools as community learning centers. It has often been argued that schools have traditionally operated as enclaves with little interaction between them and the rest of the community. They are "daytime enclaves that most students and teachers leave only for lunches or special outings," places that "Community members rarely enter" (Curtis, Livingstone, and Smaller, 1992, p. 113). By serving as community learning centers (see Parson, 1990), schools can make an important contribution to the development of the public sphere. They would provide educational services to members of the community at large. Furthermore, the community, in which the school is located can be conceived of as a learning community.

Schools, especially state schools, are public resources. Their conception as community learning centers can therefore be seen as an attempt to make democratic use of public resources, rendering them accessible to and more popular with a wider section of the local community than is the case at present. This invites parallels with the PT's conception of popular public schools. There is also an economic argument to be made given that the cost per capita of public resources in a microstate such as Malta is higher than that incurred in larger states. One must make better and maximum use of resources lest these resources become idle capital for several hours during the day and entire months during the calendar year.

There are also powerful pedagogical arguments to be made for conceiving of schools as community learning centers. It is not only adult members of the community who benefit from such schools but also children. In forging strong links between schools and the community, one would be creating greater space for the involvement of more stakeholders, such as parents, in the educational process. This has the potential to forge closer ties between schools and their pupils' immediate home environment. In the words of Francisco, a teacher in one of São Paulo's popular public schools:

There is no point in handing children books to read if they are not understanding what is happening on their own street. So only [by] departing from her [the child's] daily life experience can we form a critical citizen and [instill] the idea of the right to citizenship. (O'Cadiz et al., 1998, p. 189)

Recall Freire's statement (see chapter 4) that the learners'"concrete localization" constitutes the starting point "for the knowledge they create of the world" (Freire, 1994, p. 85) or the much cited phrase from *Pedagogy of the Oppressed:* "The starting point for organizing the program content of education or political action must be the present, existential, concrete situation, reflecting the aspirations of the people" (Freire, 1970b, 1993, p. 95). The surrounding community provides a significant part of the culture in which the children are immersed. This culture provides them with an important framework of relevance. The community can therefore serve as an important learning resource for the teaching of children during the morning and early afternoon hours. There are teachers for whom this is not necessarily a new challenge. From conversations I carried out with older members of the teaching community in Malta's public education sector, when I visited schools throughout the past year to evaluate student teachers on their practicum,[15] I was told about their previous experiences in inviting community members to share with children their firsthand and, in many instances, professional knowledge of a specific topic included in the syllabus.

The idea of developing schools as community learning centers, however, has implications for the initial and ongoing formation of teachers. It would seem appropriate for student teachers, especially at primary (elementary) level, to be initiated into the task of researching the community in question prior to the start of their teaching practice (practicum) session. Knowledge of the school's surrounding community can serve as an important teaching tool. It can help render what is taught more culturally relevant and meaningful to pupils. This derives from the unmistakably Freirean approach to work in the cultural circles; those involved as educators in the cultural circles were to spend some time in the community where they were going to be engaged. The intention is for the educators, working in tandem with other members of the circle, including learners, to immerse themselves in the culture of the community, expose themselves, often through informal conversations, to the people's speech patterns, and gain access to their universe of knowledge (see chapter 3), jotting down various aspects of the people's life in their notebooks (see Freire, 1970b, 1993, pp. 110–111).

The idea of pupils researching the community in which they will be carrying out their practicum is, in my view, an important aspect of their initial formation as educators. This development owes its origin to a group of faculty members whose pedagogical thinking has been inspired by Freire.[16]

This is not to say that teaching should begin and end with the community. That would smack of basismo. National and international perspectives remain crucial to the broadening of the child's universe of knowledge. What is being called for, here, is a more inclusive approach whereby, to provide one example, a lesson on houses, delivered at primary level, would involve an appreciation of not only international types of houses, through foreign textbook illustrations (a form of cultural invasion), but also the types of houses available in the surrounding community. Items and surroundings that are familiar to the children in their everyday life gain legitimacy by becoming part of the school's official knowledge (see Gandin and Apple, 2002, p. 105, with regard to the transformation of official knowledge in the Porto Alegre experience). Of course, the one great challenge in this context, and in relation to subjects such as houses, is to relate the issue to a social theme within the school's surrounding community. The theme would serve as a codification, as with the interdisciplinary approach used in the popular public school project in São Paulo. The issue of social housing and of tragic deaths caused by poor and decrepit housing remains a very relevant one in this context, as is the theme of homelessness in most contexts worldwide. Of course, in a polarized society (in terms of party politics) as is Maltese society, there is always the risk that the use of such themes would be viewed with suspicion by those who support the party in government, as they would regard the introduction of these themes by teachers as a way of criticizing government social policy. In contrast, PT detractors regarded the use of similar social issues as generative themes in São Paulo as subtle propaganda by the party in municipal government.

There is also a challenge for heads of school (principals in the United States) that have an important part to play in the whole project. They would have to handle effectively many of the logistics involved in allowing children to leave the school premises, under their teacher's care, to observe things and visit places, within the surrounding locality, that relate to matters being taught as part of the subject syllabus and school curriculum. Heads of school also need to collaborate with other stakeholders and personnel, particularly the coordinator entrusted with the task of running programs held on the school premises after conventional hours. It is heartening to see the area of education and the community being included in the university's evening diploma course in Educational Administration and Management, the formal qualification intended for those aspiring to take up an administrative position inside Maltese schools, especially the position of head of school (principal in the United States). This course targets prospective heads of school and assistant heads (vice-principals).

The idea of developing schools as community learning centers poses a number of challenges for those working in and around them. It is not only teachers and heads who face these challenges. Many other stakeholders are being called on to face this challenge. Parents feature prominently among the stakeholders, as I have had occasion to show in a previous section. Different stakeholders need to collaborate and to do so not on their own narrow terms. There is also the challenge for local councils and school councils to avail themselves of this opportunity and work together to help transform the school culture for this purpose. They need to ensure that funds available for physical adjustments to the building are secured to render the place accessible to and suitable for learners of different ages.

One cannot expect adults to learn in an environment meant to accommodate children. And where it is necessary to build new schools, the local councils and school councils should ensure that these schools are designed as multipurpose community learning sites. The emphasis placed on the school councils' and the local councils' active role in this venture should not imply a decrease in the state's major responsibilities in this regard. The councils' action should also include making legitimate demands on the state to honor these responsibilities. As with the popular public schools in São Paulo and with any project elsewhere concerned with social justice, education is regarded as a right, something to which each citizen is entitled. It is conceived of as a public good that needs to be safeguarded and, in certain contexts, retrieved, given that this right is constantly threatened by the New Right's onslaught on the public sector, an onslaught born out of a conviction that the services traditionally provided by this sector are ripe for commodification and privatization.

Many of the foregoing issues are being borne in mind and discussed in the current preparatory course in community learning, commissioned by the National Curriculum Council in Malta, on the basis of recommendations by the relevant Focus Group, and held under the aegis of the University of Malta. The course is intended to prepare prospective personnel wanting to fulfill an active role in changing the face of the school by transforming it into a community learning center. As with São Paulo's *Grupos de Formação*, those who are to be involved as community workers, adult educators, teachers, and other cultural workers in schools that want to be developed as community learning centers are being provided with the opportunity to be prepared for and collectively reflect on this challenging task.

THE MUSEUM AS AN ALTERNATIVE SITE OF PRACTICE—A FREIREAN PERSPECTIVE

The sites of educational practice are multiple and therefore it is possible to adopt a Freirean perspective in areas that rarely feature in the everburgeoning literature on or inspired by the ideas of the Brazilian educator. In this section, I will focus briefly on a topic on which a close colleague, Carmel Borg, and I have written articles over the last few years, the latest of which in collaboration with another colleague, Bernard Cauchi (Borg, Cauchi, and Mayo, 2003). The area in question is that of the museum, which is conceived of by all three of us as a site of cultural politics and, borrowing from Henry Giroux, public pedagogy. As Carmel Borg and I have argued, the situation concerning museums is not so far removed from that regarding the curriculum. We have argued that through the curriculum, legitimacy is accorded to some forms of knowledge to the detriment of others (Borg and Mayo, 2000a, p. 81). We also argue that

museums have a similar role. Like established curricula, they too give legitimacy to particular forms of cultural production, creating "official knowledge". Like curricula, they are caught up in the politics of knowledge and *representation.* (p. 81)

We go on to argue that museums, like curricula, are selections from the cultures of society, which therefore lead the critical viewer or museum educator to pose the problem concerning their "cultural arbitrary" and therefore refrain from viewing museums as repositories of neutral knowledge (Borg and Mayo, 2000a). We dwell in our work on the Eurocentric and class bias of museums making reference not only to Maltese museums, because the papers focus in their entirety on museums in Malta, but also to international examples provided by, for instance, MOMA and the American Crafts Museum that are situated across the road from each other in New York. The juxtaposition of what strikes us as highbrow cultural production on the one hand and subaltern and popular production on the other renders the ideas of Paulo Freire most relevant:

MOMA (Museum of Modern Art) in New York houses paintings, sculpture, architectural displays . . . displays of aspects of film history and a display of designs of cars, modern furniture and office equipment. The last mentioned are strongly associated with the corporate world, whereas the designs of different crafts (e.g., the work of the Women of Colour Quilters Network) are displayed in a different museum (the American Craft Museum) across the road from MOMA. The debate regarding whether such forms of cultural production should be separated or not is an important feature of the "culture wars" that have characterized the struggle for democratic renewal in North America. These "wars" often revolve around class, gender, race and ethnicity issues. They can easily revolve around issues relating to production, e.g., corporate power on the one hand and subsistence economies or cooperatives on the other. (Borg and Mayo, 2000a, p. 86)

What we are confronted with, in this context, are the cultural productions deriving from two different social milieus, the milieu of the dominant and the milieu of the subaltern. As with the mainstream curriculum, we witness a politics of inclusion and exclusion. Freire's ideas, as well as those of other exponents of critical pedagogy, besides ideas emerging from the field of cultural studies, become relevant in this context. They furnish the critical pedagogue, who makes use of the museum as an alternative pedagogical site, and most notably the critical museum educator, given that museum education is a growing area in a number of places throughout the world (see Chadwick and Stannett, 1995, 2001), with tools for a problem posing pedagogical approach. It is an approach that entails the posing of such questions within "the realm of cultural politics," as "Whose culture shall be the official one and whose shall be subordinated? What culture shall be regarded as worthy of display and which shall be hidden? Whose history shall be remembered and whose forgotten? What images of social life shall be projected and which shall be marginalized? What voices shall be heard and which be silenced? Who is representing whom and on what basis?" (Jordan and Weedon, 1995, p. 4).

The Museum offers us opportunities not only for simply ideology critique but also for struggling collectively and lobbying for the conversion of such sites of public pedagogy into really democratic and inclusive public spaces. Like schools, museums are culturally selective in a manner that is not innocent. They often decontextualize artifacts by extricating them from the surroundings to which they belonged in the first place. Museums could, however, be conceived of the way Freire and other critical pedagogues conceive of schools and other institutions—sites of contestation. In our published papers, Carmel Borg and I have come up with suggestions on how to render museums more inclusive and embrace the subaltern voices of the surrounding community's inhabitants. We have focused for this purpose on specific types of museums, notably ethnographic or folklore museums as well as maritime museums. Our most recent study, with Bernard Cauchi, deals with the country's national maritime museum located in a region closely connected to Malta's maritime history and therefore a museum that is surrounded by a community that includes elderly members who, in their younger years, had earned their living at sea at a time when a substantial part of the country's economy revolved around the British naval presence in Malta. The museum is located in the historic maritime city of Birgu (Vittoriosa).

Besides providing an account of its permanent exhibition, we also explore possibilities for this museum to develop into a popular public place that embraces the voices of the subaltern alongside those of dominant groups reflected in memorabilia, models, and uniforms relating to the time of either the ruling Sovereign Military Order of St. John or the colonizing British occupational force. We have argued that space should be accorded to the universe of knowledge of common folk who engage in recreational pursuits and specific forms of creative cultural production that can be traced back to the time when most economic life centered around harbor activity. We suggest, for instance, that ample space be accorded to representations connected with the popular regatta (rowing contest held on September 8, a national feast day), an event that captures the popular imagination in this part of the country.

Among other things, we also proposed the use of recent technology to capture the oral popular history of this region, thus giving prominence to the voices of those who for long have been immersed in what Freire would call the culture of silence:

> . . . oral history offers great opportunities for capturing the authentic voice of the seafaring community that traditionally belonged to the localities surrounding the Malta Maritime Museum. The community where the Museum is situated provides an invaluable wealth of real Maritime experiences. There are no indications within the Maritime museum of an urgency to record and share such genuine experiences. (Borg, Cauchi, and Mayo, 2003, p. 105)

Furthermore, the display concerning what was, for several years, the major source of livelihood in this region[17] and in the country, namely the dockyard, is also found lacking when it comes to the affirmation and representation of subaltern popular voices. It is argued,

> The section in question also overlooks a very important aspect of critical and emancipatory museology, namely the concept of *voice*. Within the dockyard display, expert knowledge is privileged over other community-based ways of knowing. The harsh reality of dockyard life, the disabilities endured through years of exhaust inhaling, grit blasting and other dangerous emissions, the death of several workers, the various struggles for worker emancipation, the anxiety generated by intermittent work, are basically sanitised in a display which fails to foreground real faces and genuine voices. Secondary sources were privileged over the primary source of the workers' voice. (Borg, Cauchi, and Mayo, 2003, p. 104)

These are just a few examples of the suggestions that emerged from our research concerning museums that are conceived of as sites of cultural politics. These suggestions are made not to detract from the fine work that characterizes museums such as the National Maritime Museum, work that testifies to the commitment of a very energetic, enterprising, knowledgeable, and dedicated group of museum personnel. The suggestions have been made with a view to providing signposts to render museums more democratic and, in Freire's words, popular public spaces that accord prominence to many of the voices that have been submerged in official centers of cultural representation.

The focus here has been on democratizing displays and spaces offered by the museum and this is only a brief selection of issues raised in our published work on the subject (Borg and Mayo, 2000a; Borg, Cauchi, and Mayo, 2003). However, we have also written our papers in a way that provides proposals for a critical pedagogical approach to museum education. The emphasis on the critical museum educator as cultural worker leads us to view the various elements on display in these museums as codifications that can serve as the basis for a discussion of wider issues concerning different aspects of the country's reality. Rather than simply indulging in ideology critique, the museum educator qua critical pedagogue avails herself or himself of a folklore museum such as the one situated in a village in Gozo to once again help develop a problem posing approach and thus prevent the viewer from engaging in simply a "nostalgic trip to a much simpler world" (Borg and Mayo, 2000a, p. 86). On the contrary, the critical educator

provides opportunities for confronting a range of socio-economic issues associated with the exhibits. Thus, for example, a room containing traditional fishing implements can stimulate discussions on the loss of fishing communities, the deskilling of fishermen through technology, fishing wars in the Mediterranean, sea pollution, overfishing and malpractices in fishing, the depletion of fishing stocks, the economic, ecological and social effects of fishing farms. . . . Such discussions not only challenge the traditional status of the objects, as conveyors of static knowledge with no connection with the present . . . but also problematise the myth that such objects are culturally neutral and value free. (Borg and Mayo, 2000a, p. 86)

The process should be one in which the educator does not treat the visitor as an empty receptacle to be filled with images and knowledge and therefore an object of the cultural transmission process. Not that the visitor is ever a passive recipient. Neither should one assume, in a rather patronizing manner, that the visitor requires the challenge of a critical museum educator to engage in a critical reading of the texts on display. Many visitors do this irrespective of any promptings whatsoever by external agents. What is being called for, however, is the development of the museum and other centers as democratic public spaces that allow possibilities for different meanings to be exchanged, appropriated, and negotiated. This can hopefully enable the visitor to be a subject in a process of coinvestigation involving the museum educator and the visitor mediated by the exhibit. In such a context, knowledge would be not static but dynamic resulting from the dialogue, surrounding the object of coinvestigation, engaged in by both museum educator and visitor.

The bias throughout the preceding discussion concerning museums is toward popular forms of knowledge. This is in keeping with much of Freire's writing that is available in English. Our work on museums also focuses on that which is constructed as highbrow, and an example of this is provided in the previous chapter, where I reproduced an argument made with respect to one of the main attractions on the island—a cathedral that is typical of several churches in Southern Europe, churches that serve as museums. They are repositories of different forms of highbrow culture, notably priceless works of art. In this chapter, I indicated, bor-

rowing from other published work (Borg and Mayo, 2000a), how these
centers can be availed of for a critical reading of a country's much-
celebrated artistic heritage, a heritage that often reflects an unmistakably
Eurocentric and racist brand of cultural politics. A critical approach to
museum education would also entail a critical confrontation with the
highbrow, something that is missing from Freire's own writing. In Freire's
work, emphasis is placed almost exclusively on the popular, with the culture of the dominant hardly featured, except for discussions concerning
standard language as opposed to dialect. As Schugurensky (1998) noted,

> It has also been argued that although Freire's cultural analysis is illuminating, it is
> limited because he rarely ventured beyond the confines of popular culture, and
> thus did not incorporate an examination of the dominant culture into his
> approach. (p. 24)

This omission in Freire's work, which occurs despite Freire's insistence
that popular knowledge represents only the starting point of the pedagogical encounter, invites interesting comparisons with the work of
Gramsci (Mayo, 1999a, pp. 142, 180), whose writings, among other things,
pose the issue of the critical appropriation by the working class of the
dominant culture.

In previous work (Mayo, 1999a, pp. 97–98), I pointed out that Antonio
Gramsci was politically active in a city that had all the makings of a typi-
cally Western European metropolis, including a well-developed civil society and a tradition of industrial organization. Furthermore, Gramsci had
worked for some time as a journalist dealing, among other things, with cultural affairs. Many of his pieces on theatre, literature, and the figurative arts,
available in anthologies of his writings, were originally written by Gramsci
as reviews for newspapers. Gramsci was, as a result of his work as cultural
critic, ideally placed to observe the various forms of artistic production that
were on display in the Italy of his time. In his analysis of cultural production, Gramsci focuses on both aspects of the high and low divide, although
he was always ready to avoid presenting them as binary opposites because
he often indicated the intersections and dialectical relationships that exist
between them. This all tied in with his search for a synthesis between the
potentially emancipatory aspects of the various types of cultural production. This synthesis is sought with a view to establishing the basis for a proletarian culture. It is this search that led him to express an interest in, for
instance, works like Dostoyevski's novels, which draw on serial fiction and,
in so doing, reveal the interplay between the popular and the artistic. For
Gramsci, a critical appropriation of the dominant, established culture is central to the emergence of a new subaltern and, in his case, proletarian culture.

It [*creating a new culture*] also, and most particularly, means the diffusion in a critical form of truths already discovered, their "socialisation" as it were, and even
making them the basis of vital action, an element of co-ordination and intellectual
and moral order. (my italics) (Gramsci, 1971, p. 325)

Critical appropriation would, in this case, include making use of the
spaces associated with the dominant culture to provide critical readings of
the specific constructions of reality found within them. I would emphasize
the point made by adult educator, Denis Haughey, who states, with
respect to radical education, inspired, in his specific case, by Gramsci's
writings, that one of the competencies "largely lacking in contemporary . . . practice[18] is the ability to function fluently in the language of the
dominant culture so as not to be relegated to the periphery of political life"
(Haughey, 1998, p. 211). It is a point that also echoes Freire's view that
members of subordinated social groups learn the standard language not
to remain on the margins of political life.

Can museums therefore become centers for critical literacy in which the
world can be read? Some museums have greater potential to do this than
others, and this explains my specific choice of museums in this section.
These museums can be more representative in the forms of cultural production they display and hence more socially accessible, particularly to
members of subaltern groups. Social and physical accessibility are two
issues that are given prominence in the collaborative work with my colleagues (see Borg and Mayo, 2000a). These museums, however, have
potential for developing the kind of knowledge—popular knowledge—
that is given prominence in Freire's work. The great challenge remains
that of transforming into democratic and accessible public spaces those
museums that have traditionally been repositories of different features of
the dominant culture (e.g., art galleries). The challenge becomes more formidable in that one is confronted by the issue of how to render high status
forms of knowledge accessible to subaltern groups without rendering this
knowledge an object of domination. The challenge, from a Gramscian perspective, would be to render such knowledge an object of critical appropriation. It is these sorts of questions that seem to be missing from Freire's
work that is available in the English language and that are overlooked in
much of the Freire-inspired literature also in English. As I have indicated
in chapter 2, these questions do not feature in the otherwise splendid
account by O'Cadiz et al. (1998) of the curricular reforms taking place in
the São Paulo schools at the time when Freire was Education Secretary in
this city. I feel that one of the many formidable challenges facing Freire-
inspired educators is that of exploring ways and means by which subaltern groups can gain accessibility to and learn to function critically in the

language of the dominant culture not to remain on the margins of political life and to contribute to a wide-ranging process of social transformation involving several sites of practice.

CONCLUSION

The brief synoptic discussion of these projects and specific sites of practice, drawing from more amplified published work, represents a modest attempt to indicate some pathways for educators to tread in a bid to engage in education for transformative action on the lines suggested by Freire and other critical pedagogues. Some of these attempts, occurring in specific geographical and social contexts, with their obvious limit situations, serve to show that there are pockets of transformative education practice that provide a counterdiscourse to the dominant one of technical rationality and marketability developed within the context and logic of capitalist reorganization. Others constitute spaces that, despite prima facie appearing exclusive and possibly elitist to some, as in the case of museums, allow possibilities for a critical approach to the coinvestigation of knowledge.

The discussion in this chapter represents an attempt on my part to show how Freire's ideas can be brought to bear on the development of different educational projects and on analysis of the cultural politics manifest in a specific site of public pedagogy, the museum in this case. My overriding concern, with respect to the issues raised in all four of the sections of this chapter, is with the democratization and revitalization of public institutions and spaces based on the conviction, shared by Freire, that all four of the sites concerned can be conceived of as sites of struggle and contestation. As with public schooling in São Paulo, when Freire was Education Secretary in this city, these different sites have the potential to provide popular public spaces.

With respect to at least two of these projects, specifically the first two dealt with in this chapter, the challenge is for these specific efforts at the local level to be combined with more comprehensive international efforts if they are to make a contribution to larger and more global efforts for social transformation. It is possibly in the exploration of the means of articulating local efforts with the more global ones that one encounters the greatest challenge for a genuinely transformative action, forged in the struggle for greater social justice and the radically democratic revitalization of the public sphere. The broader context of workers' education, occurring within the international labor movement, constitutes an important larger context for the first effort involving the WPDC. The context for the second effort (parental involvement in a state primary school), and possibly, depending on the way this develops, even the third one (schools as community learning centers), can be found in the emerging international movement for parental involvement in education and the larger movement for the democratization of public schooling. Many of these movements constantly face the ever-so-pernicious threats of co-optation and appropriation intended to make them fit into the current hegemonic framework. Nevertheless, they still hold out the promise of a context wherein people can participate as social actors or subjects, rather than two-dimensional objects (consumers, producers), in their specific sites of practice within the public sphere.

NOTES

1. These were the Malta Drydocks, Melita Knitwear, and Cargo & Handling.

2. See the interview with Professor Vanek on cooperative economics that appeared in the magazine *New Renaissance,* Vol. 5, No.1. http://www.ru.org/51cooper.html.

3. I am indebted to the former WPDC director, Professor Edward Zammit, for this information.

4. Sampaio was contacted by the University authorities at Cornel for this purpose in view of the fact that his name had appeared with those of Freire's close collaborators in *Pedagogy of the Oppressed.* Information provided in taped interview with Plinio Sampaio.

5. Plinio Sampaio's words extracted from taped interview carried out at his residence in São Paulo in 1998.

6. More recently, I have been invited and accepted to join the WPDC's Board.

7. The University has an extension campus in Gozo, the second largest and second most inhabited island in the Maltese archipelago.

8. This is an example of the kind of voices reproduced in my research on the WPDC. More voices of this type are available in Mayo (1997c, 2003), two chapters that provide a more in depth account of the situation at this particular center.

9. For a revealing account of the difficulties and challenges involved in providing a transformative education within the formal system, see chapter 6 of Allman (2001), entitled "Freirean Critical Education in an Unlikely Context" (pp. 187–216).

10. The next seven lines are extracted (with slight modifications) from McLaren and Mayo (1999).

11. I am indebted to my close friend and collaborator, Carmel Borg, for raising this point with me when providing feedback on an earlier version of this chapter.

12. See the draft document, Vella et al. (1998, pp. 17–18).

13. For a more detailed discussion on this, see Borg and Mayo (2001b).

14. Action plan provided by Focus Group regarding "Schools as Community Learning Centres" and "Parental Participation in Schools," National Curriculum Council.

15. *Teaching practice* is the term we use in Malta.

16. The idea was probably first floated around at the 1997 conference, "Tomorrow's Teachers," organized by the University of Malta's Faculty of Education to explore directions that the Faculty's initial teacher education program should take.

17. This is the Cottonera region that is closely connected to the island's Grand Harbour.

18. Haughey refers specifically to adult education practice in this context, but his point may well apply to the education of marginalized sectors of the population in general, including schooling.

Bibliography

Abdi, A. (2001). Identity in the philosophies of Dewey and Freire: Select analyses. *Journal of Educational Thought, 35*(2), 181–200.

Adams, F. (1972). Highlander Folk School: Getting information, going back and teaching it. *Harvard Educational Review, 42*(4), 97–119.

Allman, P. (1988). Gramsci, Freire and Illich: Their contribution to education and socialism. In T. Lovett (Ed.), *Radical adult education—a reader* (pp. 85–113). London: Routledge.

Allman, P. (1994). Paulo Freire's contributions to radical adult education. *Studies in the Education of Adults, 26*(2), 144–161.

Allman, P. (1996). Freire with no dilutions. In H. Reno and M. Witte (Eds.), *37th Annual AERC Proceedings*. Tampa: University of Florida.

Allman, P. (1999). *Revolutionary social transformation: Democratic hopes, political possibilities and critical education*. Westport, CT and London: Bergin & Garvey.

Allman, P. (2001). *Critical education against global capitalism: Karl Marx and revolutionary critical education*. Westport, CT and London: Bergin & Garvey.

Allman, P. (with Mayo, P., cavanagh, c., Lean Heng, C. and Haddad, S.) (1998). Introduction. " . . . the creation of a world in which it will be easier to love." *Convergence, XXI*(1 & 2), 9–16.

Apitzsch, U. (1995), Razzismo ed Atteggiamenti Verso gli Immigrati Stranieri. Il Caso della Repubblica Federale Tedesca. In *Quaderni dei Nuovi Annali* (pp. 67–76). Messina: University of Messina, 33.

Apple, M. W. (1991). Response, as the discussant, in the session "The Work of Paulo Freire as Secretary of Education in São Paulo." *Educational Policy and Social Change in Brazil*, AERA, Chicago: Teach 'em Inc. (audiotape).

Araújo Freire, A. M. (1997). A bit of my life with Paulo Freire. *Taboo: The Journal of Culture and Education, 2*, 3–11.

Araújo Freire, A. M. (1998). Paulo Freire: To touch, to look, to listen. *Convergence (A Tribute to Paulo Freire), 31*, 3–5.

Arnove, R. F. (1986). *Education and revolution in Nicaragua.* New York: Praeger.

Arnove, R. F. (1994). *Education as contested terrain. Nicaragua, 1979–1993,* Boulder, CO: Westview.

Aronowitz, S. (1993). Paulo Freire's radical democratic humanism. In P. McLaren and P. Leonard (Eds.), *Paulo Freire: A critical encounter* (pp. 8–24). London and New York: Routledge.

Aronowitz, S. (1998). Introduction. In P. Freire, *Pedagogy of Freedom: Ethics, Democracy and Civic Courage* (pp. 1–19). Lanham, MD: Rowman & Littlefield.

Aronowitz, S., and Giroux, H. (1991), *Postmodern education.* Minneapolis: University of Minnesota Press.

Baldacchino, G. (1993). Bursting the bubble: The pseudo-development strategies of microstates. *Development and Change, 24,* 29–51.

Baldacchino, G., and Mayo, P. (1996). Adult continuing education in small and island states: The case of Malta. *Convergence, 29*(2), 22–35.

Banna, P. (2000). Politiche Interculturali e ruolo del Ente locale. In G. Pampanini (Ed.), *Un Mare di Opportunita': Cultura e Educazione nel Mediterraneo del lll Millenio* (pp. 245–249). Rome: Armando Editore.

Barton, D. (1994). Globalisation and Diversification: Two Opposing Influences in Local Literacies. *Language and Education, 8,* 3–7.

Betto, F. (1986). *Fidel Castro. La Mia Fede. Cristianesimo e Rivoluzione in un'intervista con Frei Betto,* Balsamo: Edizioni Paoline.

Betto, F. (1999). Liberation theology: No longer a ghetto in the church (Frei Betto interviewed in São Paulo by Carmel Borg and Peter Mayo). *The Sunday Times* (Malta), 17/10/99, 44–45.

Betto, F., and Freire, P. (1986). *Una scuola chiamata vita.* Bologna: E.M.I.

Bloch, E. (1986). *The principle of hope,* Cambridge, MA: MIT Press.

Borg, C. (1991). Curriculum evaluation. In C. J. Farrugia (Ed.), *A national minimum curriculum for Malta* (pp. 46–49). Malta: University of Malta, Foundation for International Studies, Ministry of Education.

Borg, C. (1995). *Hegemony as educational practice: Catholicism, traditionalism and the fate of the progressive historical bloc in Malta—a Gramscian analysis.* Ph.D. thesis, Ontario Institute for Studies in Education/University of Toronto.

Borg, C., Camilleri, J., Mayo, P., and Xerri, T. (1995). Malta's national curriculum: A critical analysis. *International Review of Education, 41,* 337–356.

Borg, C., Cauchi, B., and Mayo, P. (2003). Museums' education and cultural contestation. *Journal of Mediterranean Studies, 13*(1), 89–108.

Borg, C., and Dharsey, Z. (1994). View from the margins—reflecting on issues of global transformation. *Trans/forms Insurgent Voices in Education, 1,* 20–36.

Borg, C., and Mayo, P. (1994). Invisible indentity/ies: The Maltese community in Metro-Toronto. In R. G. Sultana and G. Baldacchino (Eds.), *Maltese society: A sociological inquiry* (pp. 211–223). Malta: Mireva Publications.

Borg, C., and Mayo, P. (2000a). Maltese museums, adult education and cultural politics. *Education & Society, 18*(3), 77–97.

Borg, C., and Mayo, P. (2000b). Reflections from a third age marriage. A pedagogy of hope, reason and passion. An interview with Ana Maria (Nita) Araújo Freire. *McGill Journal of Education, 35*(2), 105–120.

Borg, C., and Mayo, P. (2001a). From "adjuncts" to "subjects": Parental involvement in a working class community. *British Journal of Sociology of Education*, 22(2), 245–266.

Borg, C., and Mayo, P. (2001b). Social difference, cultural arbitrary and identity: An analysis of a new national curriculum document in a non-secular environment. *International Studies in Sociology of Education*, 11(1), 63–84.

Borg, C., and Mayo, P. (2002a). Making sense of a postcolonial context: A Freirean perspective. *Journal of Postcolonial Education*, 1(1), 101–125.

Borg, C., and Mayo, P. (2002b). Towards an anti-racist agenda in education: The case of Malta. *World Studies in Education*, 2(2), 47–64.

Borg, C., Mayo, P., and Sultana, R. G. (1997). Revolution and reality: An interview with Peter MacLaren. In W. Pinar (Ed.), *Curriculum towards new identities* (pp. 355–376). New York: Garland Publishing.

Bourdieu, P., and Passeron, J. C. (1990). *Reproduction in education, society and culture* (2nd ed.). Newbury Park, CA: Sage.

Bray, M. (1992). *Making small practical: The organisation and management of ministries of education in small states*. London: Commonwealth Secretariat.

Bruss, N., and Macedo, D. (1985). Toward a pedagogy of the question: Conversations with Paulo Freire. *Journal of Education* (Boston), *167*, pp. 7–21.

Burtchaell, J. T. (1988). *A just war no longer exists: The teaching and trial of Don Lorenzo Milani*. Notre Dame, IN: University of Notre Dame Press.

Cacucci, P. (1998). *Io, Marcos: Il nuovo Zapata racconta* (M. Duran de Huerta, ed.). Milan: Giangiacomo Feltrinelli Editore.

Cardenal, F., and Miller, V. (1982). Nicaragua 1980: The battle of the ABCs. *Harvard Educational Review, 15*(1), 1–26.

Carnoy, M., and Torres, C. A. (1990). Education and social transformation in Nicaragua. In M. Carnoy and J. Samoff (Eds.), *Education and social transition in the third world* (pp. 315–317). Princeton, NJ: Princeton University Press.

Castles, S., and Wustenberg, W. (1979). *The education of the future: An introduction to the theory and practice of socialist education*. London: Pluto.

CEC. (2002). *Official Journal of European Communities*, 20/7/2002. Call for Proposals EAC/ 41/02.

Chadwick, A., and Stannett, A. (Eds.). (1995). *Museums and the education of adults*. Leicester: NIACE.

Chadwick, A., and Stannett, A. (Eds.). (2001). *Museums and adults learning: Perspectives from Europe*. Leicester, NIACE.

Chomsky, N. (1999). *Latin America. From colonization to globalization* (Chomsky in conversation with H. Dietrich). Melbourne and New York: Ocean Press.

Chu, D.-C. (1980). *Chairman Mao: Education of the proletariat*. New York: Philosophy Library.

City Secretariat of Education of Porto Alegre. (1999). *Cycles of Formation. Politic-Proposal for the Citizen's School*. Porto Alegre: Prefeitura de Porto Alegre.

Coben, D. (1998). *Radical heroes: Gramsci, Freire and the politics of adult education*. New York: Garland.

Commissione Nazionale sull' Educazione Interculturale. (1998). *Mappa dei progetti italiani sul Mediterraneo*. Rome: Ministero della Pubblica Istruzione.

Curtis, B., Livingstone, D. W., and Smaller, H. (1992). *Stacking the deck: The streaming of working class kids in Ontario schools.* Toronto: Our Schools/Our Selves.

Darder, A. (2002). *Reinventing Paulo Freire: A pedagogy of love.* Boulder CO: Westview.

Darmanin, M. (1993). More things in heaven and earth: Contradictions and cooptation in education policy. *International Studies in Sociology of Education, 3,* 147–167.

de Figueredo-Cowan, M., and Gastaldo, D. (Eds.). (1995). *Paulo Freire at the Institute.* London: Institute of Education/University of London.

Dei, G. (1997). *Anti-racism education: Theory and practice.* Halifax, NS: Fernwood Publishing.

Dekadt, E. (1970). *Catholic radicals in Brazil.* Oxford: Oxford University Press.

Dewey, J. (1964). *Democracy and education.* New York: Macmillan.

Dolci, D. (1966). *Poverty in Sicily.* Middlesex: Penguin.

Elias, J. (1994). *Paulo Freire: Pedagogue of liberation.* Melbourne, FL: Krieger.

Ellsworth, E. (1989). Why doesn't this feel empowering? Working through the repressive myths of critical pedagogy. *Harvard Educational Review, 59,* 297–324.

El Saadawi, N. (1997). *The Nawal El Saadawi reader.* London: Zed Books.

El Saadawi, N. (1999). *A daughter of Isis. The autobiography of Nawal El Saadawi.* New York: St. Martin's Press.

Elsheikh, M. (1999). Le omissioni della cultural italiana. In I. Siggillino (Ed.), *L'Islam nella Scuola* (pp. 30–45). Milan: Editore Franco Angeli.

Escobar, M., Fernandez, A. L., and Guevara-Niebla, G. (with Freire, P.). (1994). *Paulo Freire on higher education: A dialogue at the National University of Mexico.* Albany, NY: SUNY Press.

Fabbri, F., and Gomes, A. M. (1995). La mia pedagogia: Paulo Freire risponde a professori e studenti bolognesi. In M. Gadotti, P. Freire, and S. Guimarães, *Pedagogia: dialogo e conflitto* (B. Bellanova and F. Telleri, eds.) (pp. 92–103). Torino: Societa' Editrice Internazionale.

Fallaci, N. (1993). *Vita del Prete Lorenzo Milani.* Milan: Biblioteca Universale Rizzoli.

Fanon, F. (1952). *Black skin, white masks.* London & Sydney: Pluto.

Fanon, F. (1963). *The wretched of the earth.* New York: Grove.

Feinberg, W., and Torres, C. A. (2001). Democracy and education: John Dewey and Paulo Freire. In J. Zajda (ed.), *Education & society* (pp. 59–70). Melbourne: James Nicholas Publishers.

Fischman, G. (1999). Review of *Teachers as cultural workers: Letters to those who dare teach. Comparative Education Review, 43,* 556–559.

Flecha, R. (1990). Spanish society and adult education. *International Journal of Lifelong Education, 9*(2), 99–108.

Flecha, R. (1992). Spain. In P. Jarvis (Ed.), *Perspectives on Education and Training Adults* (pp. 190–203). Leicester: NIACE.

Foley, G. (1994). Adult education and capitalist reorganisation. *Studies in the Education of Adults, 26,* 121–143.

Foley, G. (1999). *Learning in social action: A contribution to understanding informal education.* London and New York: Zed Books.

Fondazione Laboratorio Mediterraneo. (Ed.). (1997). *Obiettivi e Mezzi per il parternariato Euromediterraneo: Il Forum Civile EuroMed.* Naples: Magma.

Freire, P. (1970a). *Cultural action for freedom.* Cambridge, MA: Harvard University Press.

Freire, P. (1970b). *Pedagogy of the oppressed.* New York: The Seabury Press.

Freire, P. (1970b, 1993). *Pedagogy of the oppressed* (30th anniversary ed.). New York: Continuum.

Freire, P. (1971). To the coordinator of a cultural circle. *Convergence, IV*(1), 61–62.

Freire, P. (1972). Education: Domestication or liberation? *Prospects, 2,* 173–181.

Freire, P. (1973). *Education for critical consciousness.* New York: Continuum.

Freire, P. (1974). Authority versus authoritarianism. Audiotape, in series: *Thinking with Paulo Freire.* Sydney: Australian Council of Churches.

Freire, P. (1976). Literacy and the possible dream. *Prospects, 6,* 68–71.

Freire, P. (1978). *Pedagogy in process: The letters to Guinea Bissau.* New York: Continuum.

Freire, P. (1981). The people speak their word: Learning to read and write in São Tomé and Princípe. *Harvard Educational Review, 51*(1), 27–30.

Freire, P. (1985). *The politics of education.* Westport, CT: Bergin & Garvey.

Freire, P. (1991). The work of Paulo Freire as secretary of education in São Paulo. In *Educational policy and social change in Brazil* (audiotape). Chicago: Teach 'em Inc.

Freire, P. (1993). *Pedagogy of the city.* New York: Continuum.

Freire, P. (1994). *Pedagogy of hope.* New York: Continuum.

Freire, P. (1995a). Learning to read the world. Paulo Freire in conversation with Carlos Torres. In C. A. Torres (Ed.), *Education and social change in Latin America* (pp. 175–181). Melbourne: James Nicholas Publishers.

Freire, P. (1995b). The progressive teacher. In M. de Figueredo-Cowan and D. Gastaldo (Eds.), *Paulo Freire at the Institute* (pp. 17–24). London: Institute of Education/University of London.

Freire, P. (1995c). Reply to discussants. In M. de Figueredo-Cowan and D. Gastaldo (Eds.), *Paulo Freire at the Institute* (pp. 61–67). London: Institute of Education/University of London.

Freire, P. (1996). *Letters to Cristina: Reflections on my life and work.* New York: Routledge.

Freire, P. (1997a). *Pedagogy of the heart.* New York: Continuum.

Freire, P. (1997b). A response. In P. Freire, with J. W. Fraser, D. Macedo, T. McKinnon, and W. T. Stokes (Eds.), *Mentoring the mentor: A critical dialogue with Paulo Freire* (pp. 303–329). New York: Peter Lang.

Freire, P. (1998a). *Pedagogy of freedom: Ethics, democracy and civic courage.* Lanham, MD: Rowman & Littlefield.

Freire, P. (1998b). *Politics and education.* Los Angeles, CA: UCLA Latin American Center Publications.

Freire, P. (1998c). *Teachers as cultural workers: Letters to those who dare teach.* Boulder, CO: Westview.

Freire, P. (2001). *Pedagogia da Indignação. Cartas pedagogicas e outros escritos.* São Paulo: Editora UNESP.

Freire, P., and Faundez, A. (1989). *Learning to question: A pedagogy of liberation.* Geneva: World Council of Churches.

Freire, P. (with Fraser, J. W., Macedo, D., McKinnon, T., and Stokes W. T.). (Eds.). (1997). *Mentoring the mentor: A critical dialogue with Paulo Freire.* New York: Peter Lang.

Freire, P., and Gadotti, M. (1995). Prefazione all'edizione italiana (preface to the Italian edition). In M. Gadotti, P. Freire, and S. Guimarães, *Pedagogia: Dialogo e conflitto* (Pedagogy: Dialogue and conflict) (B. Bellanova and F. Telleri, Eds.) (pp. 5–7). Torino: Societa' Editrice Internazionale.

Freire, P., and Macedo, D. (1987). *Literacy: Reading the word and the world.* Westport, CT: Bergin & Garvey.

Freire, P., and Macedo, D. (1993). A dialogue with Paulo Freire. P. McLaren and P. Leonard (Eds.), *Paulo Freire: A critical encounter* (pp. 169–176). New York and London: Routledge.

Freire, P., and Macedo, D. (1995). A dialogue: Culture, language and race. *Harvard Educational Review, 65*(3), 377–402.

Freire, P., and Macedo, D. (2000). Scientism as a form of racism. In S. Steiner, M. Krank, P. McLaren, and R. Bahruth (Eds.), *Freirean pedagogy, praxis and possibilities: Projects for the new millennium* (pp. 33–40). New York: Falmer.

Gaber-Katz, E., and Watson, G. M. (1991). *The land that we dream of—a participatory study of community-based literacy.* Toronto: OISE.

Gadotti, M.(1994). *Reading Paulo Freire: His life and work,* Albany, NY: SUNY Press.

Gadotti, M. (1996). *Pedagogy of Praxis: A dialectical philosophy of education,* Albany, NY: SUNY Press.

Gadotti, M., Freire, P., and Guimarães, S. (1995). *Pedagogia: Dialogo e conflitto* (B. Bellanova and F. Telleri, Eds.). Torino: Societa' Editrice Internazionale.

Gajardo, M. (1998). Despedida a Paulo Freire. *Convergence, XX1*(1 & 2), 40–49.

Gandin, L. A., and Apple, M. W. (2002). Thin versus thick democracy in education: Porto Alegre and the creation of alternatives to neo-liberalism. *International Studies in Sociology of Education, 12*(2), 99–115.

Gelpi, E. (1999). Review of *Convergence,* Vol. XXX, Nos. 2/3 (special issue on the transnational dimension of adult education). *Mediterranean Journal of Educational Studies, 4*(2), 262–263.

Giordmaina, J. (Ed.). (2000). *Proceedings: National curriculum on its way. A conference on the Implementation of the National Curriculum, Malta 9–11 June 2000.* Malta: Ministry of Education, Education Division, Faculty of Education—University of Malta.

Giroux, H. (1981). Hegemony, resistance and the paradox of educational reform. *Interchange, 12,* 3–26.

Giroux, H. (1985). Preface. In P. Freire, *The politics of education* (pp. xi–xxv). Westport, CT: Bergin and Garvey.

Giroux, H. (1988). *Teachers as intellectuals.* Westport, CT: Bergin & Garvey.

Giroux, H. (1992). *Border crossings, cultural workers and the politics of education.* New York and London: Routledge.

Giroux, H. (1993a). Literacy and the politics of difference. In C. Lankshear and P. McLaren (Eds.), *Critical literacy, politics, praxis and the postmodern* (pp. 367–377). Albany, NY: SUNY Press.

Giroux, H. (1993b). Paulo Freire and the politics of postcolonialism. In P. McLaren and P. Leonard (Eds.), *Paulo Freire: A critical encounter* (pp. 177–188). New York & London: Routledge.

Giroux, H. A. (1996). *Disturbing pleasures.* New York: Routledge.

Giroux, H. A. (1999). *The mouse that roared: Disney and the end of innocence.* Lanham, MD: Rowman & Littlefield.

Giroux, H. A. (2000). *Stealing innocence: Corporate culture's war on children.* New York: Palgrave.

Giroux, H. A. (2001). *Public spaces/private lives: Beyond the culture of cynicism.* Lanham, MD: Rowman & Littlefield.

Goulet, D. (1973). Introduction. In P. Freire, *Education for critical consciousness* (pp. vii–xiv). New York: Continuum.

Gramsci, A. (1971). *Selection from the prison notebooks* (Q. Hoare and G. Nowell Smith, eds.). New York: International Publishers.

Gramsci, A. (1995). *The southern question* (P. Verdicchio, ed. and trans.). West Lafayette, IN: Bordighera Incorporated.

Gutierrez, F., and Prado, C. (2000). *Ècopedagogia e cittadinanza planetaria.* Bologna: E.M.I.

Habib, H. (1979). *Libya: Past and present.* Malta and Tripoli: Aedam Publishing House Ltd.

Hall, B. L. (1998). "Please don't bother the canaries": Paulo Freire and the International Council for Adult Education. *Convergence, 31*(1/2), 95–104.

Hart, M. (1992). *Working and educating for life: Feminist and international perspectives on adult education.* London and New York: Routledge.

Hartung, A., and Ohlinger, J. (1972). *Quotational bibliography on Paulo Freire* (Prepared for a joint graduate seminar on Paulo Freire). Columbus: The Ohio State University.

Haug, F. (Ed.). (1987). *Female sexualization: A collective work of memory.* London: Verso.

Haughey, D. (1998). From passion to passivity: The decline of university extension for social change. In S. M. Scott, B. Spencer, and A. Thomas (Eds.), *Learning for life: Canadian readings in adult education* (pp. 200–212). Toronto: Thompson Educational.

Hickling-Hudson, A. (1999). Beyond schooling: Adult education in postcolonial societies. In R. F. Arnove and C. A. Torres (Eds.), *Comparative education: The dialectic of the global and the local* (pp. 233–255). Lanham, MD: Rowman & Littlefield.

Holst, J. D. (1999). The affinities of Lenin and Gramsci: Implications for radical adult education theory and practice. *International Journal of Lifelong Education, 18,* 407–421.

Holst, J. D. (2001). *Social movements, civil society, and radical adult education.* Westport, CT: Bergin & Garvey.

hooks, b. (1989). *Talking back: Thinking feminist, thinking black.* Toronto: Between the Lines.

hooks, b. (1993). bell hooks speaking about Paulo Freire: The man, his works. In P. McLaren and P. Leonard (Eds.), *Paulo Freire: A critical encounter* (pp.146–154). New York & London: Routledge.

hooks, b. (1994a). *Teaching to transgress.* New York: Routledge.

hooks, b. (1994b). *Feminist theory: From margin to centre.* Boston: South End Press.

Horton, M., and Freire, P. (1990). *We make the road by walking: Conversations on education and social change.* Philadelphia: Temple University Press.

IPF. (2000). *Institutional curriculum (Curriculo institucional) 2000: Project, profile and trajectory (Projeto, perfil e percurso).* São Paulo: Instituto Paulo Freire.

Ireland, T. (1987). *Antonio Gramsci and adult education: Reflections on the Brazilian experience.* Manchester: Manchester University Press.

Jarvis, P. (1987). Paulo Freire. In P. Jarvis (Ed.), *Twentieth-century thinkers in adult education* (pp. 265–279). New York: Routledge.

Jordan, G., and Weedon, C. (1995). *Cultural politics: Class, gender, race and the postmodern world.* Oxford (UK) and Cambridge (USA): Blackwells.

Jules, D. (1993). The challenge of popular education in the Grenada revolution. In C. Lankshear and P. McLaren (Eds.), *Critical literacy, politics, praxis and the postmodern* (pp. 133–165). Albany, NY: SUNY Press.

Kane, L. (2000). Popular education and the landless people's movement in Brazil (MST). *Studies in the Education of Adults, 32*(1), 36–50.

Kane, L. (2001). *Popular education and social change in Latin America.* London: Latin American Bureau.

Kester, G. (1980). Transition to workers' self-management: Its dynamics in the decolonising economy of Malta. The Hague: Institute of Social Studies.

Kidd, R., and Kumar, K. (1981). Coopting Freire: A critical analysis of pseudo-Freirean adult education. *Economic and Political Weekly, XVI* (1&2), 27–36.

Kirkwood, G., and Kirkwood, C. (1989). *Living adult education: Freire in Scotland.* Philadelphia: Open University Press.

La Belle, T. J. (1986). *Non formal education in Latin America and the Caribbean—stability, reform or revolution?* New York: Praeger.

Laboratorio Mediterraneo. (1997). Obiettivi e Mezzi per il parternariato Euromediterraneo. *Il Forum Civile EuroMed.* Naples: Magma.

Lankshear, C., and McLaren, P. (1993). Introduction. In C. Lankshear and P. McLaren (Eds.), *Critical literacy, politics, praxis and the postmodern* (pp. 1–56). Albany, NY: SUNY Press.

Larrain, J. (1983). *Marxism and Ideology.* Atlantic Highlands, NJ: Humanities Press.

Larson, M. S. (1977). *The rise of professionalism: A sociological analysis.* Berkeley: University of California Press.

Lawton, D. (1984). Curriculum and culture. In M. Skilbeck (Ed.), *Readings in school-based curriculum development* (pp. 275–289). London: Harper and Row.

Lê Thánh Khôi. (1999). *Educazione e Civilta'. Le Società di Ieri* (G. Pampanini trans.). Rome: Armando Editore.

Lê Thánh Khôi. (2000). Il Mediterraneo e il dialogo fra le civilta. In G. Pampanini (Ed.), *Un mare di opportunita'. Cultura e educazione nel Mediterraneo del lll Millenio* (pp. 49–60). Rome: Armando Editore.

Ledwith, M. (1997). *Participating in transformation: Towards a working model of community empowerment.* Birmingham: Venture Press.

Ledwith, M. (2001). Community work as critical pedagogy: Re-envisioning Freire and Gramsci. *Community Development Journal, 36*(3), 171–182.

Leonard, P. (1993). Critical pedagogy and state welfare—intellectual encounters with Freire and Gramsci, 1974–86. In P. McLaren and P. Leonard (Eds.),

Paulo Freire: A critical encounter (pp. 155–168). New York and London: Routledge.

Lima, L. (1992). Portugal. In P. Jarvis (Ed.), *Perspectives on adult education and training in Europe* (pp. 178–189). Leicester: NIACE.

Lind, A., and Johnston, A. (1986). *Adult literacy in the third world.* Stockholm: SIDA.

Livingstone, D. W. (1983). *Class, ideologies & educational futures.* Sussex: Falmer.

London Edinburgh Weekend Return Group. (1979). *In and against the state.* London: Pluto.

Lorde, A. (1984). *Sister outsider.* Trumansburg, NY: The Crossing Press.

Macedo, D. (1994). Preface. In P. McLaren and C. Lankshear (Eds.), *Politics of liberation: Paths from Freire* (pp. xiii–xviii). London and New York: Routledge.

Macedo, D. (1998). Foreword. In P. Freire, *Pedagogy of freedom* (pp. XI–XXXII). Lanham, MD: Rowman & Littlefield.

Mannheim, K. (1936). *Ideology and utopia* (L. Wirth and E. Shils, trans.). New York: Harcourt, Brace & World.

Marshall, J. (1997). Globalization from below: The trade union connections. In S. Walters (Ed.), *Globalization, adult education & training: Impacts & issues* (pp. 57–68). London: Zed Books.

Martin, D. (1998). Learning from the south. *Convergence* (a tribute to Paulo Freire), *31,* 117–127.

Marx, K., and Engels, F. (1970). *The German ideology* (C. J. Arthur, ed.). London: Lawrence and Wishart.

Marx, K., and Engels, F. (1978). *The Marx-Engels reader* (R. Tucker, ed.). New York: Norton.

Matvejevic, P. (1997). Address. In *Laboratorio Mediterraneo.Obiettivi e Mezzi per il parternariato Euromediterraneo. Il Forum Civile EuroMed* (pp. 122–123). Naples: Magma.

Mayo, M. (1987). *Imagining tomorrow. Adult education for transformation.* Leicester: NIACE.

Mayo, P. (1993). Review of The Texts of Paulo Freire by Paul V. Taylor. *Adults Learning, 4,* 283.

Mayo, P. (1994). State sponsored adult literacy programmes in Malta—a critical review. *Language and Education, 8,* 31–39.

Mayo, P. (1996). Review of Paulo Freire: Pedagogue of Liberation by John Elias. *Convergence, 29,* 63–68.

Mayo, P. (1997a). Reflections on Freire's work: A Maltese contribution. *Taboo: The Journal of Culture and Education, 2,* 120–123.

Mayo, P. (1997b). Tribute to Paulo Freire (1921–1997). *International Journal of Lifelong Education, 16,* 365–370.

Mayo, P. (1997c). Workers' education and democracy. In G. Baldacchino and P. Mayo (Eds.), *Beyond schooling: Adult education in Malta* (pp. 309–332). Malta: Mireva.

Mayo, P. (1999a). *Gramsci, Freire and adult education: Possibilities for transformative action.* London: Zed Books.

Mayo, P. (1999b). Towards a critical multiculturalism in the Mediterranean: Reflections on the conference: Il Mare che Unisce. Scuola, Europa e Mediterraneo (The sea that unites: School, Europe and the Mediterranean). *Mediterranean Journal of Educational Studies, 4*(1), 117–122.

Mayo, P. (2000). Marxism's impact on adult education. *Educational Practice and Theory, 22*(2), 95–110.

Mayo, P. (2001). Julius Nyerere (1922–1999) and education—a tribute. *International Journal of Educational Development, 21*(3), 193–202.

Mayo, P. (2002, September). Antonio Gramsci and Paulo Freire: Some connections and contrasts. Paper presented at the Third Paulo Freire Research Conference, University of California at Los Angeles.

Mayo, P. (2003). In and against the state: Gramsci, a "war of position" and adult education. In T. Clayton (Ed.), *Rethinking hegemony.* Melbourne: James Nicholas Publishers.

McIlroy, J. (1993). Community, labour and Raymond Williams. *Adults Learning, 4,* 276–277.

McLaren, P. (1994). *Life in schools* (2nd ed.). New York and London: Longman.

McLaren, P. (1995). *Critical pedagogy and predatory culture: Oppositional politics in a postmodern era.* London and New York: Routledge.

McLaren, P. (1997a). Paulo Freire's legacy of hope and struggle. *Taboo: The Journal of Culture and Education, 2,* 33–38.

McLaren, P. (1997b). *Revolutionary multiculturalism pedagogies of dissent for the new millennium.* Boulder, CO: Westview.

McLaren, P. (2000). *Che Guevara, Paulo Freire and the pedagogy of revolution.* Lanham, MD: Rowman & Littlefield.

McLaren, P. (2002). Afterword. A legacy of hope and struggle. In A. Darder, *Reinventing Paulo Freire: A pedagogy of love* (pp. 245–253). Boulder, CO: Westview.

McLaren, P., and Allen, R. L. (1998). Review of R. Paulston (Ed.), *Social cartography: Mapping ways of seeing social and educational change. Comparative Education Review, 42*(2), 225–228.

McLaren, P., and Da Silva, T. T. (1993). Decentering pedagogy: Critical literacy, resistance and the politics of memory. In P. McLaren and P. Leonard (Eds.), *Paulo Freire: A critical encounter* (pp. 47–89). New York and London: Routledge.

McLaren, P., and Lankshear, C. (Eds.). (1994). *Politics of liberation: Paths from Freire.* London and New York: Routledge.

McLaren, P., and Leonard, P. (Eds.). (1993). *Paulo Freire: A critical encounter.* London and New York: Routledge.

McLaren, P., and Mayo, P. (1999). Value commitment, social change and personal narrative. *International Journal of Educational Reform, 8,* 397–408.

Melo, A. (1985). From traditional cultures to adult education: The Portuguese experience after 1974. In K. Wain (Ed.), *Lifelong education and participation* (pp. 38–48). Malta: University of Malta Press.

Mies, M., and Shiva, V. (1993). *Ecofeminism.* London: Zed Books.

Milani, B. (2002). From opposition to alternatives. Postindustrial potentials and transformative learning. In E. O'Sullivan, A. Morrell, and M. A. O'Connor (Eds.), *Expanding the boundaries of transformative learning: Essays on theory and praxis* (pp. 47–58). New York and Basingstoke: Palgrave.

Miles, A. (1996). *Integrative feminisms: Building global visions, 1960s–1990s.* New York and London: Routledge.

Miles, A. (1998). Learning from the women's movement in the neo-liberal period. In S. M. Scott, B. Spencer, and A. Thomas (Eds.), *Learning for life: Canadian readings in adult education* (pp. 250–258). Toronto: Thompson Educational.

Mills, C. W. (1959). *The sociological imagination.* New York: Oxford University Press.

Ministero della Pubblica Istruzione. (1998). Mappa dei progetti italiani sol mediterraneo. Rome: Ministero della Pubblica Istruzione.

Ministry of Education. (2000). *Creating the future together: National minimum curriculum.* Floriana: Ministry of Education.

Moatassime, A. (2000). Mediterraneo fra plurilinguismo e pluriculturalità. In G. Pampanini (Ed.), *Un Mare di Opportunita': Cultura e Educazione nel Mediterraneo del lll Millenio* (pp. 111–114). Rome: Armando Editore.

Morgagni, E. (1995). Anno 1989: Paulo Freire, "dottore in Pedagogia", honoris causa, dell' Alma Mater Studiorum di Bologna. In M. Gadotti, P. Freire, and S. Guimarães, *Pedagogia: dialogo e conflitto* (B. Bellanova and F. Telleri, eds.) (pp. 86–91). Torino: Societa' Editrice Internazionale.

Morrow, R. A., and Torres, C. A. (1995). *Social theory and education: A critique of theories of social change and cultural reproduction.* Albany, NY: SUNY Press.

Morrow, R. A., and Torres, C. A. (2000). Gramsci and popular education in Latin America: From revolution to democratic transition. In C. Borg, J. A. Buttigeg, and P. Mayo (Eds.), *Gramsci and education* (pp. 179–200). Lanham, MD: Rowman & Littlefield.

Morrow, R. A., and Torres, C. A. (2002). *Reading Freire and Habermas: Critical pedagogy and transformative social change.* New York and London: Teachers College Press.

Nairn, T. (1982). Antonu su Gobbu. In A. Showstack Sassoon (Ed.), *Approaches to Gramsci* (pp. 159–179). London: Writers and Readers Publishing Cooperative Society.

Ngugi Wa Thiong'o. (1981). *Decolonising the mind: The politics of language in African literature.* Oxford: James Currey & Heinemann.

Nyerere, J. K. (1968). *Uhuru Na Ujamaa: Freedom and socialism.* London: Oxford University Press.

Nyerere, J. K. (1979a). Adult education and development. In H. Hinzen and V. J. Hundsdorfer (Eds.), *The Tanzanian experience: Education for liberation and development* (pp. 49–55). Hamburg: Unesco Institute for Education; London: Evans Brothers.

Nyerere, J. K. (1979b). Education never ends. In H. Hinzen and V. J. Hundsdorfer (Eds.), *The Tanzanian experience: Education for liberation and development* (pp. 33–42). Hamburg: Unesco Institute for Education; London: Evans Brothers.

O'Cadiz, M., Wong, P. L., and Torres, C. A. (1998). *Education and democracy: Paulo Freire, social movements and educational reform in São Paulo.* Boulder, CO: Westview.

O'Sullivan, E. (1999). *Transformative learning: Education for the 21st century,* London and New York: Zed Books; Toronto: University of Toronto Press.

O'Sullivan, E., Morrell, A., and O'Connor, M. A. (Eds.). (2002). *Expanding the boundaries of transformative learning: Essays on theory and praxis.* New York and Basingstoke: Palgrave.

Ozga, J., and Lawn, M. (1981). *Teachers, professionalism and class: A study of organised teachers.* Brighton: Falmer.

Paiva, V. (1995). Catholic populism and education in Brazil. *International Review of Education, 41*(3–4), 151–175.

Pallavicini, S.A.W. (1998, October). *Identita e differenze.* Paper presented at the conference Il Mare ele Unisce Scuole, Europa e Mediterraneo, Sestri Levante, Italy.

Pampanini, G. (Ed.). (2000). *Un mare di opportunita'. Cultura e educazione nel Mediterraneo del lll Millenio.* Rome: Armando Editore.

Parson, S. (1990). Lifelong learning and the community school. In G. Poster and A. Kruger (Eds.), *Community education in the western world* (pp. 29–38). London and New York: Routledge.

Pecorini, G. (1996). *Don Milani! Chi Era Costui?* Milan: Baldini & Castoldi.

Peters, J. M., and Bell, B. (1987). Horton of highlander. In P. Jarvis (Ed.), *Twentieth century thinkers in adult education.* London and New York: Routledge.

Ransome, P. (1992) *Antonio Gramsci: A new introduction.* Hemel Hempstead, UK: Harvester Wheatsheef.

Retamal, G. (1981). *Paulo Freire, christian ideology and adult education in Latin America* (Newland Papers No. 5). Hull: University of Hull.

Rikowski, G. (2001). *The battle in Seattle: Its significance for education.* London: Tufnell Press.

Roberts, P. (ed.) (1999). *Paulo Freire, politics and pedagogy: Reflections from Aotearoa-New Zealand.* Palmerston North: Dunmore Press.

Roberts, P. (2000). *Education, literacy, and humanization exploring the work of Paulo Freire.* Westport, CT: Bergin & Garvey.

Runté, R. (1995). Is teaching a profession? In G. Taylor and R. Runté (Eds.), *Thinking about teaching: An introduction* (pp. 288–299). Toronto and Montreal: Harcourt Brace Canada.

Said, E. (1978). *Orientalism.* New York: Random House.

Said, E. (1993). *Culture and imperialism.* London: Vintage.

Saul, A. M. (1995). Municipal educational policy in the city of São Paulo, Brazil (1988–1991). In C. A. Torres (Ed), *Education and social change in Latin America* (pp. 155–162). Melbourne: James Nicholas Publishers.

Schugurensky, D. (1996). Paulo Freire: From pedagogy of the oppressed to pedagogy of hope. In H. Reno and M. Witte (Eds.), *37th annual AERC proceedings.* Tampa: University of Florida.

Schugurensky, D. (1998). The legacy of Paulo Freire: A critical review of his contributions. *Convergence, XXI*(1 & 2), 17–29.

Schugurensky, D. (2002a). From south to north: Can the participatory budget be exported (Daniel Schugurensky interviewed by Angie Gallop). Retrieved from http://www.rabble.ca, November 1–9.

Schugurensky, D. (2002b). Transformative learning and transformative politics: The pedagogical dimension of participatory democracy and social action. In E. O'Sullivan, A. Morrell, and M. A. O'Connor (Eds.), *Expanding the boundaries of transformative learning: Essays on theory and praxis* (pp. 59–76). New York and Basingstoke: Palgrave.

Scuola di Barbiana. (1996). *Lettera a una professoressa.* Florence: Libreria Editrice Fiorentina.

Shor, I. (Ed.). (1987). *Freire for the classroom: A sourcebook for liberatory teaching.* Portsmouth, NH: Boyton/Cook Publishers.

Shor, I. (1992). *Empowering education: Critical teaching for social change.* Chicago: University of Chicago Press.

Shor, I. (1997). What is critical literacy. *Journal for Pedagogy, Pluralism & Practice, 4*(1), http://www.lesley.edu/journals/JPPP/4/shor.html.

Shor, I. (1998). The centrality of beans: Remembering Paulo. *Convergence, XXI*(1 & 2), 75–80.

Shor, I., and Freire, P. (1987). *Pedagogy for liberation dialogues on transforming education.* Westport, CT: Bergin & Garvey.

Stefanos, A. (1997). African women and revolutionary change: A Freirian and feminist perspective. In P. Freire with J. W. Fraser, D. Macedo, T. McKinnon, and W. T. Stokes (Eds.), *Mentoring the mentor: A critical dialogue with Paulo Freire* (pp. 243–271). New York: Peter Lang.

Stefanos, A. (2002). Gender equity and nationalism in Eritrea: Challenges to women's consciousness and emancipation. *Journal of Postcolonial Education, 1*(1), 67–99.

Steiner, S., Krank, M., McLaren, P., and Bahruth, R. (Eds.). (2000). *Freirean pedagogy, praxis, and possibilities: Projects for the new millennium.* New York and London: Falmer.

Street, B. V. (1994). What is meant by local literacies? *Language and Education. 8,* 9–17.

Stromquist, N. (1997). *Literacy for citizenship: Gender and grassroots dynamics in Brazil.* Albany, NY: SUNY Press.

Sultana, R. G. (1994). L-ghalliema, il-genituri u l-kunsilli ta' l-iskejjel: bini ta' pont fuq bahar jaqsam? In R. G. Sultana (Ed.), *Genituri u ghalliema ghal edukazzjoni ahjar: Gwida ghal shubija gdida* (pp. 7–16). Malta: Mireva.

Sultana, R. G. (1995). Adult education and the politics of knowledge: The relevance of Malta's Dun Gorg Preca. *International Journal of Lifelong Education, 15*(4), 276–285.

Sultana, R. G. (1996). The Mediterranean, education and the millennium. *Mediterranean Journal of Educational Studies, 1*(1), i–xi.

Sultana, R. G., and contributors. (1997). *Inside/outside schools: Towards a critical sociology of education in Malta.* Malta: PEG Publications.

Sultana, R. G. (1999). The Euro-Mediterranean region and its universities: Trends, issues and prospects. *Mediterranean Journal of Educational Studies, 4*(2), 7–49.

Taylor, P. V. (1993). *The texts of Paulo Freire.* Buckingham: Open University Press.

Telleri, F. (Ed.). (2002). *Il Metodo Paulo Freire. Nuove technologie e sviluppo sostenibile.* Bologna: CLUEB.

Torres, C. A. (1982). From the pedagogy of the oppressed to a Luta Continua—the political pedagogy of Paulo Freire. *Education with Production, 2,* 76–97.

Torres, C. A.(1990). *The politics of nonformal education in Latin America.* New York: Praeger.

Torres, C. A. (1993). From the pedagogy of the oppressed to a Luta Continua—the political pedagogy of Paulo Freire. In P. McLaren and P. Leonard (Eds.), *Paulo Freire: A critical encounter* (pp. 119–145). London and New York: Routledge.

Torres, C. A. (1994). Paulo Freire as secretary of education in the municipality of São Paulo. *Comparative Education Review, 38,* 181–214.

Torres, C. A. (Ed.). (1995). *Education and social change in Latin America.* Melbourne: James Nicholas Publishers.

Torres, C. A. (1998a). *Democracy, education and multiculturalism: Dilemmas of citizenship in a global world.* Lanham, MD, Rowman & Littlefield.

Torres, C. A. (1998b). *Education, power, and personal biography. dialogues with critical educators.* New York and London: Routledge.

Torres, R. M. (1986). Education and democracy in revolutionary Grenada. *Access, 5,* 1–43.

Tunnerman, C. (1983). *El pensamiento pedagogico de sandino.* Managua: Ministry of Education.

Unsicker, J. (1986). Tanzania's literacy campaign in historical-structural perspective. In R. F. Arnove and H. Graff (Eds.), *National literacy campaigns in historical and comparative perspective.* New York: Plenum.

Vanek, J. (1977). Education and the practice of self-management. In *Democracy in the workplace* (pp. 15–26). Washington, DC: Strongforce.

Vella, M., Agius, L., Bencini, J., Borg, C., Buttigieg, J., Cachia, G., et al. (1998). *Kurrikulu Nazzjonali Gdid ghall-Edukazzjoni f' Malta bejn l-eta' ta' 3 u 16 'l sena.* Floriana: Ministry of Education and National Culture.

Verdicchio, P. (1995). Introduction. In A. Gramsci, *The southern question* (P. Verdicchio, Trans.) (pp. 1–13). West Lafayette, IN: Bordighera Inc.

Viezzer, M. (1990). La poblacion marginada, objeto del ano internacional de la alfabetizacion (interview with Paulo Freire). *Convergence, XXIII*(1), 5–8.

Von Freyhold, M. (1982). Some observations on adult education in Tanzania. In H. Hinzen, and V. H. Hundsdorfer (Eds.), *The Tanzanian experience: Education for liberation and development* (pp. 162–167). Hamburg: Unesco Institute for Education, London: Evans Brothers.

Wain, K. (1991). *The Maltese national curriculum. A critical evaluation.* Malta: Mireva.

Wain, K., Attard, P., Bezzina, C., Camilleri, R., Darmanin, M., Farrugia, C. J., et al. (1995). *Tomorrow's schools: Developing effective learning cultures.* Floriana: Ministry of Education and Human Resources.

Walters, S., Borg, C., Mayo, P., and Foley, G. (2004). Economics, politics and adult education. In G. Foley (Ed.), *Dimensions of adult learning: Adult education and training in a global era.* Sydney: Allen and Unwin.

Weiler, K. (1991). Freire and a feminist pedagogy of difference. *Harvard Educational Review, 61,* 449–474.

West, C. (1993). Preface. In P. McLaren and P. Leonard (Eds.), *Paulo Freire: A critical encounter* (pp. xiii–xiv). London and New York: Routledge.

Young, R. J. C. (2003). *Postcolonialism: A very short introduction.* Oxford: Oxford University Press.

Youngman, F. (1986). *Adult education and socialist pedagogy.* Kent: Croom Helm.

Zachariah, M. (1986). *Revolution through reform—a comparison of Sarvodaya and conscientisation.* New York: Praeger.

Zammit Marmara', D. (1997a). Manwel Dimech's search for enlightenment. In G. Baldacchino and P. Mayo (Eds.), *Beyond schooling: Adult education in Malta* (pp. 5–22). Malta: Mireva.

Zammit Marmara', D. (1997b). A voice in the wilderness: Manwel Dimech and the education of the Maltese proletariat. In R. G. Sultana and contributors (Eds.), *Inside/outside schools: Towards a critical sociology of education in Malta* (pp. 457–477). Malta: PEG Publications.

Index

ABOUT THE AUTHOR

PETER MAYO is Associate Professor, Education, University of Malta. He is co-editor of the *Journal of Postcolonial Education* and the author of several books and articles concerning the work of Paolo Freire, Antonio Gramsci, and other works on adult education.